MW00675289

The
Eclectic
Gourmet
Guide to
Atlanta
2nd Edition

Also available from MENASHA RIDGE PRESS

The Eclectic Gourmet Guide to Atlanta

2nd Edition

Jane Garvey

MENASHA
RIDGE
PRESS

Every effort has been made to ensure the accuracy of information throughout this book. Bear in mind, however, that prices, schedules, etc., are constantly changing. Readers should always verify information before making final plans.

Menasha Ridge Press, Inc.
P.O. Box 43673
Birmingham, Alabama 35243

Distributed by The Globe Pequot Press

Cover and text design by Suzanne H. Holt
Cover art by Michele Natale

ISBN 0-89732-369-6
Library of Congress Cataloging in Publication Data:
Garvey, Jane, 1943–
The eclectic gourmet guide to Atlanta / Jane Garvey.—2nd ed.
    p. cm.
Includes index.
ISBN 0-89732-369-6 (alk. paper)
1. Restaurants—Georgia—Atlanta—Guidebooks. I. Title.

TX907.3.G42 A8544 2001
647.95758'231—DC21

                                                  CIP
                                          2001030846

Manufactured in the United States of America

10 9 8 7 6 5 4 3 2 1

Second Edition

CONTENTS

acknowledgments

This book is the work of many people, and it must be dedicated to them all. First, it is dedicated to the chefs and staffers of Atlanta restaurants who do their level best day in and day out to produce what in their view is the best cooking they can imagine. And it's dedicated to Menasha Ridge Press, whose staff members always have been great companions in the task of producing this volume.

Then there are the myriad friends and family who have accompanied me to sundry restaurants, given their input, and searched out and reported back to me new restaurants they felt I should explore. Without my team of "spies," I could never cover this exploding restaurant scene. On one evening in search of yet another worthy spot, I literally put 100 miles round trip on the odometer, going from east Atlanta to its far northwestern 'burbs.

Our family always has been food focused. My grandfather grew first-class fruits and vegetables for a living. They had to be perfect before they went to market, so his tomatoes were the juicy kind, the sort you could peel without immersing them in hot water. My great grandfather was a butcher, and his granddaughter, my mother, remained steadfast in her standards for what constituted good meat. After all, her idea of an after-school snack was a quick steak. Before dinner.

Without this family, I wouldn't have the standards I possess. So this book is dedicated to them, because they knew that good food isn't just sustenance, it's a way of life. Sharing this background, my siblings and cousins all make great restaurant spies. The nephews, Sam and Adam, now 16 and 12, have grown into great dining companions, savoring Thai, Korean, or

Chinese at a moment's notice, perfectly at ease handling chopsticks. They prove you can teach children the value of good food, and the link between cuisine and culture. And boy, are they tough critics!

Mother always had high standards for good cooking, whether done at home or enjoyed at restaurants. If you were to ask her what she would like for dinner, she'd say, "Something tasty." Usually, it took several more queries before you could unearth what that might be on any given day. It could be a simple dish of slow-braised pork in sauerkraut with mashed potatoes and a glass of beer—and don't dare serve it in a frosted mug—or anything from Veni Vidi Vici, perhaps her favorite Atlanta restaurant. Our last lunch there the month before she passed away last year, she savored as best she could a bit of bean soup, a piatti piccoli of shrimp, and some panna cotta. We were going to share this, and after she put her spoon into it, she looked up at me and asked: "And what are you having?" I got the point. And got out of the way. So I dedicate this book to Mother, who was always on the lookout for "something tasty." Within its pages, I hope you, too, will find something tasty.

about the author

Jane F. Garvey has been writing about food and wine for one publication or another for the past decade and a half. But food and wine are companion interests to culture, art, history, and travel, which also are subjects about which she has written. Jane has lived in Georgia for more than 40 years, most of them in the Atlanta area. She has seen the Atlanta restaurant scene grow from a day in which chefs couldn't serve sweetbreads to one in which sushi bars are now as commonplace as hamburger joints.

In past lives, Jane has taught Spanish language and literature at the college level, worked in real estate sales, and edited design and lifestyle magazines. Freelance writer is her fourth, and best, career to date. And writing about food and wine is the most savored subject.

The Eclectic Gourmet Guide to

Atlanta

2nd Edition

GETTING IT RIGHT

A lot of thought went into this guide. While producing a dining guide may appear to be a straightforward endeavor, I can assure you that it is fraught with peril. I have read dining guides by authors who turn up their noses at anything except four-star French restaurants (of which there are a whole lot fewer than people think). Likewise, I have seen a guide that totally omits Thai and Indian restaurants—among others—because the author did not understand those cuisines. I have read guides absolutely devoid of criticism, written by "experts" unwilling to risk offending the source of their free meals. Finally, I've seen those books that are based on surveys and write-ins from diners whose credentials for evaluating fine dining are mysterious at best and questionable at least.

How, then, do you go about developing a truly excellent dining guide? What is the best way to get it right?

If dining guides are among the most idiosyncratic of reference books, it is primarily because the background, taste, integrity, and personal agenda of each author are problematical. The authors of most dining guides are vocational or avocational restaurant or food critics. Some of these critics are schooled professionals, with palates refined by years of practical experience and culinary study; others are journalists, often with no background in food criticism or cooking, who are arbitrarily assigned the job of reviewing restaurants by their newspaper or magazine publisher (although it is occasionally possible to find journalists who are also culinary professionals). The worst cases are the legions of self-proclaimed food critics who mooch their way from restaurant to restaurant, growing fat on free meals in exchange for writing glowing reviews.

Ignorance of ethnic cuisine or old assumptions about what makes for haute cuisine particularly plague authors in cities without much ethnic variety in restaurants, or authors who have been writing for years about the same old, white linen, expense-account tourist traps. Many years ago in Lexington, Kentucky, for example, there was only one Chinese restaurant in town and it was wildly successful—in spite of the fact that it was Chinese in name only. Its specialty dishes, which were essentially American vegetable casseroles smothered in cornstarch, were happily gobbled up by loyal patrons who had never been exposed to real Chinese cooking. The food was not bad, but it was not Chinese either. Visitors from out of town, inquiring about a good local Chinese restaurant, were invariably directed to this place. As you would expect, they were routinely horrified by the fare.

While you might argue that American diners are more sophisticated and knowledgeable nowadays than at the time of the Lexington pavilion, the evidence suggests otherwise. In Las Vegas, for instance, a good restaurant town with a number of excellent Italian eateries, the local Olive Garden (a chain restaurant) is consistently voted the city's best Italian restaurant in a yearly newspaper poll. There is absolutely nothing wrong with the Las Vegas Olive Garden, but to suggest that it is the best Italian restaurant in the city is ludicrous. In point of fact, the annual survey says much more about the relative sophistication of Las Vegas diners than it does about the quality of local Italian restaurants.

But if you pick up a guide that reflects the views of many survey respondents, a *vox populi* or reader's choice compendium, that is exactly the problem. You are dependent on the average restaurant-goer's capacity to make sound, qualitative judgments—judgments almost always impaired by extraneous variables. How many times have you had a wonderful experience at a restaurant, only to be disappointed on a subsequent visit? Trying to reconcile the inconsistency, you recall that on your previous visit, you were in the company of someone particularly stimulating, and that perhaps you had enjoyed a couple of drinks before eating. What I am getting at is that our reflections on restaurant experiences are often colored by variables having little or nothing to do with the restaurant itself. And while I am given to the democratic process in theory, I have my doubts about depending entirely on survey forms that reflect such experiences.

There are more pragmatic arguments to be made about such eaters' guides as well. If you cannot control or properly qualify your survey respondents, you cannot ensure their independence, knowledge, or critical sensitivity. And, since literally anyone can participate in such surveys, the ratings can be easily slanted by those with vested interests. How many bogus responses would it take to dramatically upgrade a restaurant's rating in a survey-based, big-city dining guide? Forty or even fewer. Why? Because the publisher receives patron reports (survey responses, readers' calls) covering more restaurants than can be listed in the book. Thus the "voting" is distributed over such a large number of candidate restaurants that the median number of reports for the vast majority of establishments is 120 or fewer. A cunning restaurant proprietor who is willing to stuff the ballot box, therefore, could easily improve his own rating—or lower that of a competitor.

So my mission in the *Eclectic Gourmet Guides* is to provide you with the most meaningful, useful, and accessible restaurant evaluations possible. Weighing the alternatives, I have elected to work with culinary experts, augmenting their opinions with a carefully qualified survey population of totally independent local diners of demonstrated culinary sophistication. The experts I have sought to author the *Eclectic Gourmet Guides* are knowledgeable, seasoned professionals; they have studied around the world, written cookbooks or columns, and closely follow the development of restaurants in their cities. They are well versed in ethnic dining, many having studied cuisines in their native lands. And they have no prejudice about high or low cuisine. They are as at home in a Tupelo, Mississippi, catfish shack as in an exclusive French restaurant on New York's Upper East Side. Thus the name *Eclectic Gourmet*.

Equally important, I have sought experts who make every effort to conduct their reviews anonymously, and who always pay full menu prices for their meals. We are credible not only because we are knowledgeable, but also because we are independent.

You, the reader of this *Eclectic Gourmet Guide,* are the inspiration for and, we hope, the beneficiary of our diligence and methodology. Though we cannot evaluate your credentials as a restaurant critic, your opinion as a consumer—of this guide and the restaurants within—is very important to us. Please tell us about your dining experiences and let us know whether you agree with our reviews.

Eat well. Be happy.

Bob Sehlinger

dining in ATLANTA

For a perspective on how dining in Atlanta has changed over the last almost half-century, a quick glance at *Gourmet* magazine's 1948 "Guide to Good Eating" reveals a city almost entirely devoted to its Southern culinary heritage. In many restaurants, alcohol was not served. The French Cafe, later known as Emile's French Cafe, probably constituted the city's most adventurous dining spot.

In the 1960s, a few Chinese restaurants appeared, serving chiefly Chinese-American food. Ding Ho, which stood on Cain Street (now International Boulevard), was probably the best of the bunch. But nothing then hinted at the current burst of Asian restaurants—authentic, good ones—lining the Buford Highway and Peachtree Industrial Boulevard, popping up all over south and east Cobb County, and spreading even south of the city. Most ironically, today's plethora of Thai restaurants probably started in Gwinnett County, whose denizens are not assumed to savor extraordinary or challenging fare.

Today, Atlanta's restaurateurs win national awards. Two restaurants, Bacchanalia and Horseradish Grill, made *Bon Appétit* magazine's list of ten best new restaurants in the country the year of their respective openings. Bacchanalia's culinary team, Anne Quatrano (she now handles their new Floataway Cafe) and Clifford Harrison, has been named by *Food and Wine* magazine as among the country's best chefs. Canoe made the pages of *Esquire* magazine in 1996 as one of the ten best new restaurants in the nation. In 1996 Gunther Seeger, former star at the Ritz-Carlton, Buckhead, and now operating his own restaurant (see Seeger's, page 257), was named James Beard Best Chef in the Southeast. *Esquire* also named his eponymous restaurant "Best New Restaurant" in the nation the year it opened (1998). And in 2001, Seeger's was awarded Relais & Chateaux' Relais Gourmands designation, the only free-standing restaurant to be so honored in 2001.

New in 2000, BluePointe and Aria took honors in *Esquire* magazine's line-up of best new restaurants. Numerous local chefs have been invited to perform their culinary wonders at the James Beard House. Increasingly, the city's ethnic restaurants expand the range of cuisines available in town, as well as pursue authenticity within established cuisines.

There are other developments to watch. Since this guide's last edition (1997), the metro north area has exploded in fine dining restaurants. Within the last year, even the south side has begun to develop fine dining establishments. Also sneaking into the far suburban areas are ethnic restaurants—mostly Asian—bringing the delights of Malayan, Thai, and Japanese cuisine to the farthest points of metropolitan Atlanta.

Is Atlanta now culinary nirvana? Not quite. For one thing, service hasn't kept pace with gastronomic sophistication. Too often, service personnel know nothing about the dishes on the menu, nor can they make intelligent recommendations.

Anyone interested in wine will likely find wine service maddeningly ignorant except in the most elegant of restaurants. In one supposedly sophisticated establishment, my recent request for a dry sherry as an apéritif brought the offer of a pair of vintage ports. "See me after dinner," I said.

A similar experience befell me only a few months ago, causing me to get on a soapbox on the subject. However, the alternatives offered were, instead of a pair of ports, two sweet red wines, a sweet Rasteau and a Banyuls! While the error—assuming sherries by definition are sweet—is the same, the suggested substitutes attest to the increasing adventurousness of Atlanta's wine lists. The two proposed wines, by the way, are great for after dinner with chocolate. This episode did not occur in vaunted Buckhead, but in downtown Decatur, which, since the last edition, has bloomed as a dining destination.

Still, in the years since the last edition, wine lists have become increasingly exciting, with unusual varietals, such as Viognier and Pinot Blanc as alternatives to the ubiquitous (and often boring) Chardonnay, and more exploration of Italian varietals and French Rhône wines over Merlot and Cabernet Sauvignon.

By-the-glass wine lists have improved markedly, frequently reaching into these more unusual choices, and many restaurants have added sections of good half-bottle choices. Increasingly, wine lists are being constructed with the restaurant's food in mind, although it's still frustrating to find inappropriate choices at the city's Asian restaurants. More restaurants are taking the trouble and expense to provide decent glassware to enhance the enjoyment of wine. Service, however, is still an issue, as staffers tend to drift into what once was a profession from student lives and other careers, viewing restaurant service as a stopgap career. But perhaps that, too, is changing, as here and there one finds the occasional committed professional dedicated to service as a way of life.

In addition to the growth in authentic Asian restaurants, the most dramatic changes have come in the presentation of regional Southern cooking. Believe it or not, fried chicken has achieved a vogue in fine Atlanta restaurants that your grandmother would never have imagined. Chef Scott Peacock at Watershed in Decatur saw his fried chicken on the cover of *Food and Wine* magazine in the year 2000, and now he has to rustle up as many as 90 portions for its regular Tuesday menu appearance. "It's all gone by 8 P.M., too," he says with a tone of amazed exhaustion.

We've seen collard greens and black-eyed peas, made tangy with intriguing seasonings rather than the customary fat meat, come to new heights. Or depths, if you're a traditionalist. A recently seen (clearly Northern) penchant for softening the characteristic bitter tang of collards with the addition of honey would drive grandma to distraction. So if you, like us, occasionally want the good ol' dishes prepared in the downhome, standard ways, they're out there, and we've pointed the way in this chapter to some of the better sources.

A few cuisines are still missing in Atlanta—Portuguese, Indonesian, and Afghanistani, for instance. But by and large, you can find just about anything your palate could possibly yearn for or your purse can pay for. And that, too, is changing. Coming in the fall of 2001 is Kyma, a new, upscale Greek restaurant from none other than Pano Karatassos of Buckhead Life Restaurant Group.

TOURIST PLACES

You may have heard of these tourist places, which should be considered only as a last resort. Meals here are often overpriced, and food generally falls beneath the standard of that served in lesser-known restaurants. This is not to say you won't get a lovely steak or a good meal in any of these places, but there is more creative food to be had elsewhere.

Atlanta Grill, the Ritz-Carlton
81 Peachtree Street, NE, at Ellis Street, Downtown
(404) 659-0400, ext. 6450

How to fall from grace to the sea after spending countless dollars on a out-of-context redesign? The idea was to make the dining space more casual, more enticing—and indeed customers do come—but the New Orleans–inspired interior somehow doesn't fit its Atlanta setting. That aside, the problem is that the food, service, and wine stewardship simply don't make the grade. Should you dine here, skip any dish pitched as a "Southern Specialty" and stick to the grill side of the menu. The simple grilled salmon, for instance, is excellent. So is the cream of lima bean soup, if that happens to be available.

Cheesecake Factory

3024 Peachtree Road, NW, Buckhead   (404) 816-2555
Perimeter Mall, 4400 Ashford Dunwoody Road
　　Dunwoody   (678) 320-0201

Cheesecake is the draw, but folks throng for other dishes, too, despite the fact that pretty much everything is made off-site and shipped in. The company claims the Buckhead location is one of the nation's busiest restaurants, and certainly the lines outside attest to its enduring popularity. But there is much better food to be had elsewhere for less money. Even in the cheesecake department. Serious culinary work it's not. Still, kids love the place.

Dante's Down the Hatch

3380 Peachtree Road, NE   (404) 266-1600

This longtime stalwart is a favorite of many folks, but you need to like fondue and then some. The chocolate fondue experience is excellent, and worth gathering a gang to savor, as no one person can make off with all of it. (This must be ordered in advance.) And it's a great place to listen to music. But unless you want fondue on fondue, make it dinner elsewhere then saunter over here to catch the music and the chocolate. Following a recent disastrous fire, owner Dante Stephensen had to scramble to get the wharf portion open by spring 2001 and hoped to have the rest done by later in the year. Call ahead to be sure of the status.

Dave & Buster's

2215 D&B Drive, off Northwest Parkway, I-75 at Delk Road
　　(Exit 261), Marietta (770) 951-5554
4000 Venture Drive, I-85 (Exit 103 if northbound,
　　Exit 104 if southbound), Duluth (770) 497-1152

This pair of game-focused enterprises attracts families, although they're designed for adults. But families come. The pizzas and quesadillas make good kid food, and the char-grilled top sirloin steak for $13.95 is a good value. The kids dine happily, and the grown-ups appreciate the quality/value ratio: Entrees range from $9.95–16.95 (rib eye). Then it's off, armed with Power Cards, to play games upstairs. Billiards are available for grown-ups.

ESPN Zone

3030 Peachtree Road, NW, Buckhead   (404) 682-3776

Sports-themed commission art, abundant TVs, and a huge wall TV with smaller side screens in a space where "Zone Throne" seating is equipped with surround-sound individualized channel selection listening. Gobs of games upstairs attract families from all over. The place throbs. The food is decent, if not great. Everything is served in mega portions, so the quite tasty spinach dip could easily serve a table. Sandwiches rule, but cooked dishes—again in large portions—are good for hefty appetites. The duet of eight-ounce pork chops is just one example.

Gladys Knight & Ron Wiggins Chicken and Waffles

529 Peachtree Street, NE, between Renaissance Parkway and Linden Avenue, Midtown   (404) 874-9393

Chef Reginald Washington explains how chicken and waffles became linked in Harlem back during the days of the 1920s Harlem Renaissance, when an old gentleman had a place that was open late and served entertainers. He had a waffle iron and did fried chicken. Voilà. There's better fried chicken almost anywhere around town, and the food generally is just fair. But the place, dotted with Gladys Knight's image and memorabilia, is sharp and features cool music. It's open weekends until 4 A.M., making it quite tasty when you're famished late at night.

Justin's

2200 Peachtree Road, at Colonial Homes Drive   (404) 603-5353.

Rapper Sean "Puffy" Combs (Puff Daddy) named this large emporium for his son. Numerous restaurants preceded it, but this one likely will survive. It's a mecca for nicely dressed young folks out on the town; they come for the lengthy martini list and the ambiance. The food, which includes both Southern and Caribbean dishes, is, frankly, just fair and expensive. Tender local palates couldn't deal with the authentic heat levels of the Caribbean dishes, so the kitchen toned it back. Better Jamaican/Caribbean fare is to be found over on Memorial Drive anyway. The best deal is the Wednesday $10.95 buffet, which draws from the menu's bi-cuisine character. Still, it's a fun place and a likely stop for Hollywood glitterati in town, just in case you're into star spotting.

Sylvia's

241 Central Avenue, SW, Downtown   (404) 529-9692

Sylvia's is the work of the dynamic, South Carolina–born Sylvia Woods, now a resident of Harlem, New York, where she has a successful eponymous soul-food operation. Transplanting her success to Atlanta, the restaurant serves Southern food in stylish surroundings. Appealing as it does to the denizens of City Hall and the State Capitol Building, it has been successful. But this interpretation of Southern food is so short of the mark, and so expensive, it's not to be recommended. For much better barbecue, hit any of the spots indicated on the list below.

New Places

Oh my! So many new restaurants not only in the last three years, but also in the last year. The pace of openings has us hyperventilating to keep up. Still too new to know well, but very promising at press time, are the following:

Aangan

763-C DeKalb Industrial Way, Decatur   (404) 294-8989

The Decatur area of DeKalb County is rapidly becoming mecca for folks seeking really good, authentic Indian food. This is one of the newcomers and one of the best of the bunch. The excellent lunch buffet offers unusual dishes and is one grand deal, costing $7-8 depending on which day you dine there—the weekends being more expensive because seafood is added to the mix.

Agavé

242 Boulevard, at Carroll Street, Cabbagetown   (404) 588-0006

Jack Sobel's dream of offering Atlantans the authentic Southwestern food he grew up with has become a reality in this freshly launched operation in one of the city's gentrifying neighborhoods. From the posole to the huevos rancheros, the tastes of the Southwest dominate. Yet there are touches from other regions as well, such as the diablo crawfish pasta and seared rare tuna.

Andaluz

903 Peachtree Street, NE, at 6th Street, Midtown   (404) 875-7013

An authentic tapas and wine bar, with a chef from Barcelona and a nearly all-Spanish wine list, leaves Atlanta Hispanophiles eager for more. Tapas range from $3–15, and there's a hefty paella to share with at least two persons. *Atlanta* magazine called tapas the Best New Trend for 2000.

Andiamo Italian Bistro

1044 Greenwood Avenue at N. Highland Avenue   (404) 892-3555
An intimate neighborhood bistro that's been beautifully redone to reflect
the warmth of Italy, Andiamo has strength in starters (lovely calamari, for
instance), but the main courses are going to require major rethinking.
How do you want your veal or chicken? A la Marsala? A la Parmigiana?
Specials sound appealing. The Baldelli brothers are experienced restaurateurs and know how to do this. They'll get it right.

Angelo and Maxie's

Peachtree Point Plaza Building, 1545 Peachtree Street, Suite 101
(404) 870-0060
This first outpost of an established Big Apple steakhouse has lots of glitz
and glass, but will need to acquire some polish to do business in the
South. The ambient noise level (i.e., its "music") is obnoxious. If you're
deaf or dining on the patio, you might enjoy one of their huge steaks (a
24-ounce porterhouse, for instance) or the 10-ounce salmon fillet.
Atlanta magazine called this the Best New Steakhouse in 2000.

Atlantic Star

Ice House Lofts, 105 Sycamore Place, Decatur   (404) 377-8384
Stylishly linking old industrial elements (brick walls and rough textures)
with contemporary values in dining spaces, Fariba and Tommy Todd
have kept a good reign on the design and on the character of the food.
Nothing is pretentious, from the goat cheese croquette on red onion
marmalade to the pork shoulder with mac 'n' cheese. Delicious spot.
I predict a hit.

Bitter End Seafood Restaurant

Sandy Plains Village, 4651 Woodstock Road, Suite 305, Roswell
(770) 645-6564
A tiny space is devoted to selling fresh raw fish and seafood, steaks and
lamb, as well as prepared meals to go. After that, it's table service all the
way, with very fine fish dishes, crab cakes and good desserts. The pleasant
atmosphere sports a casual, Caribbean-beach theme (umbrellas and such
indoors) and lots of nautical artifacts lying about, including some repli-
cated tall ships.

Bradley Street Fish House

210 Adamson Square, Carrollton   (770) 838-1111
Good cooking is spreading to the outlying metro area towns, as this

newcomer proves. Inventive appetizers and great desserts are the highlights to date.

Brio Tuscan Grille

2964 Peachtree Road, Buckhead   (404) 760-0014

All restaurant roads seem to lead to Atlanta: Based in Columbus, Ohio, this Atlanta unit of a Tuscan-style trattoria also has a bakery within the store. Tuscan specialties include a delicious flatbread pizzetta with wild mushrooms and caramelized onions. The steaks are excellent, as are the veal and salmon.

Cabernet

5575 Windward Parkway, Alpharetta   (770) 777-5955

A handsome steakhouse, Cabernet burned to the ground just hours before it was to open, then was completely rebuilt. The undaunted owners have crafted an attractive dining spot with emphasis on very fine steaks, lamb, and fish. The good wine list supports the kitchen's efforts. A pricey place, but still should do well.

Cherry

1051 W. Peachtree Street, NW, at 11th Street, Midtown
    (404) 872-2020

Renovating an early 20th-century Midtown residence, owners Dee Grimes, Ray Sieradzki, Tom Nahas, and Paul Gibbs executed some nifty design features, such as a second-story deck that wraps around the one side and front. Nifty food, too, including sushi and dishes that reflect Asian as well as South American influences. Plus cherry cobbler, of course.

Chimayo

Brookhaven Station, 4058 Peachtree Road   (404) 760-0255

This stylish Southwestern restaurant brings not only a comfortable, cozy ambiance to Brookhaven, but also some distinctive dining and very friendly service. The wine list needs work, but over time is likely to improve, as the owners seem quite willing to do just that.

Cino Grille

Avenue East Cobb Shopping Center, 4475 Roswell Road,
    Suite 1410, at Johnson Ferry Road, Marietta   (770) 509-5522

Southwestern fare rules in a classy, contemporary environment that offers friendly service and tasty dishes. Interesting pastas, much for vegetarians to enjoy, and Southwestern seasonings abound.

Coast 92
Roswell Crossing Shopping Center
  625 Crossville Road, Roswell   (770) 649-6739
From brothers Harold and Richard Marmulstein of dick & harry's (see page 154) comes this classy seafood operation designed to bring sushi, New England fried clams, and Southern fried catfish all under one roof. It's casual, more regional (New England and Southern), and mostly devoted to seafood. Clam bellies (deep-fried soft-shell clams) and classic diner tapioca pudding for dessert are outrageously good.

Eurasia Bistro
  129 E. Ponce de Leon Avenue, Decatur   (404) 687-8822
From Donald Mui, who also owns Northlake Thai Restaurant (see profile on page 223), this newcomer to Decatur will have almost the same menu. It should be just as popular as the Northlake location.

Fandango's
Shoppes of Dunwoody,
  5500 Chamblee Dunwoody Road, Dunwoody   (770) 671-9758
Tapas representing different ethnic foods rather than just Spanish fare mark this newcomer's menu. The Spanish ambiance comes from the soft, golden stucco-finished walls, with a wood-beamed ceiling, wrought-iron light fixtures, and a tiled bar. Flamenco guitar music entertains during happy hour, and later there's dance music.

Fogo di Chão
  3101 Piedmont Road, Buckhead (404) 995-9982
A classic Brazilian churrascaria brings Brazilian fare to Atlanta. The fixed-price lunch and dinner ($19 and $35 respectively) focuses on meats on long skewers, presented by young Brazilian men dressed as guachos. The food is very, very good. This should be a hit.

Fontaine's Oyster House
  1026½ N. Highland Avenue, Virginia-Highland   (404) 872-0869
A fun, exuberant spot created with the classic New Orleans oyster bar in mind, Fontaine's jams with Virginia-Highlanders seeking oysters and seafood of all kinds. Stick with the Creole fare and skip dessert. The bar scene continues till the wee hours, with food stopping at midnight, although oysters are served until 1 A.M.

Fresco
Shops at Eagle Point, 2990 Eagle Drive, Woodstock
  (770) 924-0036 or (770) 924-8061

The 'burbs are brighter thanks to this large, family-oriented, packed dining establishment purveying Italian fare. Some excellent dishes, such as pasta with creamy walnut basil sauce, and some not so good dishes, such as very dry roast chicken, point to a kitchen that's got some work to do. Best bets for the moment are entrees that have to be cooked to order and pastas.

Fritti

311 N. Highland Avenue, Inman Park   (404) 523-6678
The practically perfect pizza parlor, Fritti is joined at the hip with its slightly older sibling, Sotto Sotto (see page 264). Riccardo Ullio's classy updo of a former garage has a wood-burning oven, a sheltered outdoor dining space, and a warm, delicious-smelling atmosphere. Fried things—the meaning of the word "fritti"—and pizzas with zingy, imaginative toppings will make this one a winner.

¡Fuego! Latin Café

Carlisle Commons, 10970-A State Bridge Road, Suite 4, Alpharetta
   (770) 753-4477
A fun, casual tapas bar with comfortable upholstered seating in front of a fireplace for conviviality.

Goldfish

Perimeter Mall, 4400 Ashford Dunwoody Road, Dunwoody
   (770) 671-0100
Open in June 2000, Tom Catherall's newest venture (see also Tom Tom, Prime, Star Steaks & BBQ, and Noche) focuses on fresh fish so good you can savor it grilled, medium rare. Excellent stone-ground grits as a side dish, Key lime pie for dessert, plus a very fine wine list make this one suitable for destination dining—not just post shopping. A sure hit.

Gordon Biersch

848 Peachtree Street, 6th–7th, Midtown   (404) 870-0805
A slightly overdone sound system makes one take refuge on the sheltered patio that surrounds the dining room of this brewpub. Once safely outside, however, one can savor a wide range of dishes from the eclectic menu that draws from a multitude of cuisines. Good brews, too, especially the IPA.

Gulf Coast Grill

Medlock Crossing Shopping Center, 970 Medlock Bridge Road,
   Suite 100, Duluth   (678) 474-9244
Good fresh fish simply prepared is the hallmark of this newcomer. Gulf fish—grouper, for instance—is excellent. Shrimp are frozen but still good, breaded to order before being fried. Nice service.

Hampton House

29 E. Main Street, Hampton   (770) 946-3111

Part special-events place and part restaurant, the Hampton House brings better dining to a part of the metro area that's never really had it before. No wine service, because the city is dry, but you can bring your own and pour it yourself (they can't touch it) without paying a corkage fee.

Haru Ichiban

Mall Corners Shopping Center, 3646 Satellite Boulevard, Duluth
    (770) 622-4060

In its short life to date, this splendid outpost of Japanese cooking near Gwinnett Place mall has garnered much respect for its inventive merging of the traditional and the contemporary.

Isabella's Ristorante Italiano

Peachtree Suwanee Crossing Shopping Center,
    360 Peachtree Industrial Boulevard at
    Lawrenceville-Suwanee Road, Suwanee   (770) 614-1672

Open in October 2000, this new venture brings authentic Italian fare to the farthest northern suburbs. Suwanee now savors the same kind of Italian fare that Buckhead enjoys at Antica Posta (see page 100) and Dunwoody at Il Fornaio (see page 202). Butternut squash–filled ravioli with butter and sage, gnocchi al pesto, pappardelle with duck sauce, grilled tuna steak with balsamic reduction sauce, and panna cotta. This is where? Suwanee? Yoooo!!!

Legacy 1931

Brookwood Village, 1931 Peachtree Road, Buckhead
    (404) 355-5993

Replacing Paul Luna's vaunted Luna Sí, Legacy 1931, chef/owner Chuck Morgan serves lunch and dinner. The seasonal contemporary American menu shows influences of Spanish, Italian, and French cooking.

Marisquería 7 Mares

3009 Buford Highway, near N. Druid Hills Road, Atlanta
    (404) 477-0311

Extraordinary quality and freshness mark all the food at this authentic Mexican restaurant. Mariachi music makes dinner conversation a bit strained from time to time, but it's fun and the food is excellent. Check out that freshly made salsa with the bits of fish in it—sort of like a ceviche salsa. A second location is in the works.

McCormick & Schmick's

600 Ashwood Parkway, Dunwoody   (770) 399-9900

Fish, fish, and more fish is delivered twice daily, so often the menu is printed twice daily. Best bets from this Portland, Oregon–based operation are the fresh "finners," simply grilled, and the steamed mussels or clams. One hopes for a better wine list.

Meritage

3125 Piedmont Road, NE, Buckhead   (404) 231-6700

Christian Favalli, son of Sergio and Inge Favalli of La Grotta (see page 207), and Chef Patrick Kelly form the team behind this stylish operation in the former location of Bacchanalia's first home. Dishes feature Asian touches without going overboard, and, of course, Italian nuances flourish. A roasted onion and goat cheese fontina tart with black olive sauce is just one example. The really good wine list needs a boost from a good rosé, but otherwise shows guts and good taste.

Monty's Stone Crab Seafood Restaurant

3400 Wooddale Drive, behind the Swissôtel, Buckhead
  (404) 495-9115

Stone crab claws in three sizes, from large to larger to mega large, are the mainstay of this new Florida-based (of course) operation. Claws may be savored as appetizers or as main dishes with the traditional creamy mustard sauce. The she crab soup is awesome. This restaurant is near Lenox Square.

Noodle

205 E. Ponce de Leon Avenue, Decatur   (404) 378-8622

Lenny, Lina, and Lili Shou, all siblings, are Koreans of Chinese descent. Their second restaurant, Noodle spans the Asian world with Thai, Vietnamese, Japanese, Chinese, and Korean dishes. It's wicked cheap, good dining, and it's a hit with Decaturites.

On Main Restaurant & Bar

968 Main Street, Conyers   (770) 761-1787

In a fine old Victorian residence, June Price and her children, Jennifer and Mark Gallagher, have brought a new dining standard to Conyers, serving such dishes as confit of duck and chicken and dumplings (singularly rich and delectable), and making nearly all their own desserts. There's a surprising, ample wine list with many choices by the glass. Who would have thought they'd ever see Prosecco poured here? But here it is. Lunch, brunch, and dinner are served.

Oscar's

3725 Main Street, College Park   (404) 766-9688

Two former staffers of Mumbo Jumbo (see page 223)—owner/designer Oscar Morales and chef Todd Immel—have renovated a historic space and offer southsiders a taste of fine, casual, contemporary American dining. On their first Friday, they hit 150 covers, and more than 450 people attended the opening. Reservations are already essential for weekends.

Philippe's

10 Kings Circle, NE, Peachtree Hills   (404) 231-4113

Philippe Haddad, a native of Belgium, and Bill Swearingen, his boss at The Abbey, teamed up to do this neighborhood bistro, which has been a hit from the start. Haddad pays homage to his Belgian roots with dishes like beef stew cooked in Flemish dark beer, waterzooi of shellfish, and moules et frites (Belgian-style mussels and french fries). A nice balcony, a good private room for parties, and a friendly bar make this a likely neighborhood winner.

Portofino

3199 Paces Ferry Place, NW, Buckhead   (404) 231-1136

American fare with an Italian accent leads to such dishes as Italian piccoli piatti (tapas), pastas, and a pizza or two. The wine list is heavy on Italian (about a quarter) but also has a good number of Californian, French, Australian, and South American wines. From the folks who own Toulouse (see page 275), the former Asti Trattoria now has an enclosed porch area, up-lit tray ceilings, a separate bar area, and a modern but warm interior.

Puras Tortas

Plaza Mexico shopping center

2078 Beaver Ruin Road, Suite 100, Norcross   (770) 849-9698

Carlos Chávez, who also owns Fonda San Carlos (see page 167), is passionate about authenticity. And that goes for elaborate dishes as well as these simple feasts of layered meats and cheeses on freshly baked bread. They're a staple of Mexico City, where Chávez was born. Fancy grilled chicken with thin onions, a slice of queso fresco and a layer of black refried beans—topped with mole poblano sauce! Food like this could make the word "torta" as widely understood as the word "sandwich."

Ria's Bluebird

421 Memorial Drive at Cherokee Avenue, Grant Park

(404) 521-3737

Ria Pell's stylish diner took shape over seven arduous months, finally opening in October 2000. Breakfast and lunch (until 4 P.M.) are the only services, but they're worth coming out for. Imagine prosciutto and Brie sandwiches with homemade fig jam. Soups are terrific. This is a sure winner.

Roxx Tavern & Diner

1824 Cheshire Bridge Road   (404) 892-4541

How to run a major fast-food joint out of town: This former McDonald's has been completely recast as a casual dining spot that has the neighbors delighted. *Atlanta* magazine called it Best New Patio Action for 2000.

Satay Ria

1861 Peachtree Road, NE, Buckhead   (404) 609-0990

Ethnic diversity in Atlanta restaurants continues to spread in new directions, as Malaysian restaurants develop new locations. This newcomer combines Malaysian and Thai food in a nice environment and offers a decent wine list.

Shingaar Palace

3364 Chamblee-Tucker Road, Chamblee   (770) 458-4466

Northern Indian cuisine served in an elegant surrounding has pushed this newcomer to the top of the charts in its genre. *Atlanta* magazine called it the Best Indian Restaurant 2000.

Spice

793 Juniper Street, at 5th Street, Midtown   (404) 875-4242

After a multi-million dollar renovation—more like a reconstruction— Spice opened to crowds drawn by its sleek contemporary design. The food gambles with oddly crossed ingredients—a pineapple salsa on the Georgia white shrimp turns the shrimp's texture gummy—while other dishes, such as the doughnut dessert with a tiny cup of coffee, are delightful. Time will work out the kinks.

Stetson's Steak House

657 Atlanta Street, Roswell   (770) 552-1776

Steaks are the main draw at this Roswell newcomer housed in a historic building that once contained the Roswell City Jail.

Taqueria del Sol

1200-B Howell Mill Road, NW, West Side   (404) 352-5811

A classy taco joint from the same folks that run Sundown Café, this is the place for a quick, tasty lunch crafted from freshly made ingredients.

Savor fish tacos, rotisserie chicken enchiladas, well-flavored turnip greens, and tangy jalapeño cole slaw.

10th and Myrtle

230 10th Street at Piedmont Avenue, Midtown   (404) 685-9233
From the same folks who brought Atlanta the River Room, Vinings Inn, and Bridges comes this new entry into Midtown's burgeoning dining scene. The stylishly modern interior proudly offers a great view of the Midtown skyline and streetscape. Bars upstairs and down fill with folks looking for a casual spot for drinks and a nibble. Lunch and dinner menus offer completely different dishes, making this almost two restaurants in one.

Terra di Siena

654 Peachtree Street, NE, at Ponce de Leon Avenue, next to the
    Fox Theatre, Midtown (404) 885-7505
A lively young team sets in motion rigorously authentic Tuscan cooking. Filled with unusual Italian wines, the two-story wine tower rises to the occasion. This is the perfect spot for pre-theater dining, where you can savor rabbit-wrapped foie gras on arugula and housemade Tuscan cookies with vin santo for dessert.

Village Tavern

11555 Rainwater Drive at Westside Drive, Alpharetta
    (770) 777-6490
The first venture outside of its home state for this Winston-Salem, North Carolina–based company is a good addition to the suburban dining scene. House-smoked salmon is very good indeed, and fish is fresh and properly cooked. Good wines list, too, with taste-size pours to foster customer curiosity.

Willie Rae's

25 N. Park Square, Marietta   (770) 792-9995
A mélange of Cajun and Mexican dishes shapes a menu that seems unfocused but attracts an enthusiastic audience nonetheless.

CHANGING PLACES

Indigo closed on the last day of the millenium (2001) and became **Star**. Tom Catherall remains as owner. Steaks and barbecue. 1397 N. Highland Avenue, NE, (404) 876-0676.

The Peasant Corporation is breaking up. Selling off **City Grill,** 50 Hurt Plaza, Hurt Building, Downtown, (404) 524-2489, and **Dailey's,** 17 International Boulevard, NE, Downtown, (404) 681-3303, to former company president Karen Bremer. Former corporate stalwarts Maureen Kalmanson and Pamela Furr bought **The Pleasant Peasant,** where the company was founded nearly 30 years ago, 555 Peachtree Street, NE, at Linden Avenue, Midtown (404) 874-3223, and the **Peasant Uptown,** 3500 Peachtree Street, NE, Phipps Plaza, Buckhead (404) 261-6341. **The Public House** in Roswell, 605 Atlanta Street, (770) 992-4646, was sold to Greg Cherry. At the moment, the new owners are just settling in with their new acquisitions and plan to keep a steady course, although Bremer is restoring some of the old popular recipes to Dailey's. But none plans a name change or radical departure from past successful formulae. As we went to press, Kalmanson and Furr purchased the **Midtown Mick's,** bringing their total to three, while Kalmanson with two other partners purchased **Decatur and Bennett Street Mick's.** With these changes, perhaps Mick's will restore food quality to what had become a flagging operation.

Il Localino, a neighborhood trattoria founded at 467 N. Highland Avenue, NE, (404) 222-0650, opened in 1998, then expanded, nearly went bump in the night, and closed. It finally is under new management. One hopes stability finally finds a home here. The place is charming, and with new management has found new vigor and new clientele, but the food just doesn't seem as good. Take charge of your order here: If you want fish, make sure the kitchen knows you want it not overcooked. Don't leave the chef to his/her own devices. Garlic levels can be quite assertive, so take charge of that, too. And ask if there are any unusual wine choices in the house. We were finally offered a Prosecco, an Italian sparkling wine, even though none was indicated on the list.

Just before presstime, Joël Antunes, the famed chef of the **Dining Room at the Ritz-Carlton, Buckhead,** announced his departure to open, as did his predecessor, an eponymous restaurant in Buckhead. To be named **Joël,** the restaurant will open in The Piazza at Paces, a mixed-use development near the intersection of W. Paces Ferry Road and Northside Parkway. Included in the development is a 64-unit luxury condominium, The Borghese, and luxury apartments, providing Antunes with plenty of prospective hungry patrons. From the restaurant's windows, one will enjoy a magnificent garden view. "I want to do a cuisine with a lot of taste, with high-quality ingredients, and also a comfortable cuisine," he says. He likes a simple cuisine, but one that reflects the many places around the world where he's cooked. Moreover, he's striking for reasonable prices, more around $50-60 per person at dinner rather than over $100. The plan is to offer breakfast, lunch, and dinner. The place will have its own bakery to bake its own bread and pastries. Opening is scheduled for August 2001. 3290 Northside Parkway, (404) 233-3500.

Meanwhile, back at the Ritz, plans call for a complete renovation to be finished by summer's end in 2001. A search is on for a top-flight chef to keep the culinary tradition going at the Dining Room. Call (404) 237-2700 for details. The Ritz-Carlton, Buckhead, is located at 3434 Peachtree Road, NE.

The Sandy Springs original location of **La Paz** began to slowly change focus in 2001 to feature homestyle, regional Mexican cooking with the input and consultation of Laura Caraza, a highly regarded culinary and television personality in Mexico. In addition to regional specialties, the regular menu still is available. The remaining locations will continue to operate with the current menu while adding selections from this regional, homestyle Mexican repertoire as it develops to test them out. Sample dishes from the new menu include sopa de camarón (soup of grilled shrimp, squash and tomato); pollo pibil (chicken breast daubed with a Yucatecan seasoning paste), and cocada, a dessert of coconut, cream, and cane sugar. Some thought also is being given to converting this location into a restaurant/nightclub designed to appeal to Latin families. 6410 Roswell Road, Sandy Springs, (404) 256-3555.

Still owned by Boyd Barrow and Fred Lauff, the 12,000-square-foot **Atlanta Beer Garten** closed and was reformatted into three different operations: The patio area became **Clutch Cargo's,** open only in good weather; the front of the interior became **Bayou LaRoux's,** a Cajun operation serving gumbo, po' boy sandwiches, jambalaya, and similar dishes; and the back room is restyled as **Go Lounge** for live music four to five nights a week. The place continues to brew its own beers, producing a specialty brew for each area. 3013 Peachtree Road, NE, at Pharr Road, Buckhead, (404) 261-9898.

Zac's, listed in the last edition, sold its charming site to Renée Moog and René Chandia, who opened **Mosaic,** devoted to Mediterranean and Latin American cuisine (he's from Chile). Sample dishes include mussels whose flavors change every day, the Mosaic Seafood Antipasto (mussels, shrimp, and smoked salmon with a fennel/onion salsa), and paella on Thursdays. The pair inherited Zac's stellar banana pudding; it's still on the menu and remains popular. There's a lovely outdoor patio for fair-weather dining, and good art (for sale) lines the walls. Exhibitions change frequently. Live music and tango are featured on the last Thursday of the month. The far end of the Shops at 308 W. Ponce de Leon Avenue, Decatur, (404) 373-9468.

More Recommendations

♦ Best Bagels

Bagel Palace Deli and Bakery
Toco Hills Shopping Center,
 2869 N. Druid Hills Road   (404) 315-9017

Goldberg's Bagel Company
West Paces Shopping Center, 1272 W. Paces Ferry Road, NW
 at Northside Parkway, Buckhead   (404) 266-0123
Roswell-Wieuca Shopping Center, 4383 Roswell Road, NE   (404)
 256-3751
Georgetown Shopping Center, 4520 Chamblee-Dunwoody Road
 (770) 455-1119
Atlanta magazine Best Bagels 2000; *Atlanta Business Chronicle,*
Best Deli, 2001.

♦ Best Bakeries

Alon's
1394 N. Highland Avenue, NE, Virginia-Highland   (404) 872-6000

Basket Bakery at the Village Corner
6055 James B. Rivers/Memorial Drive, Stone Mountain
 (770) 498-0329
German specialties, breads, and great cookies

The Bread Garden
549 Amsterdam Avenue, NE, Morningside   (404) 875-1166

The Bread Market
1937 Peachtree Road, NE   (404) 352-5252

Break of Day Bakery & Café
Wisdom Pointe Shopping Center, 290 N. GA 74, Peachtree City
 (770) 632-7600

Bruehwiler's Bakery
334 Sandy Springs Circle, NW   (404) 255-8200
Swiss and German-style bakery, with a general European flavor.

Buckhead Bread Company and Corner Café
3070 Piedmont Road, NE, at E. Paces Ferry Road,
   Buckhead   (404) 240-1978

E. 48th Street Italian Market
Williamsburg at Dunwoody Shopping Center,
   2462 Jett Ferry Road, Suite 340,
   at Mt. Vernon Highway, Dunwoody   (770) 392-1499

Flying Biscuit
1655 McLendon Avenue, NE, Candler Park   (404) 678-8888
1001 Piedmont Avenue, Suite 103, at 10th Street,
   Midtown   (404) 874-8887

German Bakery
2914 White Boulevard off Lawrenceville Highway, Decatur
   (404) 296-4336

Hong Kong Bakery
Asian Square, 238 A Buford Highway, Doraville   (770) 452-1338

Joli-Kobe Bakery
The Prado Shopping Center, 5600 Roswell Road, Sandy Springs
   (404) 843-3257

La Piccolina
2834 Franklin Street, Avondale Estates (404) 296-1624

Mondo
750 Huff Road, NW, at Howell Mill Road, West Side
   (404) 603-9995

Royal Caribbean Bakery
4859 Memorial Drive, Stone Mountain   (404) 299-7714

Southern Sweets
186 Rio Circle off E. Ponce de Leon Avenue, Decatur
   (404) 373-8752

Sweet Auburn Bread Company
Sweet Auburn Curb Market, 209 Edgewood Avenue, SE,
   Downtown (404) 525-2248

Theo's Brother's Bakery
12280 Houze Road, Alpharetta   (770) 740-0360

♦ Best Balance among Food, Price, and Setting

BluePointe
The Pinnacle Building, 3455 Peachtree Road, Buckhead
   (404) 237-9070

Canoe
4199 Paces Ferry Road, NW   (770) 432-2663
Located on the banks of the Chattahoochee River.

City Grill
50 Hurt Plaza, Downtown   (404) 524-2489
Posh interior.

Nikolai's Roof
Hilton Atlanta Hotel, 255 Courtland Street, NE,
  and Harris Street, NE   (404) 221-6362
View of skyline.

Ray's on the River
6700 Powers Ferry Road, SE, Marietta   (770) 955-1187
Located on the banks of the Chattahoochee River.

◆ Best Barbecue

ACE Barbecue Barn
30 Bell Street, NE off Auburn Avenue   (404) 659-6630

Anderson's Old-Fashion Bar-B-Q
65 Willis Mill Road, SW   (404) 696-8144
More than 35 years in business. Open late Friday and Saturday.

B.B.Q. Corner
5385-I New Peachtree Road, Chamblee   (770) 451-7277
Asian Square, 5150 Buford Highway   (770) 451-2888
Good Chinese barbecue, including duck and pork; rough English.

Bobby & June's Kountry Kitchen
375 14th Street, Midtown   (404) 876-3872

Corky's
1605 Pleasant Hill Road, Duluth   (770) 564-8666
Only Memphis-style dry-rub ribs recommended.

Daddy D'z
264 Memorial Drive, SE, at Hill Street, Grant Park
  (404) 222-0206
Atlanta magazine, the *New York Times,* and *USA Today* have all
  recognized the barbecue here. Friday and Saturday catch 'cue
  and blues from 9 P.M. to midnight.

Dean's Barbecue
9480 S. Main Street, Jonesboro   (770) 471-0138
More than a half-century of practice and tradition means the pork
  is cooked at least 15 hours before it's on anybody's plate. Done
  the right way, in other words.

Dusty's
1815 Briarcliff Road, NE   (404) 320-6264

Fat Matt's Rib Shack
1811 Piedmont Road, NE near Cheshire Bridge Road
  (404) 607-1622

Recent maddening inconsistencies have one loving the ribs one day
and finding them dry and overcooked them the next, as well as
despising the Brunswick stew one day (tasting horribly of canned
ingredients) and lapping it up the next. Still wildly popular, it's a
music venue as well as a 'cue joint.

Harold's
265 GA 54, Jonesboro   (770) 478-5880
171 McDonough Boulevard, SE   (404) 627-9268
So many folks like this, we've included it, but it's not one of our
favorites. Cornbread and Brunswick stew are worth the trip,
however. Gourmet magazine picked it for best barbecue in 2000.

Jimmy's Smokehouse Bar-B-Q
4420 Centerville Highway, Snellville   (770) 972-1625
Operates out of a pair of trailers, no seating, exquisite smoked pork
shoulder, Friday and Saturday only.

The Rib Ranch
25 Irby Avenue, NW off W. Paces Ferry Road, Buckhead
(404) 233-7644
2063 Canton Highway at Sandy Plains Road, Marietta
(770) 422-5755

Slope's BBQ
34 Crossville Road, Roswell   (770) 518-7000
5865 Gateway Drive, behind the Goodyear Tire Store, Alpharetta
(678) 393-1913
10020 GA 92, Suite 100, near the Ingles Shopping Center at GA 5,
Woodstock   (770) 516-6789
Carolina-style 'cue. Fine Brunswick stew, perhaps the city's best.

Spiced Right
5364 Lawrenceville Highway, Lilburn   (770) 564-0355
A raft of trophies attest to its successes in competition.

Williamson Brothers Bar-B-Q
1425 Roswell Road, Marietta   (770) 971-3201 or (770) 971-7748
1600 Marietta Highway, Canton   (780) 345-9067
A lot of folks' favorite.

◆ Best Bar Food and Appetizers

Andaluz
903 Peachtree Street, NE at 6th Street, Midtown   (404) 875-7013

Café Tu Tu Tango
East Village Square, 220 Pharr Road, NE   (404) 841-6222

Eclipse di Luna
764 Miami Circle, NE off Piedmont Road   (404) 846-0449

Eno
800 Peachtree Street, NW at 5th Street, Midtown   (404) 685-3191
Little plates of tasty delectables make for delightful noshing while
   sipping a fine wine or two.

Fadó
3035 Peachtree Road, NE at Buckhead Avenue   (404) 841-0066

Fandango's
Shoppes of Dunwoody, 5500 Chamblee Dunwoody Road,
   Dunwoody   (770) 671-9758

¡Fuego! Latin Café
Carlisle Commons, 10970-A State Bridge Road Suite 4, Alpharetta
   (770) 753-4477

Fuzzy's Place
2015 N. Druid Hills Road, NE at Buford Highway
   (404) 321-6166

The Grape
Vinings Jubilee Shopping Center, 4300 Paces Ferry Road, Suite 244
   (770) 803-WINE

Loca Luna
114 6th Street, NE, Midtown   (404) 875-4494

Mi Spia
4505 Ashford Dunwoody Road, Park Place across from Perimeter
   Mall, Dunwoody   (770) 393-1333

Manuel's Tavern
602 N. Highland Avenue, NE, Poncey-Highland   (404) 525-3447
Great chicken wings, steak sandwich, beer-steamed hot dogs.

Mumbo Jumbo
89 Park Place, Downtown   (404) 523-0330

The Righteous Room
1051 Ponce de Leon Avenue   (404) 874-0939
Healthy bar food—wouldja believe?

TomTom a Bistro and Sushi Bar
Lenox Square Mall, one level above the Food Court, 3393
   Peachtree Road, NE   (404) 264-1163

Veni Vidi Vici
41 14th Street, NE at Spring Street   (404) 875-8424

Vino!
2900 Peachtree Road, NE   (404) 816-0511

◆ Best Breakfasts and/or Lunches

American Roadhouse
842 N. Highland Avenue, NE   (404) 872-2822

Blue Ribbon Grill
4006 LaVista Road, NE, Northlake   (770) 491-1570

Bobby & June's Kountry Kitchen
375 14th Street, NW   (404) 876-3872

BluePointe
The Pinnacle Building, 3455 Peachtree Road, Buckhead, Atlanta
   (404) 237-9070

Buckhead Bread Company and Corner Cafe
3070 Piedmont Road, NE   (404) 240-1978
A popular breakfast-cum-meeting spot.

The Cafe, Ritz-Carlton, Buckhead
3434 Peachtree Road, NE across from Lenox Mall   (404) 237-2700
Breakfast, lunch, dinner—you name it.

Café Alsace
121 E. Ponce de Leon Avenue, Decatur   (404) 373-5622
Homemade quiche and salad for lunch in the French manner—
   with a glass of wine—make a perfect taste treat.

Canton House
4825 Buford Highway, Chamblee   (770) 936-9030
Dim sum on Saturday and Sunday is a cultural and culinary experience without peer.

Crescent Moon
174 W. Ponce de Leon Avenue, Decatur   (404) 377-5623

East Village Grille
248 Buckhead Avenue, NE   (404) 233-3345
All-day breakfast and late night from 10 P.M.–midnight.

Eclipse di Luna
764 Miami Circle   (404) 846-0449

Einstein's
1077 Juniper Street, NE   (404) 876-7925

Flying Biscuit Café
1655 McLendon Avenue, NE, Candler Park   (404) 687-8888
1001 Piedmont Avenue, Suite 103, at 10th Street, Midtown
   (404) 874-8887

Java Jive Coffee House and Café
790 Ponce de Leon Avenue, NE, Virginia-Highland
   (404) 876-6161
Noble pancakes, especially the pumpkin ones made just a couple of
   times a year.

Liza's Café
2201 American Industrial Way, Chamblee   (770) 452-7001
This charming Victorian house harbors a welcoming respite spot
   for ladies at lunch. It's not the best food on the planet by far, but
   it's respectable and ideal for the lunch bunch.

OK Cafe
1284 W. Paces Ferry Road, NW   (404) 233-2888
Stick to the breakfast stuff and simple fare at lunch. Beware the
   honey-imbued collard greens; they're way off the mark. Only
   Yankees, who don't understand collard greens, like them. *Atlanta*
   magazine dubbed it the Best Breakfast/Power Breakfast 2000.

R. Thomas Deluxe Grill
1812 Peachtree Road, NE at Piedmont Road   (404) 881-0246

Ria's Bluebird
421 Memorial Drive at Cherokee Avenue, Grant Park
   (404) 521-3737
Breakfast and lunch are the only meals served. Lovely work in a
   very unexpected place.

Royal China
3295 Chamblee-Dunwoody Road, Chamblee   (770) 216-9933
Dim sum, especially on Sunday.

Roy's Classic Diner
6000 Buford Highway, Norcross   (770) 242-7211

Silver Skillet
200 14th Street, NE   (404) 874-1388
Country-style breakfast.

Taqueria del Sol
1200-B Howell Mill Road, NW, West Side   (404) 352-5811
Atlanta magazine called it Best New Hang-Out for the Margarita
   and Taco Crowd 2000. Wicked good, wicked cheap lunches draw
   crowds.

Thumbs Up Diner
573 Edgewood Avenue, SE, Old Fourth Ward   (404) 223-0690
Atlanta magazine's Best Comeback 2000. The old favorite resur-
   faced and relocated itself in a funky intown neighborhood.

White House
3172 Peachtree Street   (404) 237-7601

◆ Best Brew Pubs

Buckhead Brewery
1757 Rock Quarry Road, Stockbridge   (770) 389-8112
872 Buford Highway, GA 400 (Exit 14), Cumming
   (770) 887-6070

Five Seasons Brewing Company
The Prado, 5600 Roswell Road, Suite 21   (404) 255-5911

John Harvard's Brew House
3045 Peachtree Road, NE at Buckhead Avenue   (404) 816-BREW
1456 Holcomb Bridge Road, Roswell   (770) 645-BREW

Max Lager's
320 Peachtree Street, Downtown   (404) 525-4400

Rock Bottom Brewery
3242 Peachtree Street, NW, Buckhead   (404) 264-0253

U.S. Border Brewery and Cantina
12460 Crabapple Road, Suite 106, Alpharetta   (770) 772-4400

◆ Best Burgers

Blue Ribbon Grill
4006 LaVista Road, NE, Northlake   (770) 491-1570

Carey's Place
1021 Cobb Parkway, SE, Marietta   (770) 422-8042

The Downwind Restaurant & Lounge
DeKalb Peachtree Airport, Clairmont Road, Chamblee
    (770) 452-0973
The mushrooms burger—a huge two-hander stuffed with sautéed
    mushrooms—is awesome.

The Earl
East Atlanta Village, 488 Flat Shoals Avenue   (404) 522-3950
A music venue with a classy burger.

The Vortex Bar & Grill
878 W. Peachtree Street, Midtown   (404) 875-1667
438 Moreland Avenue, NE, Little Five Points   (404) 688-1828
Veggie burgers are also available.

Fuddruckers
Ten metro Atlanta locations; check the phone book for the nearest
    location.

Johnny Rockets
5 W. Paces Ferry Road, NW   (404) 231-5555
Several other locations; check the phone book for the nearest
    location.

R. Thomas Deluxe Grill
1287 Peachtree Road, NE, at Piedmont Road   (404) 881-0246

Roxx Tavern & Diner
1824 Cheshire Bridge Road   (404) 892-4541

Watershed
406 W. Ponce de Leon Avenue, Decatur   (404) 378-4900

◆ Best Coffees and Desserts

Aurora Coffee
992 N. Highland Avenue   (404) 607-1300
468 Moreland Avenue, NE, Little Five Points   (404) 523-6856
1572 Piedmont Road, NE at Monroe Drive, Morningside
    (404) 607-9994
Atlanta magazine called it Best Espresso Bar/Best Coffee 2000.

Cafe Intermezzo
Park Place, 4505 Ashford Dunwoody Road, NE, Dunwoody   (770)
    396-1344
1845 Peachtree Road, NE   (404) 355-0411

Caribou Coffee
Numerous locations are found throughout the metro area; check
    the phone book for the nearest location.

Coffee Plantation Toco Hill
2205-F LaVista Road, NE   (404) 636-1038

Continental Park Café
941 Main Street, Stone Mountain   (770) 413-6448

E. 48th Street Italian Market
2462 Jett Ferry Road, Suite 340, Dunwoody   (770) 392-1499

Harvest Moon
Centennial Village Plaza, 2300 Holcomb Bridge Road, Suite 410,
    Roswell   (770) 641-9607

Jake's
676 Highland Avenue, NE, Old Fourth Ward   (404) 523-1830
This total coffee experience begins with ice cream. Get your favorite
    house-made flavors here (make mine ginger). Relax in the upstairs
    living room–style space or out on the deck with a magnificent
    view of the downtown skyline. Espresso, cappuccino, latte—and
    the "world-famous" J. D. Rothschild Gourmet Hot Chocolate are
    good go-withs. Good lunch spot and a gourmet market.

Java Monkey
205 E. Ponce de Leon Avenue, Decatur   (404) 378-5002

Joe Muggs
3275 Peachtree Road, NE at Piedmont Road, Buckhead
    (404) 364-9290
More than a coffeehouse, it's also a newsstand and bookstore. Read,
    relax, and taste some of the good things to eat. Baked goods are
    not made on site, but they're yummy.

Liza's Café
2201 American Industrial Way, Chamblee   (770) 452-7001
A wealth of quite delectable pastries and good espresso make this a
   fine stop-in for a treat.

Michael's Coffees
2899-F DeKalb Industrial Way, Decatur   (404) 294-1111
Michael Harris will custom-roast coffees while you wait.

Mondo Baking
750 Huff Road, NW, West Side   (404) 603-9995

Sacred Grounds
510 Flat Shoals Avenue, East Atlanta Village   (404) 223-0089
123-B Luckie Street, NW, between Cone and Spring streets,
   Fairlie-Poplar, Downtown (404) 588-0666
The company's wholesale bakery, Cake Walk (next door), does all
   the pastries for this operation.

San Francisco Coffee Roasting Company
1192 N. Highland Avenue, NE, Virginia-Highland   (404) 876-8816

Starbuck's
The national coffee chain arrived with a bang, and opened locations all over the place. Some locations (such as Peachtree Battle)
   have sofas and comfy chairs in which to relax.

Virginia's
112 Krog Street, Inman Park   (404) 827-9005
Not just a coffee-and-dessert place; this is also a restaurant.

◆ Best Delis

Bruehwiler's Bakery
334 Sandy Springs Circle, NW   (404) 255-8200
German delicatessen items.

E. 48th Street Italian Market
2462 Jett Ferry Road, Dunwoody   (770) 392-1499

Quality Kosher Emporium
2153 Briarcliff Road, NE   (404) 636-1114
Hammond Square Shopping Center, 5942 Roswell Road,
   Sandy Springs   (404) 705-8643
This strictly kosher deli closes at 3 P.M. on Fridays.

Salumeria Taggiasca
Sweet Auburn Curb Market, 209 Edgewood Avenue, Downtown
   (404) 524-0006

Sausage World and Deli
5363 Lawrenceville Highway, Lilburn   (770) 925-4493

This is a place to shop and take home uniquely flavored sausages to cook and enjoy, not a place to dine. Call ahead to make sure somebody's available.

St. Charles Deli
2470 Briarcliff Road, NE, Loehman's Plaza   (404) 636-5201

◆ Best Ethnic Dining

Indian
Aangan
763-C DeKalb Industrial Way, Decatur   (404) 294-8989

Brazilian
Fogo di Chão
3101 Piedmont Road, Buckhead (404) 995-9982

Vietnamese
Biên Thùy
Northwoods Plaza, 5095 F Buford Highway
  at Shallowford Road, Doraville   (770) 454-9046

Chinese—dim sum
Canton House
4825 Buford Highway, Chamblee   (770) 936-9030

Mexican
Fonda San Carlos
Maxim Shopping Center, 2077 Beaver Ruin Road, Suite 170,
  Norcross   (770) 797-2828

Korean
Hae Woon Dae
Treasure Village Shopping Center, 5805 Buford Highway, Suite 5,
  Doraville   (770) 451-7957

Jamaican
Kool Runnings
4977 Memorial Drive, Stone Mountain   (404) 508-0277

Peruvian
Macchu Picchi
Northeast Plaza Shopping Center, 3375 Buford Highway
  (404) 320-3226

Chinese—Szechuan
Little Szechuan
5091-C Buford Highway, at Shallowford Road,
  Northwoods Plaza   (770) 451-0192

Persian

Mirage
Abernathy Square Shopping Center, 6631C Roswell Road,
  at Abernathy Drive, Sandy Springs   (404) 843-8300

Ethiopian

Queen of Sheba
1594 Woodcliff Drive, Suite G   (404) 321-1493

Dominican

Santo Domingo
5310 Buford Highway   (770) 452-3939

◆ Best Fish and Seafood

Atlanta Fish Market
265 Pharr Road, NE near Peachtree Road   (404) 262-3165

Blue Ridge Grill
1261 W. Paces Ferry Road, NW at Northside Parkway,
  Buckhead   (404) 233-5030
Horseradish-crusted grouper and trout with bacon-cabbage hash.

Brasserie Le Coze
Lenox Square Mall, 3393 Peachtree Road, NE
  ground level next to Neiman Marcus   (404) 266-1440
Skate wing in browned butter, mussels—glorious. You get a fish
  knife and a sauce spoon to savor every drop.

Coast 92
Roswell Crossing Shopping Center, 625 Crossville Road
  Roswell   (770) 649-6739

Embers Seafood Grill
234 Hildebrand Drive, NW near Roswell Road, Sandy Springs
  (404) 256-0977

Goldfish
Perimeter Mall, 4400 Ashford Dunwoody Road, Dunwoody
  (770) 671-0100

Gulf Coast Grill
Medlock Plaza, 9700 Medlock Bridge Road, Duluth
  (678) 474-9244

Marra's Grill: Fresh Seafood and Great Steaks
1782 Cheshire Bridge Road, NE   (404) 874-7347 or
  (404) 874-7363

McCormick & Schmick's Seafood Restaurant
600 Ashwood Parkway off Ashford Dunwoody Road, Dunwoody
  (770) 399-9900

A newcomer from the West Coast brings a Pacific Northwest
   approach to seafood and fish.

McKinnon's Louisiane
3209 Maple Drive, NE   (404) 237-1313

Mumbo Jumbo
89 Park Place near Woodruff Park   (404) 523-0330

Oyster King
3003 Cobb Parkway, Kennesaw   (404) 974-8361

Pricci
500 Pharr Road, NW at Maple Drive   (404) 237-2941
Sea bass and vegetables in parchment.

South City Kitchen
1144 Crescent Avenue, Midtown   (404) 873-7358
Crab hash, shrimp, and scallops over stone-ground grits with garlic
   gravy. Catfish Reuben.

Stringer's Fish Camp
3384 Shallowford Road, NE near Buford Highway
   (770) 458-7145
Old-fashioned, Southern-style fried seafood, but they can grill, too.

◆ Best Game

Abruzzi
Peachtree Battle Shopping Center, 2355 Peachtree Road, NE,
   Buckhead   (404) 231-6700
All kinds, depending on the market: venison and quail regularly,
   sometimes boar.

Bacchanalia
1198 Howell Mill Road, NW, West Side   (404) 365-0410
Squab.

The Cabin
2678 Buford Highway, NE   (404) 315-7676
Venison, buffalo, elk, etc.

dick and harry's
Holcomb Woods Village Shopping Center, 1570 Holcomb Bridge
   Road, Roswell   (770) 641-8757
A wide variety, including emu and occasionally wild boar.

The Food Studio
King Plow Arts Center, 887 W. Marietta Street, Studio K-102
   (404) 815-6677
Venison.

SoHo
Vinings Jubilee Shopping Center, 4200 Paces Ferry Road, NW
(770) 801-0069
Elk.

South City Kitchen
1144 Crescent Avenue, Midtown   (404) 873-7358
Quail.

◆ Best Getaway Dining

Breezes
9000 Holiday Road, Lake Lanier Islands   (770) 945-8921
Make it a weekend and stay in one of the rooms with private
enclosed hot tubs. There also is a new steakhouse called Fairways,
where one may enjoy lunch or dinner after a round of golf.

Barnsley Gardens, Woodlands Grill and Rice House
597 Barnsley Gardens Road, Adairsville   (770) 773-7480
Fine dining in one of the state's most attractive and unusual resorts.
Barnsley Gardens is a 19th-century antebellum estate lovingly
preserved by Prince Hubertus Fugger and his photographer wife,
Alexandra. Lodgings are in cottages designed in the manner of
Andrew Jackson Downing, whose ideas also influenced the land-
scaping and village-like feel. There are two good restaurants and a
beer garden.

Bernie's at Nacochee Valley Guesthouse
229 GA 16, Sautee, outside of Helen   (706) 878-3830
Dinner only Thursday—Monday. Bring your own wine; they've got
the glasses. No credit cards, but personal checks accepted. Wonderful food from the hands of a Culinary Institute of America
graduate.

Callaway Gardens
US 27, Pine Mountain, I-85 south to I-185, Exit 42, (800) 225-5292
The recent acquisition of a bevy of French chefs has drastically raised
the quality of the food at this rural resort just a short drive (one
hour) south of Atlanta. Imagine riding a bicycle along paths that
glide through azalea gardens, then sitting down in the Georgia
Room to feast on foie gras and duck, with muscadine ice cream
for dessert. Not bad. Other restaurants feature more casual fare.

Countryside Café
3909 Steve Tate Highway, Marble Hill   (770) 893-3389
John and Cindy Lupi's lovely country-style restaurant is a mecca for
folks enjoying the mountains. The menu changes frequently, and
there's a good wine list, but you may bring your own and pay a
very fair $10 corkage fee.

Glen-Ella Springs Inn

1789 Bear Gap Road, Clarkesville   (706) 754-7295 or
 (888) 455-8786

Award-winning renovation and destination with 16 rustic contemporary accommodations. Terrific food. Bring your own wine
 (corkage $2) as this is a dry county.

Le Lavandier

Forester's Square, 2616 Riverside Drive, Macon (I-75, Exit 167,
 Pierce Avenue)   (912) 738-9919

Some of the best French food in the state. Period. Good wine list.
 Nice surroundings and excellent service.

Nacoochee Grill

7277 S. Main Street, Helen   (706) 878-8020

Built in the style of a north Georgia mountain homestead, this new
 restaurant is on the grounds of Habersham Winery. Bring your
 own wine until the owners get the wine service issue worked out
 with local authorities. Venison chili stew, chicken pot pie, and
 cornmeal-dusted trout are hits. Love that masa corn hash, too.

Renée's Café

136 N. Chestatee Street, NW, Dahlonega   (706) 864-6829

A restored 19th-century residence is home to this popular
 dining spot that attracts Atlantans looking for a day's escape.
 A terrific wine bar upstairs is the scene of frequent wine-
 tasting events.

Woodbridge Inn Restaurant & Lodge

411 Chambers Street, Jasper   (706) 692-6293

A rustic setting in a historic, restored, pre–Civil War hotel sets the
 stage for simple fare, a decent, if short, wine list, and a magnificent view of the mountains. Duck á l'orange, good steaks, oysters, specials. Very popular, so make reservations.

◆ Best Healthy Dining

The Cafe, Ritz-Carlton, Buckhead

3434 Peachtree Road, NE   (404) 237-2700

In addition to "Cuisine Vitale" dishes, this restaurant also offers
 macrobiotic fare. While these dishes are no longer listed on the
 menus, they may be requested.

Marra's Grill: Fresh Seafood & Great Steaks

1782 Cheshire Bridge Road, NE   (404) 874-7347 or
 (404) 874-7363

Chef Dan Noble's "Trim Cuisine" features fresh grilled fish, stir-
 fried vegetables, and rice.

Pricci

500 Pharr Road, at Maple Drive, Buckhead (404) 237-2941
Healthy dining with a Tuscan flavor. Sea bass and vegetables
   in parchment paper makes the word "diet" float away on
   the wind.

The Spa at Chateau Elan

Haven Harbour Drive, Braselton (770) 271-6064

◆ Best Markets

Buford Highway Farmer's Market

5600 Buford Highway, Doraville (770) 455-0770
Carter Crossing, 6355 Jimmy Carter Boulevard, at Buford Highway,
   Norcross (770) 449-6262
Moved, expanded, enhanced, and wonderful—Asian and Hispanic
   products all in one spot.

E. 48th Street Italian Market

Williamsburg at Dunwoody Shopping Center,
   2462 Jett Ferry Road at Mt. Vernon Road, Dunwoody
   (770) 392-1499

Eatzi's Market and Bakery

3221 Peachtree Road, NE, Buckhead (404) 237-2266

Fresh Market

Old Alabama Square, 3005 Old Alabama Road, Alpharetta
   (770) 664-5350

Harris Teeter

Brookhaven Plaza, 3954 Peachtree Road, NE (404) 814-5990
Mt. Vernon Centre, 2480 Mt. Vernon Road, Dunwoody
   (770) 551-0990
Sage Hill Shopping Center, 1799 Briarcliff Road, NE
   (404) 607-1189
Rivermont Station Shopping Center, 8465 Holcomb Bridge Road,
   Roswell (770) 650-1000
Upscale gourmet grocery store with in-store casual dining. Briar-
   cliff Road location has a rabinically supervised kosher section.
   Since the 1997 edition, many more have opened, and more are
   nearing completion. Check the phone book for additional loca-
   tions. This is now just a sample.

Harry's Farmers Market

2025 Satellite Point, Duluth (770) 416-6900
1180 Upper Hembree Road, Alpharetta (770) 664-6300
70 Powers Ferry Road, Marietta (770) 578-4400
Fresh produce, seafood, meat, poultry, prepared dishes, bakery, wine.

International Farmers Market
5193 Peachtree Industrial Boulevard, Chamblee   (770) 455-1777
Fresh produce and grocery goods.

99 Ranch Market
Asian Square, 5150 Buford Highway, NE, Doraville
 (770) 458-8899
Asian foods.

Quality Kosher Emporium
2153 Briarcliff Road, NE   (404) 636-1114
Hammond Square, 5942 Roswell Road, Sandy Springs
 (404) 705-8643
This strictly kosher deli closes at 3 P.M. on Fridays.

Shield's Market
1554 N. Decatur Road, Emory Village   (404) 377-0204
The city's best beef, chicken, and ham.

Star Provisions
1198 Howell Mill Road, NW, West Side   (404) 365-0410
Get what you need to cook at home—foie gras, gray salt, Kobe
 steaks, exquisite cheeses—from the foks who gave us Bacchanalia.

Sweet Auburn Curb Market
209 Edgewood Avenue, NE, Downtown   (404) 659-1665
Individually owned stalls; produce and pork.

Taj Mahal Imports
1594 Woodcliff Drive, NE   (404) 321-5940
Indian food.

Whole Foods
2111 Briarcliff Road, NE at LaVista Road   (404) 634-7800
Hammond Square Shopping Center, 5930 Roswell Road
 at Hammond Drive, Sandy Springs   (404) 236-0810

Your DeKalb Farmers Market
3000 E. Ponce de Leon Avenue, Decatur   (404) 377-6400
Produce, meats, fish, ethnic exotica.

◆ Best Pizza

California Pizza Kitchen
Lenox Square, 3393 Peachtree Road, NE   (404) 262-9221
6301 Nort Point Parkway, Alpharetta   (770) 664-8246
4600 Ashford-Dunwoody Road, Dunwoody
 (just north of I-285)   (770) 393-0390
Crossover and fusion pizza, such as barbecue and Thai flavors, plus
 classic treatments.

Camelli's Gourmet Pizza Joint
699 Ponce de Leon Avenue, NE, Virginia-Highland.
 (404) 249-9020

Everybody's Famous Pizza
1040 N. Highland Avenue, NE   (404) 873-4545
1593 N. Decatur Road, NE   (404) 377-7766
The thin pizza crisps are especially good.

Fellini's Pizza
Multiple locations; check the phone book for the nearest location.

Fritti
311 N. Highlands Avenue, NE, Inman Park   (404) 523-6678
Perhaps the city's most authentic—and best.

Ferrera's Bistro
635 Atlanta Street, Roswell   (770) 640-5345
Pizza dough comes directly from New York. "It's the water," says
 owner Michael Petrucci. Whatever, it's terrific.

Franco's Pizza and Delicatessen
1740 Cheshire Bridge Road, NE   (404) 873-1577

Grant Central Pizza & Pasta
451 Cherokee Avenue, SE, Grant Park   (404) 523-8900

Grant Central Pizza East
1279 Glenwood Avenue, SE, East Atlanta Village   (404) 627-0007

Mellow Mushroom
This Atlanta-based chain does an excellent job at more locations
 around the city than sand on the beach.

Mo's Pizza
3109 Briarcliff Road, NE at Clairmont Road   (404) 320-1258
Classic New York pizza pie—no designer stuff.

Partners II
215 Northlake Drive, Peachtree City   (770) 487-9393
Southsiders choice for pizza.

Pasta Vino
Peachtree Battle Shopping Center, 2391 Peachtree Road, NE
 (404) 231-4946
Grand Pavillion Shopping Center, 11130 State Bridge Road,
 Suite F-103 at Kimbell Bridge Road   (770) 777-1213

Rocky's Brick Oven
1770 Peachtree Street, NW   (404) 876-1111
1394-D N. Highland Avenue, Virginia-Highland   (404) 870-7625

Savage Pizza
484 Moreland Avenue, NE, Little Five Points   (404) 523-0500
Imagine chicken cordon bleu pizza. Then taste it.

◆ Best Restaurants to Take Adolescents

The Café, the Ritz-Carlton Hotel, Buckhead
3434 Peachtree Road, NE across from Lenox Mall
　(404) 237-2700

California Pizza Kitchen
Lenox Square, 3393 Peachtree Road, NE　(404) 262-9221
4600 Ashford-Dunwoody Road, just north of I-285,
　Dunwoody　(770) 393-0390
6301 North Point Parkway　(770) 664-8246

Camille's
1186 N. Highland Avenue, Virginia-Highland　(404) 872-7203

Fuddruckers
Multiple locations; check the phone book for the nearest location.

Romano's Macaroni Grill
4788 Ashford-Dunwoody Road, just outside I-285, Dunwoody
　(770) 394-6676
770 Holcomb Bridge Road, just east of GA 400, Roswell
　(770) 993-7115
1565 Pleasant Hill Road, near Gwinnett Place Mall, Duluth
　(770) 564-0094

◆ Best Saturday Lunches

Aangan
763-C DeKalb Industrial Way, Decatur　(404) 294-8989

Anis Café & Bistro
2974 Grandview Avenue, NE, Buckhead　(404) 233-9889

Basil's Mediterranean Cafe
2985 Grandview Avenue, NE, Buckhead　(404) 233-9755

Biên Thùy
Northwoods Plaza, 5095 F Buford Highway, NE,
　at Shallowford Road, Doraville　(770) 454-9046

Brasserie Le Coze
Lenox Square, 3393 Peachtree Road, NE, ground level next to
　Neiman Marcus　(404) 266-1440

The Bread Market
Brookwood Village, 1937 Peachtree Road, NE　(404) 352-5252
Offers prepared foods.

Buckhead Bread Company and Corner Cafe
3070 Piedmont Road, NE　(404) 240-1978

Buckhead Diner
3073 Piedmont Road, NE   (404) 262-3336

Café Sunflower
Brookwood Square Shopping Center, 2410 Peachtree Road, NE
   (404) 352-8859
5975 Roswell Road, NE, at Hammond Drive, Hammond Springs
   (404) 256-1675
Vegetarian.

Canton House
4825 Buford Highway, Chamblee   (770) 936-9030

The Colonnade Restaurant
1879 Cheshire Bridge Road, NE, near Piedmont Road
   (404) 874-5642

Garrison's Broiler & Tap
Vinings Jubilee Shopping Center, 4300 Paces Ferry Road, NW,
   Vinings   (770) 436-0102
Medlock Crossing Shopping Center, 9700 Medlock Bridge Road,
   Duluth   (770) 476-1962
The Duluth location also does Saturday brunch.

Grazie: A Bistro
West Marietta Crossing Shopping Center, 1000 Whitlock Avenue, at
   Burnt Hickory Road, Marietta   (770) 499-8585

Haveli Indian Restaurant
490 Franklin Road, Marietta   (770) 955-4525
Gift Mart Building, 225 Spring Street, NW   (404) 522-4545

Houston's
3321 Lenox Road, NE across from Lenox Square   (404) 237-7534
Brookwood Square, 2166 Peachtree Road, NW
   at Colonial Homes Drive   (404) 351-2442
3050 Windy Hill Road, SE, Wildwood, Marietta   (770) 563-1180
3539 Northside Parkway at W. Paces Ferry Road, Buckhead
   (404) 262 7130
4701 Ashford Dunwoody Road, Dunwoody   (770) 512-7066

On Main Restaurant & Bar
968 Main Street, NE, Conyers   (770) 761-1787

Peasant Uptown
Phipps Plaza, 3500 Peachtree Street, NE, Buckhead
   (404) 261-6341

Prime
Lenox Square, 3393 Peachtree Road, NE, Buckhead
   (404) 812-0555

South City Kitchen
1144 Crescent Avenue, Midtown   (404) 873-7358

Surin of Thailand
810 N. Highland Avenue, NE   (404) 892-7789

TomTom a Bistro and Sushi Bar
Lenox Square Mall, 3393 Peachtree Road, NE,
  one level above the Food Court   (404) 264-1163

Van Gogh's
Crabapple Square Shopping Center, 70 W. Crossville Road, Roswell
(770) 993-1156

◆ Best Sunday Brunches

Babette's Cafe
573 N. Highland Avenue, NE, Poncey-Highland   (404) 523-9121

Blue Ribbon Grill
4006 LaVista Road, NE, Northlake, Atlanta   (770) 491-1570

Café Alsace
121 E. Ponce de Leon Avenue, Decatur   (404) 373-5622

The Cafe, Ritz-Carlton, Buckhead
3434 Peachtree Road, NE across from Lenox Square
  (404) 237-2700

Einstein's
1077 Juniper Street, NE   (404) 876-7925

Fadó
3035 Peachtree Road, NE   (404) 841-0066

Flying Biscuit Cafe
1655 McLendon Avenue, NE   (404) 687-8888
1001 Piedmont Avenue, Suite 103, Midtown   (404) 874-8887
Long, long waits for brunch.

Frontera Mex-Mex Grill
4606 Jimmy Carter Boulevard, Norcross   (770) 493-8341
This is the only location that does Mexican breakfast on Sunday,
  complete with very good menudo.

Heaping Bowl & Brew
469 Flat Shoals Avenue, SE, East Atlanta Village   (404) 523-8030
Brunch is offered both Saturday and Sunday and features some
  solid, unusual dishes, such as Polish eggs Benedict on pierogis.

Murphy's
997 Virginia Avenue, NE, Virginia-Highland   (404) 872-0904

Park 75 Restaurant, the Four Seasons Hotel
75 14th Street, NE   (404) 881-9898
Classy, American-style dim sum for Sunday brunch is a unique
  experience.

South City Kitchen
1144 Crescent Avenue, Midtown   (404) 873-7358

Zócalo
187 10th Street, NE, at Piedmont Avenue, Midtown
    (404) 249-7576

◆ Best Sushi Bars

Asiana Garden
Asian Square Shopping Center, 5150 Buford Highway, NE,
    Doraville   (770) 452-1677 or (770) 452-0012
Stunning eel makes a visit worthwhile.

BluePointe
The Pinnacle Building, 3455 Peachtree Road, Buckhead
    (404) 237-9070

Hanwoori
4251 N. Peachtree Road, Chamblee   (770) 458-9191
Exceptional quality and warm, friendly service.

Haru Ichiban
Mall Corners Shopping Center, 3646 Satellite Boulevard, Duluth
    (770) 622-4060.
Classy sushi makes its presence felt in Gwinnett County. Other
    dishes are clever East-meets–West dishes as well as conventional
    (but well prepared). Already recognized by *Atlanta* magazine as
    Best New Japanese 2000, and Atlanta Journal & Constitution
    reviewed 3 stars in 2000.

Misono Japanese Seafood Steakhouse
Terrace Village Shopping Center, 2500 Old Alabama Road,
    Roswell   (770) 993-3037 or (770) 993-3056
Good sushi and good grill, with fair to slow service.

Prime
Lenox Square Mall, upper level, 3393 Peachtree Road, NE
    (404) 812-0555
Start with sushi and finish with steak—the best of both worlds.
    With this restaurant, owner Tom Catherall launched sushi in all
    his restaurants (except Noche).

Ru San's
Tower Place, 3365 Piedmont Road, NE   (404) 239-9557
Clear Creek Shopping Center, 1529 Piedmont Road,
    Morningside/Ansley Park   (404) 875-7042
Windy Hill Crossing, 2313 Windy Hill Road, Marietta
    (770) 933-8315
California meets Japan, and the result is a wild assortment of crazy
    sushi, various rolls of myriad flavors.

Sa Tsu Ki
3043 Buford Highway, NE   (404) 325-5285
Probably the best service in a sushi bar, with the best quality as
    well.

Soto Japanese Restaurant
Piedmont/Peachtree Crossing Shopping Center
    3330 Piedmont Road, NE, Buckhead   (404) 233-2005
Stellar sushi and other dishes top drawer.

Sushi Avenue
308 W. Ponce de Leon Avenue, Decatur   (404) 378-8448
Decatur's entry into the sushi life is excellent.

◆ Best Vegetarian

Broadway Café
2166 Briarcliff Road, NE   (404) 329-0888
Kosher (and rabbinically supervised), meatless, gourmet dishes with a
    good wine list, including kosher wine. Fish dishes were recently
    added. Closed after 3 P.M. Fridays and closed on Saturdays.

The Café, the Ritz-Carlton, Buckhead
3434 Peachtree Road, NE   (404) 237-2700
Vegetarian and macrobiotic are available by special request, meaning
    vegetarians can actually enjoy nice circumstances and fine china
    while dining. How novel!

Café Sunflower
Brookwood Square, 2410 Peachtree Road, NW   (404) 352-8859
Hammond Springs Shopping Center, 5975 Roswell Road
    at Hammond Drive   (404) 256-1675

Harmony Vegetarian Restaurant
Orient Center, 4897 Buford Highway, NE
    at Chamblee-Tucker Road, Chamblee   (770) 457-7288
This Chinese restaurant is vegetarian.

R. Thomas Deluxe Grill
1287 Peachtree Road, NE   (404) 872-2942
Macrobiotic dishes available.

Rainbow Restaurant
North Decatur Plaza, 2118 N. Decatur Road
    at Clairmont Road, Decatur   (404) 636-5553
Sandwiches, soups, salads, and daily specials.

Soul Vegetarian
879 Ralph D. Abernathy Boulevard, SW, West End
    (404) 752-5194
652 N. Highland Avenue, NE, Poncey-Highland   (404) 875-4641

Sweet Tomatoes

6350 Peachtree Dunwoody Road, NE at Crestline Parkway,
  Dunwoody   (770) 913-0203
1125 Ernest Barrett Parkway, NW, near Town Center Mall,
  Kennesaw   (770) 429-5522
3505 Mall Boulevard, just outside Gwinnett Place Mall,
  Duluth   (770) 418-1148;
950 North Point Drive, near North Point Mall in front of Staples,
  Alpharetta   (770) 777-9500
This San Diego–based outfit does vegetarian and nonvegetarian
  food. Buffet service provides a salad bar, pasta bar, fresh fruit,
  baked potato bar, and soup bar, dishing up vegetarian and nonvegetarian dishes. House-made dressings. Vegetarian items are
  labeled.

Udipi Café

1850 Lawrenceville Highway, Decatur   (404) 325-1933.
Named for a city on the South Indian coast, Udipi features South
  Indian vegetarian specialties. The pappadams are the crispest and
  lightest anywhere. Everything is made on the premises, including
  the mango chutney.

Wall Street Pizza

Loehman's Plaza, 2470 Briarcliff Road, NE, at N. Druid Hills Road
  (404) 633-2111
Rabbincally supervised kosher pizza is vegetarian, made with soy
  "beef," soy-based sausage, and soy cheese. It's good! Also other
  similarly contrived Mediterranean/Italian dishes and good salads.

◆ Best View with Breakfast

Einstein's

1077 Juniper Street, NE, Midtown   (404) 876-7925
Brunch (Saturday and Sunday) on the porch with a view of the
  Midtown skyline; this also is a great people-watching spot. Sit on
  the porch balcony to evade the marauding, scavenging pigeons
  that other guests like to feed.

Ruth's Chris Steakhouse, Embassy Suites Hotel

Embassy Suites Hotel, 267 Marietta Street, NE, Downtown
  (404) 223-6500
Sweeping windows let the eye gather in a great view of Atlanta's
  skyline from Midtown to Downtown, plus Atlanta's Centennial
  Olympic Park in the foreground. Breakfast buffet is a great value.
  If conventions are in town during weekdays, breakfast buffet lines
  can be long.

◆ Best View with Lunch

Canoe
4199 Paces Ferry Road, NW   (770) 432-2663
Nice location on the banks of the Chattahoochee River.

◆ Best View with Dinner

Nikolai's Roof
Hilton Atlanta Hotel, 255 Courtland Street, NE and
   Harris Street, NE   (404) 221-6362
Downtown city skyline view.

◆ Best View with a Drink

Sun Dial Restaurant and Lounge
Westin Peachtree Plaza Hotel, 210 Peachtree Street, NE, Downtown
   (404) 589-7506
There is a rotating view of the downtown skyline from Sun Dial's
   lounge.

◆ Best Wicked Cheap and Bountiful

Aangan
763-C DeKalb Industrial Way, Decatur   (404) 294-8989
The delicious lunchtime buffet goes for a mere $6.95 weekdays and
   $7.95 weekends (when seafood is added to the line-up).

Bajaritos
Cherokee Plaza, 3877 Peachtree Road, NE, Brookhaven
   (404) 239-WRAP
Wraps with class.

Doc Chey's Noodle House
Emory Village, 1556 N. Decatur Road, (404) 378-8188
1424 N. Highland Avenue at Lanier Boulevard, Virginia-Highland
   (404) 888-0777.
Heaping, steaming bowls of noodles with tasty toppings.

Evans Fine Foods
2125 N. Decatur Road, Decatur   (404) 634-6294
Huge piles of excellent chicken livers, country-fried steak, vegetables,
   and cornbread. Cost is about $5 for a meat and two vegetables.

Heaping Bowl & Brew
469 Flat Shoals Avenue, East Atlanta Village (404) 523-8030
Heaping bowls—literally—of delectable pasta dishes with sundry
 savory toppings are easily shared.

Kool Korners Grocery
349 14th Street, NW, near Georgia Tech (404) 892-4424
The city's best Cuban sandwiches ($4.16–$4.55) are more than most
 of us can eat at a single sitting.

Let's Eat Café
1780 Glendale Road, Scottdale (Decatur area) (404) 297-9316
Breakfast, lunch, and dinner served in a clean but bare-bones
 atmosphere from the hands of some really friendly folks.

Mr. Delicious
1524 B Church Street, Decatur (404) 370-0031
4351 Hugh Howell Road, Tucker (770) 939-8080

Noodle
205 E. Ponce de Leon Avenue, Decatur (404) 378-8622

Piccadilly Classic American Cooking
Suburban Plaza, 2595 N. Decatur Road, at Church Street, Decatur
 (404) 373-3931
21 South DeKalb Mall, Decatur (404) 243-1191 or
 (404) 243-8053 (take-out)
This Louisiana-based operation features a long cafeteria-style line
 with traditional Southern favorites that draw the after-church
 crowd on Sundays. In the metro Atlanta area, there nearly 30
 locations. The "Dilly Plate" runs $4.99–$10. Consult the phone
 book for other locations.

Poona
1630 Pleasant Hill Road, NW, Duluth (770) 717-1053
Lunch buffet is still $5.95. Best deal for miles.

Thelma's Kitchen
Roxy Hotel, 768 Marietta Street, near Northside Drive
 (404) 688-5855
Simple, delicious food and plenty of it for small change.

Sweet Tomatoes
6350 Peachtree Dunwoody Road, NE, at Crestline Parkway,
 Dunwoody (770) 913-0203
1125 Ernest Barrett Parkway, NW, near Town Center Mall,
 Kennesaw (770) 429-5522
3505 Mall Boulevard, just outside Gwinnett Place Mall, Duluth
 (770) 418-1148
950 North Point Drive, near North Point Mall, in front of Staples,
 Alpharetta (770) 777-9500
Lunch is $6.69, dinner $7.99. All you can eat. Vegetarian and nonvegetarian dishes are attractively arranged for easy self-service.

Thomas Marketplace Restaurant
State Farmer's Market, 16 Forest Park Way, Forest Park
   (404) 361-1367
Where else can you get a platter of fresh fried green tomatoes sufficient for at least four people for $4.25, and a T-bone steak for $14?

Violette
2948 Clairmont Road, NE, east of I-85   (404) 633-3363
Dishes like a French maman would make go for wicked cheap
   prices: $6.95 at lunch and $8.95 at dinner for coq au vin. Bistro
   fare at is it was meant to be: nourishing, tasty, and not expensive.

Willy's Mexicana Grill
Paces Ferry Center, 2460 Cumberland Parkway, SE
   (770) 801-8633
2900 Delk Road, SE, Marietta   (770) 690-9975
North Decatur Center, 2074 N. Decatur Road, Decatur
   (404) 321-6060
Peachtree Center Food Court, Downtown   (404) 524-0821
Roswell-Wieuca Shopping Center, 4377 Roswell Road, NE,
   Buckhead   (404) 252-2235
Burritos with all fresh ingredients—first rate and filling.

◆ Best Wines by the Glass

Bone's
3130 Piedmont Road, NE, Buckhead   (404) 237-2663

Buckhead Diner
3073 Piedmont Road, NE, Buckhead   (404) 262-3336

The Cabin
2678 Buford Highway, NE   (404) 315-7676
About 80 by-the-glass choices of top quality.

Café Intermezzo
1845 Peachtree Road, NE   (404) 355-0411
The list is extensive, but it's irritating how often the inventory is
   out of what you've chosen.

The Dining Room, Ritz-Carlton, Buckhead
3434 Peachtree Road, NE, across from Lenox Square
   (404) 237-2700

Eno
800 Peachtree Street, NW at 5th Street, Midtown   (404) 685-3191
From the silver bowl full of Champagnes and sparkling wines to
   the two-ounce taste sizes this adventurous list is a winner.

Food 101
Belle Isle Square Shopping Center, 4969 Roswell Road, Suite 200,
   Sandy Springs   (404) 497-9700

Some 75 all-American selections by the glass get into some adventurous varietals.

The Grape
Vinings Jubilee Shopping Center, 4300 Paces Ferry Road, Suite 244 (770) 803-WINE
Combination retail shop, tasting bar, and limited sit-down dining indoors and on a patio. Enjoy small, very tasty dishes with wine. Beautifully designed. More than 100 wines by the glass.

Lo Spuntino
3005 Peachtree Road, NE, Suite D, Buckhead   (404) 237-5724
The Viansa wines of Vicki and Sam Sebastiani are featured, but others are available as well. An attached retail shop sells the wines by the bottle. Nibbles include salamis, prosciutto, and asiago cheese annointed with Cucina Viansa's basil pesto aïoli.

Portofino
3199 Paces Ferry Place, NW, Buckhead   (404) 231-1136
Heavily, but not exclusively, Italian.

Renée's Café
136 N. Chestatee Street, NW, Dahlonega   (706) 864-6829
Upstairs wine bar is the scene of many wine tastings and special events.

SoHo
4200 Paces Ferry Road, NW, Vinings   (770) 801-0069
More than 100 choices by the glass.

Toulouse
Peachtree Walk, 2293-B Peachtree Road, NE near Peachtree Memorial Drive   (404) 351-9533
The menu pairs main courses with wine choices, all of which are available by the glass.

Watershed
406 W. Ponce de Leon Avenue, Decatur   (404) 378-4900
Savor extraordinary selections by the glass—the Riedel glass, no less.

The Wine Bar, the Ritz-Carlton, Buckhead
3434 Peachtree Road, NE, across from Lenox Square (404) 237-2700
Taste through a wide range of excellent wine selections by flights and by generous pours in Riedel glassware. Enjoy superb nibbles with them. This is a most relaxing atmosphere after a hectic day.

Recommendations for Special Purpose Dining

◆ Business Dining

Bone's
3130 Piedmont Road, NE   (404) 237-2663

City Grill
50 Hurt Plaza, Downtown   (404) 524-2489

The Dining Room, the Ritz-Carlton, Buckhead
3434 Peachtree Road, NE, Buckhead   (404) 237-2700

McKendrick's
Park Place Shopping Center, 4505 Ashford Dunwoody
   Road   (770) 512-8888

103 West
103 W. Paces Ferry Road, NW, Buckhead   (404) 233-5993

◆ Quiet and Romantic Dining

The Abbey
163 Ponce de Leon Avenue, NE, Midtown   (404) 876-8532

Abruzzi
Peachtree Battle Shopping Center, 2355 Peachtree Road, NE,
   Buckhead   (404) 261-8186

The Dining Room, the Ritz-Carlton, Buckhead
3434 Peachtree Road, NE, Buckhead   (404) 237-2700

Le Saint Amour
1620 Piedmont Avenue, NE, Morningside   (404) 881-0300

Park 75 Restaurant, the Four Seasons Hotel
75 14th Street, NE, between Peachtree and Juniper streets,
   Midtown   (404) 881-9898

Pano's & Paul's
1232 W. Paces Ferry Road, NW, at Northside Drive,
   Buckhead   (404) 261-3662

South of France
2345 Cheshire Bridge Road, NE, at LaVista Road
   (404) 325-6963

◆ Late-Night Dining

ACE Barbecue Barn
30 Bell Street, NE, off Auburn Avenue, Sweet Auburn
(404) 659-6630
Get a midnight barbecue craving? Here's where you come. Ribs
with all the trimmings and everything else delectable they make
until 2 A.M. Sunday, Monday, and Wednesday and until 3 A.M.
Thursday–Saturday.

Asiana Garden
Asian Square Shopping Center, 5150 Buford Highway, NE,
Doraville   (770) 452-1677 or (770) 452-0012
Superb Korean/Japanese food is served until 2 A.M.

Atlanta Diner
2071 N. Druid Hills Road, NE   (404) 633-0024
Twenty-four-hour service with quite good food and breakfast
around the clock.

Café Tu Tu Tango
East Village Square, 220 Pharr Road, NE, Buckhead
(404) 841-6222
Open until midnight Monday–Wednesday and until 1 A.M.
Thursday–Saturday.

Fonda San Carlos
Maxim Shopping Center, 2077 Beaver Ruin Road, Suite 170,
Norcross   (770) 797-2828
Open until 4 A.M. Fridays and Saturdays, with full menu service.

Georgia Diner
1655 Pleasant Hill Road, Duluth   (770) 806-9880
Twenty-four hour service, with breakfast and full menu. Here's
where you satisfy that 2 A.M. meat-loaf craving.

Kool Runnings
4977 Memorial Drive, Stone Mountain   (404) 508-0277
Jamaican, 24 hours on Fridays and Saturdays.

Landmark Diner
3652 Roswell Road, NW, Buckhead   (404) 816-9090
Breakfast around the clock.

Marietta Diner
306 Cobb Parkway, SE, Marietta   (770) 423-9290
Breakfast dishes are the safest bets.

R. Thomas Deluxe Grill
1287 Peachtree Road, NE, at Piedmont Road   (404) 881-0246

Perfect Day

If you've only got one or two days in Atlanta and you only want to eat where you'll get very good food and distinctly local character, focus on the places below. Sure it means going whole hog. But if you spend one glorious day having breakfast, lunch, and dinner from the restaurants on this list, you'll end your day bursting with pleasure.

◆ Breakfast

Crescent Moon
174 W. Ponce de Leon Avenue, Decatur   (404) 377-5623

◆ Lunch

Horseradish Grill
4320 Powers Ferry Road, NW   (404) 255-7277
3070 Windward Plaza, Suite P, Alpharetta   (770) 442-3123

◆ Dinner

Bacchanalia
1198 Howell Mill Road, NW, West Side   (404) 365-0410

UNDERSTANDING THE RATINGS

We have developed detailed profiles for the best restaurants (in our opinion) in town. Each profile features an easily scanned heading that allows you, in just a second, to check out the restaurant's name, cuisine, star rating, cost, quality rating, and value rating.

Star Rating.   The star rating is an overall rating that encompasses the entire dining experience, including style, service, and ambiance in addition to the taste, presentation, and quality of the food. Five stars is the highest rating possible and connotes the best of everything. Four-star restaurants are exceptional, and three-star restaurants are well above average. Two-star restaurants are good. One star is used to denote an average restaurant that demonstrates an unusual capability in some area of specialization, for example, an otherwise forgettable place that has great barbecued chicken.

Cost.   Below the star rating is an expense description that provides a comparative sense of how much a complete meal will cost. A complete meal for our purposes consists of an entree with vegetable or side dish and choice of soup or salad. Appetizers, desserts, drinks, and tips are excluded.

Inexpensive	$14 or less per person
Moderate	$15–25 per person
Expensive	$26–39 per person
Very Expensive	$40 or more per person

Quality Rating.   Below the cost rating appear a number and a letter. The number is a quality rating based on a scale of 0–100, with 100 being the highest (best) rating attainable. The quality rating is based expressly on the taste, freshness of ingredients, preparation, presentation, and creativity of food served. There is no consideration of price. If you are a person who wants the best food available, and cost is not an issue, you need look no further than the quality ratings.

Value Rating.   If, on the other hand, you are looking for both quality and value, then you should check the value rating, expressed in letters. The value ratings are defined as follows:

A   Exceptional value, a real bargain
B   Good value
C   Fair value, you get exactly what you pay for
D   Somewhat overpriced
F   Significantly overpriced

Locating the Restaurant

Just below the restaurant name is a designation for geographic zone. This zone description will give you a general idea of where the restaurant is located. For ease of use, we divide Atlanta into eight geographic zones.

Zone 1   Southwest Atlanta
Zone 2   Northwest Atlanta
Zone 3   Buckhead/Sandy Springs
Zone 4   Lenox/Chamblee
Zone 5   Northeast Atlanta
Zone 6   Southeast Atlanta
Zone 7   Downtown West
Zone 8   Downtown East

If you are downtown and intend to walk or take a cab to dinner, you may want to choose a restaurant from among those located in Zones 7 or 8. If you have a car, you might include restaurants from contiguous zones in your consideration.

A Note about Atlanta's Geography

The zones are designed to cluster some of Atlanta's neighborhoods and towns in an organized way. The suburban towns, some of them as old or older than Atlanta, have been absorbed into the metroplex. Some neighborhoods have their own names, quite independent of the cities in which they're located.

The center of the city's entertainment, shopping, and dining district lies at the intersection of W. and E. Paces Ferry roads with Roswell and Peachtree roads. This community is called Buckhead, supposedly because nearby once stood a libation-dispensing entity called "The Buck's Head" tavern. There seems to be no documentation establishing its historic authenticity, so it's strictly the stuff of legend. Head north on Roswell Road, and you encounter Sandy Springs, so called because there were springs containing a lot of sand that drew folks to the area, especially for revival camp meetings. The northwestern edge of Zone 3 captures fast-growing east Cobb County, while the eastern edge dips into north Fulton County. Anything lying north of this zone, such as Kennesaw and Canton in Cobb and Alpharetta in Fulton, is "off the map" but in that direction. East of GA 400 is Zone 4, Lenox/Chamblee. Head up GA 400, turn east, and you soon come to Duluth, also off the map.

Reverse your direction out of Buckhead, going south on Peachtree Road toward Downtown, and you come to Midtown, running roughly from the teen-numbered streets down to North Avenue. Paralleling Peachtree Street, as it's known farther south, is I-75/85, which divides the Downtown/Midtown area into West and East, Zones 7 and 8, respectively.

Northeast Atlanta (Zone 5) captures everything from Morningside and Virginia-Highland to Decatur and Stone Mountain, while Northwest Atlanta (Zone 2) references that area west of I-75, including the far west Atlanta neighborhoods, Vinings, Smyrna, and Marietta. Southwest Atlanta, where you'll find the Atlanta airport and the charming historic town of College Park, is Zone 1. And Southeast Atlanta (Zone 6) wends its way along southern I-75 and I-675, through south DeKalb County.

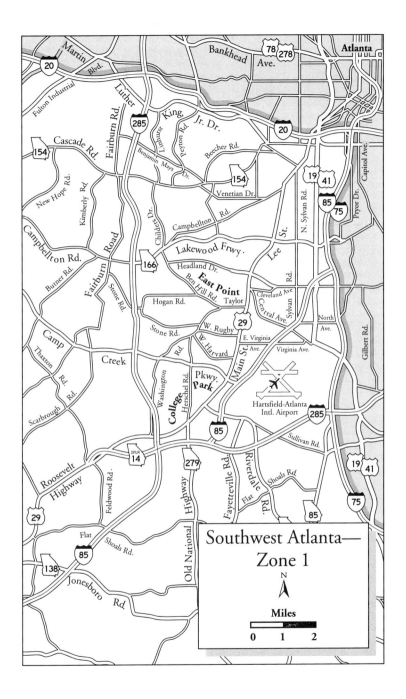

Southwest Atlanta—
Zone 1

N

Miles

0   1   2

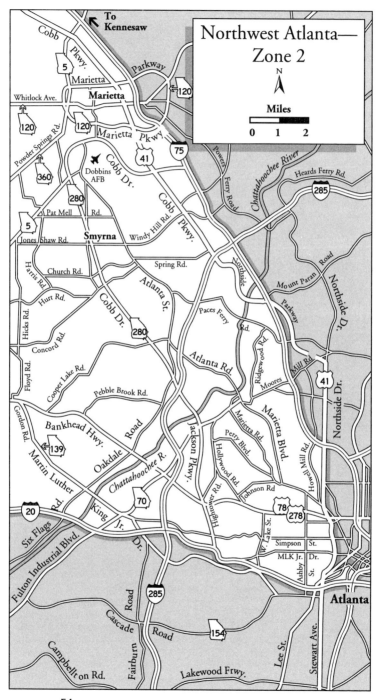

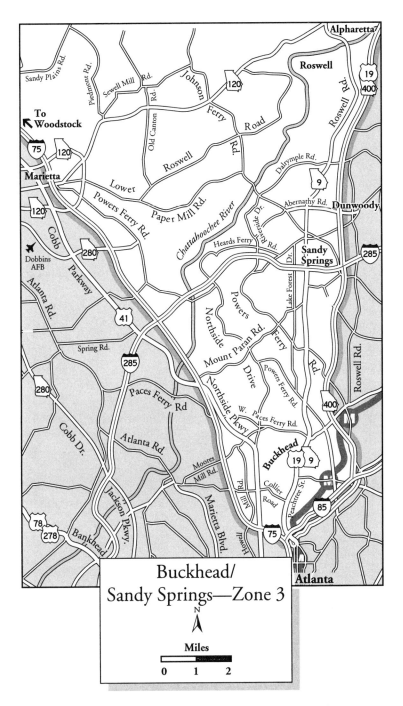

Buckhead/
Sandy Springs—Zone 3

N

Miles

0   1   2

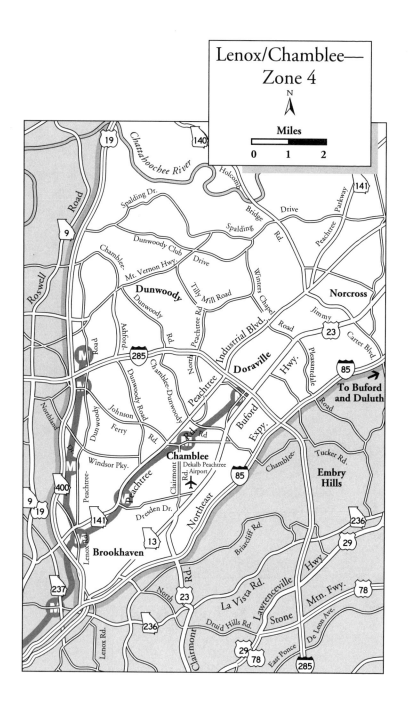

Lenox/Chamblee—
Zone 4

N

Miles

0   1   2

Chattahoochee River

Holcomb

Bridge
Drive

Spalding Dr.

Spalding Rd.

Dunwoody Club   Drive

Chamblee-

Mt. Vernon Hwy.

Peachtree Parkway

Dunwoody

Tilly Mill Road

Norcross

Jimmy

Dunwoody Rd.

North Peachtree Rd.

Winters Chapel Road

Ashford-Dunwoody Rd.

Chamblee-Dunwoody

Industrial Blvd.

Doraville

Hwy.

Carter Blvd

Pleasandale Road

**To Buford
and Duluth**

Dunwoody Ferry Rd.

Peachtree

Rd. Rd.

Buford Expy.

Johnson Ferry Rd.

Chamblee

Dekalb Peachtree
Airport

Chamblee-

Tucker Rd.

**Embry
Hills**

Windsor Pky.

Clairmont Rd.

Northeast

Peachtree

Dresden Dr.

Briarcliff Rd.

Northland

Peachtree

Brookhaven

Lenox Rd.

North Rd.

La Vista Rd.

Lawrenceville Hwy.

Stone

Mtn. Fwy.

Clairmont

Druid Hills Rd.

De Leon Ave.

East Ponce

Roswell Road

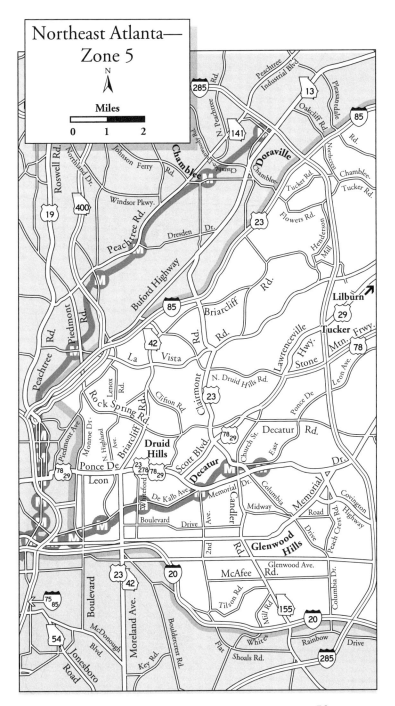

Northeast Atlanta—
Zone 5

N

Miles

0   1   2

285

13

85

Peachtree Industrial Blvd

Oakcliff Rd.

pleasantdale

Rd.

141

N. Peachtree

Chamblee

Doraville

Johnson Ferry Rd.

Chamblee-

Chamblee-Tucker Rd.

Tucker Rd.

Northeast

Roswell Rd.

Northland Dr.

Windsor Pkwy.

19

400

Flowers Rd.

23

Peachtree Rd.

Dresden   Dr.

Buford Highway

Henderson Mill

85

Briarcliff

Lilburn

29

Tucker

Mtn. Frwy.

42

Rd.

Rd.

Lawrenceville Hwy.

78

Piedmont

Rd.

Peachtree

Rd.

La   Vista

Stone

Leon Ave.

Lenox   Rd.

Clifton Rd.

Clairmont

N. Druid Hills Rd.

Ponce De

23

Rock Spring Rd.

Monroe Dr.

N. Highland Ave.

Briarcliff

78   29

Decatur   Rd.

Druid
Hills

Church St.

Decatur

Piedmont Ave.

78
29

Ponce De

Leon

23
278   78   29

Scott Blvd.

Decatur

East

Memorial

Dr.

De Kalb Ave.

Memorial

Dr.

Winneford

Candler

Ave.

Columbia

Midway

Road

Covington Highway

Boulevard

Drive

Peach Crest Rd.

Drive

2nd

Rd.

Glenwood
Hills

Columbia Dr.

23

20

McAfee   Rd.

Glenwood Ave.

42

75
85

Boulevard

Moreland Ave.

Tilson Rd.

Mill Rd.

155

20

54

McDonough Blvd.

Key Rd.

Bouldercrest Rd.

White's

Flat   Shoals Rd.

Rainbow   Drive

285

Jonesboro

Road

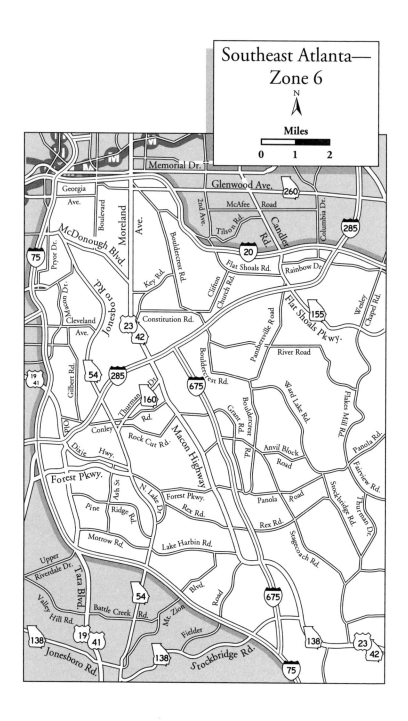

Southeast Atlanta—
Zone 6

N

Miles

0   1   2

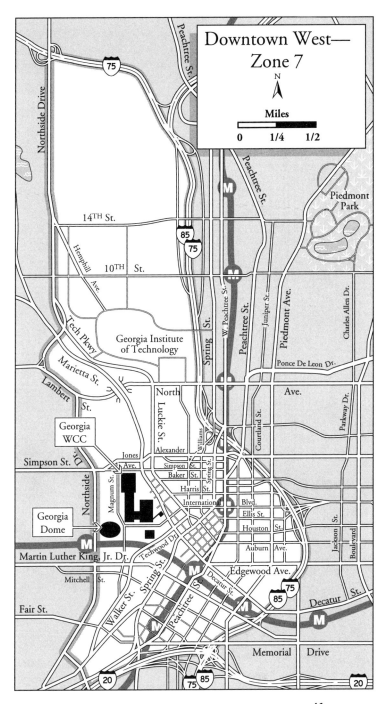

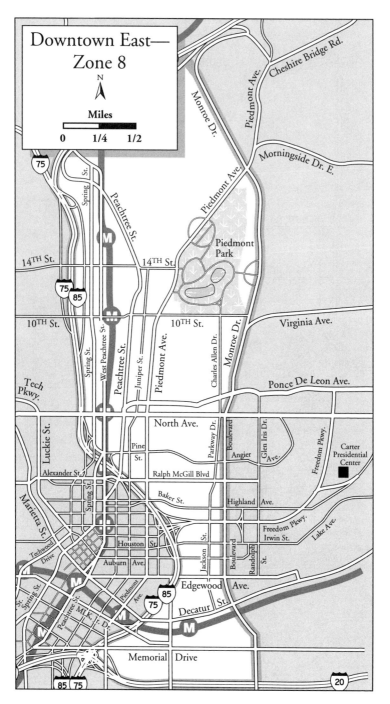

Downtown East—
Zone 8

N

Miles

| 0 | 1/4 | 1/2 |

75

Spring St.

Monroe Dr.

Peachtree St.

Piedmont Ave.

Cheshire Bridge Rd.

Piedmont Ave.

Morningside Dr. E.

Piedmont
Park

14TH St.

14TH St.

75
85

10TH St.

10TH St.

Virginia Ave.

Spring St.

West Peachtree St.

Peachtree St.

Juniper St.

Piedmont Ave.

Charles Allen Dr.

Monroe Dr.

Tech
Pkwy.

Ponce De Leon Ave.

North Ave.

Parkway Dr.

Boulevard

Glen Iris Dr.

Angier

Ave.

Freedom Pkwy.

Carter
Presidential
Center

Luckie St.

Pine
St.

Alexander St.

Ralph McGill Blvd

Spring St.

Baker St.

Highland

Ave.

St.

Freedom Pkwy.
Irwin St.

Lake Ave.

Marietta St.

Techwood
Drive

Houston

St.

Jackson

St.

Boulevard

Randolph

St.

Auburn

Ave.

St.

Spring St.

Peachtree St.

Piedmont

Ave.

M.L.K. Jr. Dr.

Edgewood

Ave.

85

75

Decatur

St.

Memorial

Drive

85 75

20

OUR pick of the best ATLANTA RESTAURANTS

Restaurants are opening and closing all the time in Atlanta, so we have tried to confine our list to establishments—or chefs—with a proven track record over a fairly long period of time. Those newer or changed establishments that demonstrate staying power and consistency will be profiled in subsequent editions.

The list is highly selective. Non-inclusion of a particular place does not necessarily indicate that the restaurant is not good, but only that it was not ranked among the best or most consistent in its genre. Detailed profiles of each restaurant are in alphabetical order.

A Note about Spelling

Most diners who enjoy ethnic restaurants have noticed subtle variations in the spelling of certain dishes and preparations from one menu to the next. A noodle dish found on almost all Thai menus, for example, appears in one restaurant as *pad thai,* in another as **Phat Thai,** and in a third as **Phad Thai.**

This and similar inconsistencies arise from attempts to derive a phonetic English spelling from the name of a dish as pronounced in its country of origin. While one particular English spelling might be more frequently used than others, there is usually no definitive correct spelling for the names of many dishes. In this guide, we have elected to use the spelling most commonly found in authoritative ethnic cookbooks and other reference works.

We call this to your attention because the spelling we use in this guide could be different from that which you encounter on the menu in a certain restaurant. We might say, for instance, that the *tabbouleh* is good at the Pillars of Lebanon, while at the restaurant itself the dish is listed on the menu as *tabouli.*

Restaurants by Cuisine

Name of Restaurant	Star Rating	Price Rating	Quality Rating	Value Rating	Zone
American					
BluePointe	★★★★★	Expensive	90	C	3
Mumbo Jumbo	★★★★	Expensive	95	C	7
Watershed	★★★★	Mod/Exp	95	C	5
Horseradish Grill	★★★★	Mod/Exp	94	C	3
Buckhead Diner	★★★★	Moderate	92	C	3
dick and harry's	★★★★	Expensive	92	C	4
Canoe	★★★★	Moderate	90	C	2
Park 75 Restaurant	★★★★	Very Expensive	90	B	8
Tiburon Grille	★★★★	Moderate	90	C	5
Toulouse	★★★★	Moderate	88	C	3
The Food Studio	★★★	Moderate	90	C	2
Greenwood's on Green Street	★★★	Mod/Exp	90	C	3
Roman Lily Cafe	★★★	Moderate	90	A	5
Sia's	★★★	Expensive	90	B	3
Breezes	★★★	Expensive	88	C	Lake Lanier
Bridges	★★★	Expensive	88	B	3
Buckhead Bread Company and Corner Cafe	★★★	Inexpensive	88	B	3
The Cabin	★★★	Expensive	88	C	5
Dish	★★★	Expensive	88	C	5
Heaping Bowl & Brew	★★★	Inexpensive	88	B	6
Sage on Sycamore	★★★	Moderate	88	C	5
The Bread Market	★★★	Inexpensive	85	C	3
Food Business	★★★	Moderate	85	B	5
R. Thomas Deluxe Grill	★★★	Inexpensive	85	C	3
Vinings Inn	★★★	Expensive	85	C	2
Crescent Moon	★★	Inexp/Mod	88	A	5
Flying Biscuit Cafe	★★	Inexpensive	88	B	5, 8
The Vortex Bar & Grill	★★	Inexpensive	88	C	5, 8
Aqua Terra	★★	Moderate	85	B	4
American Roadhouse	★★	Inexpensive	82	C	5
Blue Ridge Grill	★★	Expensive	82	C	3
Food 101	★★	Moderate	82	C	3
The Varsity	★	Inexpensive	80	A	2, 5, 8
Asian					
BluePointe	★★★★★	Expensive	90	C	3

Name of Restaurant	Star Rating	Price Rating	Quality Rating	Value Rating	Zone
Asian (continued)					
Pacific Rim Bistro	★★★	Moderate	90	B	8
Savu	★★★	Expensive	88	C	4
Barbecue					
Rockin' Rob's B-B-Q	★★★★	Inexpensive	95	A	5
Spiced Right	★★★	Inexpensive	90	B	5
ACE Barbecue Barn	★★★	Inexpensive	85	B	8
The Rib Ranch	★★★	Inexpensive	85	A	2, 3
Dusty's	★★	Inexpensive	90	A	5
Swallow at the Hollow	★★	Inexp/Mod	88	B	3
Bobby & June's Kountry Kitchen	★	Inexpensive	85	B	7
Fat Matt's Rib Shack/ Fat Matt's Chicken Shack	★	Inexpensive	85	B	5
Cajun/Creole					
Hal's	★★★	Mod/Exp	90	B	3
McKinnon's Louisiane	★★★	Moderate	88	B	3
Fuzzy's Place	★★	Inexpensive	85	A	5
California American					
Murphy's	★★★	Inexp/Mod	90	C	5
California Italian					
Mi Spia	★★★	Moderate	88	C	4
Chinese					
Yen Jing	★★★★★	Inexpensive	95	A	5
Little Szechuan	★★★★	Inexpensive	95	A+	4
Canton House	★★★	Moderate	90	B	4
Chopstix	★★★	Moderate	88	C	3
Hsu's Gourmet Chinese Restaurant	★★★	Moderate	86	C	7
Contemporary					
Seeger's	★★★★★	Very Expensive	98	C	3
The Abbey	★★★★	Very Expensive	95	C	8
Asher Restaurant	★★★★	Expensive	95	A	3
The Food Studio	★★★	Moderate	90	C	2

Name of Restaurant	Star Rating	Price Rating	Quality Rating	Value Rating	Zone
Continental					
Nikolai's Roof	★★★★★	Very Expensive	96	C	7
Mumbo Jumbo	★★★★	Expensive	95	C	7
Pano's & Paul's	★★★★	Very Expensive	94	C	3
Anthony's	★★★	Very Expensive	90	C	3
Grazie, A Bistro	★★★	Mod/Exp	90	C	2
Hal's	★★★	Mod/Exp	90	B	3
Van Gogh's	★★★	Mod/Exp	90	C	3
Kurt's	★★★	Moderate	85	C	4
Ten East Washington	★★	Moderate	85	C	Newnan
Cuban					
Mambo Cuban Restaurant	★★★	Moderate	88	C	5
Coco Loco Cuban & Caribbean Restaurant	★★	Inexp/Mod	88	B	3
Crazy Cuban	★★	Inexpensive	88	C	2
Eclectic					
Aria	★★★★★	Mod/Exp	95	A	3
Sia's	★★★	Expensive	90	B	3
Pascal's Bistro	★★★	Moderate	88	B	P'tree City
Vino!	★★★	Moderate	85	C	3
Ethiopian					
Queen of Sheba	★★★★	Inexpensive	88	A	5
European Country					
Babette's Cafe	★★★	Moderate	88	C	5
French					
Nikolai's Roof	★★★★★	Very Expensive	96	C	7
Brasserie Le Coze	★★★★	Mod/Exp	94	C	3
Le Saint Amour	★★★★	Expensive	92	C	5
Violette	★★★	Mod/Exp	90	B	5
Le Giverny Bistro	★★★	Moderate	89	B+	5
Anis Café and Bistro	★★	Mod/Exp	88	C	3
Café Alsace	★★	Inexpensive	82	B	5
French/American					
Bacchanalia	★★★★★	Mod/Exp	98	A	3

Restaurants by Cuisine (continued)

Name of Restaurant	Star Rating	Price Rating	Quality Rating	Value Rating	Zone
Fusion					
TomTom, a Bistro and Sushi Bar	★★★★	Moderate	90	C	3
Café Tu Tu Tango	★★	Inexpensive	85	C	3
German					
Vrney's Biergarten and German Grille	★★★	Inexp/Mod	88	B	4
Basket Bakery & Cafe at the Village Corner	★★	Inexpensive	82	C	5
Indian					
Haveli Indian Restaurant	★★★	Inexpensive	90	C	2, 8
Poona	★★★	Moderate	90	A	5
Udipi Cafe	★★★	Inexpensive	90	B	5
Zyka	★★★	Inexpensive	90	A	5
Irish					
Fadó Irish Pub	★★★	Moderate	88	C	3
Italian					
La Grotta Ristorante	★★★★★	Very Expensive	98	C	3, 4
Veni Vidi Vici	★★★★★	Mod/Exp	98	B	8
La Tavola Trattoria	★★★★	Expensive	95	B	5
Sotto Sotto	★★★★	Moderate	95	A	5
Antica Posta	★★★★	Expensive	92	C	3
Abruzzi	★★★★	Mod/Exp	91	C	3
Il Fornaio	★★★★	Expensive	90	B	4
Pricci	★★★★	Expensive	90	C	3
Vinny's on Windward	★★★★	Expensive	90	C	4
Grazie, A Bistro	★★★	Mod/Exp	90	C	2
Villa Christina	★★★	Mod/Exp	90	C	4
Pastificcio Cameli	★★	Moderate	88	B	6
Brooklyn Cafe	★★	Moderate	85	C	3
Nona's Italian Kitchen	★★	Moderate	85	B	3
Italian American					
E. 48th Street Italian Market	★★★★	Inexpensive	95	A	4
Ferrera's Bistro	★★★	Moderate	88	C	3
Fratelli di Napoli	★★★	Moderate	88	C	3, 4
Camille's	★★	Moderate	85	C	5

68

Name of Restaurant	Star Rating	Price Rating	Quality Rating	Value Rating	Zone
Japanese					
Kamogawa	★★★★	Very Expensive	96	C	3
Sa Tsu Ki	★★★★	Inexpensive	95	B	5
Soto Japanese Restaurant	★★★★	Expensive	95	C	3
Hashiguchi Japanese Restaurant & Sushi Bar	★★★★	Moderate	90	B	3
Circle Sushi	★★★	Moderate	88	B	3
Korean					
Yen Jing	★★★★★	Inexpensive	95	A	5
Hae Woon Dae	★★★	Moderate	93	A	4
Korean/Japanese					
Hanwoori	★★★★	Moderate	95	A	4
Asiana Garden	★★★	Inexp/Mod	90	A	4
Seoul Garden Restaurant	★★★	Inexp/Mod	90	C	5
Latin American					
Tierra	★★★	Expensive	93	B	8
Alameda	★★	Moderate	88	B	2
Lebanese/Middle Eastern					
Cedars	★★★	Moderate	91	B	3
Malaysian					
Penang	★★★★	Moderate	95	A	5
Mediterranean					
Floataway Cafe	★★★★	Expensive	93	C	5
TomTom a Bistro and Sushi Bar	★★★★	Moderate	90	C	3
Eno	★★★	Expensive	90	C	8
Basil's Mediterranean Cafe	★★★	Moderate	88	C	3
Harvest	★★★	Moderate	86	C	5
Café Lily	★★★	Moderate	85	C	5
Mexican					
Oh . . . María!	★★★★★	Moderate	95	B	3
Zócalo	★★★	Inexpensive	95	A	8
Costa del Sol	★★★	Inexpensive	92	B	4
Fonda San Carlos	★★★	Moderate	92	B	4
La Paz	★★★	Moderate	90	B	2, 3

Restaurants by Cuisine (continued)

Name of Restaurant	Star Rating	Price Rating	Quality Rating	Value Rating	Zone
Mexican (continued)					
Frontera Mex-Mex Grill	★★★	Inexpensive	85	B	4, 5
Alameda	★★	Moderate	88	B	2
Gringos'	★★	Inexpensive	88	C	5
Nuevo Laredo Cantina	★★	Inexpensive	86	A	2
Don Taco	★★	Inexpensive	83	B	4
Moroccan					
Imperial Fez	★★★★	Expensive	90	B	3
Pan Asian					
Nickiemoto's	★★★	Inexp/Mod	90	A	8
Persian					
Mirage	★★★	Moderate	90	B	3
Seafood					
Chops/The Lobster Bar	★★★★	Very Expensive	95	C	3
Atlanta Fish Market	★★★	Moderate	88	C	3
Fishmonger	★★★	Moderate	88	B	3
Marra's Grill: Fresh Seafood and Great Steaks	★★★	Moderate	88	C	5
Stringer's Fish Camp	★★★	Inexpensive	85	C	4
Pattaya Seafood Restaurant	★★	Moderate	86	C	2
Fishbone & The Piranha Bar	★★	Moderate	85	C	3
South African					
Ten Degrees South	★★★	Moderate	88	B	3
Southern					
Watershed	★★★★	Mod/Exp	95	C	5
Horseradish Grill	★★★★	Mod/Exp	94	C	3
South City Kitchen	★★★★	Expensive	93	C	8
1848 House	★★★★	Expensive	90	C	2
Anthony's	★★★	Very Expensive	90	C	3
Greenwood's on Green Street	★★★	Mod/Exp	90	C	3
Thomas Marketplace Restaurant	★★★	Inexpensive	90	A	6

70

Restaurants by Cuisine (continued)

Name of Restaurant	Star Rating	Price Rating	Quality Rating	Value Rating	Zone
Southern (continued)					
ACE Barbecue Barn	★★★	Inexpensive	85	B	8
Stringer's Fish Camp	★★★	Inexpensive	85	C	4
Swallow at the Hollow	★★	Inexp/Mod	88	B	3
Thelma's Kitchen	★★	Inexpensive	88	C	7
Agnes & Muriel's	★★	Inexp/Mod	86	C	5
Mary Mac's Tea Room	★★	Inexpensive	83	B	8
Evans Fine Foods	★★	Inexpensive	82	B	5
The Colonnade Restaurant	★★	Inexpensive	80	B	5
Son's Place	★★	Inexpensive	80	C	5
Bobby & June's Kountry Kitchen	★	Inexpensive	85	B	7
Southwestern					
Sundown Cafe	★★★	Mod/Exp	93	C	5
La Paz	★★★	Moderate	90	B	2, 3
SoHo	★★★	Expensive	89	C	2
Georgia Grille	★★★	Moderate	88	C	3
Nava	★★★	Expensive	88	D	3
Noche	★★★	Expensive	88	C	5
Azteca Grill	★★★	Moderate	85	C	1
Bajaritos	★	Inexpensive	85	A	3
Spanish/Tapas					
Eclipse di Luna	★★★	Very Inexp	88	A	3
Steak					
Bone's	★★★★★	Very Expensive	98	C	3
Chops/The Lobster Bar	★★★★	Very Expensive	95	C	3
Ruth's Chris Steak House	★★★★	Expensive	90	C	3, 7
McKendrick's	★★★★	Very Expensive	88	D	4
Marra's Grill: Fresh Seafood and Great Steaks	★★★	Moderate	88	C	5
Steak/Sushi					
Prime	★★★★	Expensive	92	C	3
Tapas					
Eclipse di Luna	★★★	Very Inexp	88	A	3
Loca Luna	★★	Inexpensive	88	A	8

Restaurants by Cuisine *(continued)*

Name of Restaurant	Star Rating	Price Rating	Quality Rating	Value Rating	Zone
Thai					
Tamarind	★★★★	Moderate	94	C	8
Annie's Thai Castle	★★★★	Inexpensive	90	A	3
Northlake Thai	★★★★	Moderate	90	A	5
Thai Chili	★★★★	Moderate	90	B	5
Surin of Thailand	★★★	Inexp/Mod	88	A	5
Sukothai	★★★	Inexpensive	85	C	2
Pattaya Seafood Restaurant	★★	Moderate	86	C	2
Vegetarian					
Mirage	★★★	Moderate	90	B	3
Café Sunflower	★★	Inexpensive	85	C	3
Vietnamese					
Biên Thùy	★★★★	Inexpensive	90	A	4

Restaurants by Star Rating

Name of Restaurant	Cuisine	Price Rating	Quality Rating	Value Rating	Zone
Five-Star Restaurants					
Bacchanalia	French/American	Mod/Exp	98	A	3
Bone's	Steak	Very Exp	98	C	3
La Grotta Ristorante	Italian	Very Exp	98	C	3, 4
Seeger's	Contemporary	Very Exp	98	C	3
Veni Vidi Vici	Italian	Mod/Exp	98	B	8
Nikolai's Roof	Continental/ French	Very Exp	96	C	7
Aria	Eclectic	Mod/Exp	95	A	3
Oh . . . María!	Mexican	Moderate	95	B	3
Yen Jing	Chinese/Korean	Inexpensive	95	A	5
BluePointe	American/Asian	Expensive	90	C	3
Four-Star Restaurants					
Kamogawa	Japanese	Very Exp	96	C	3
The Abbey	Contemporary	Very Exp	95	C	8
Asher Restaurant	Contemporary	Expensive	95	A	3
Chops/ The Lobster Bar	Steak/Seafood	Very Exp	95	C	3
E. 48th Street Italian Market	Italian American	Inexpensive	95	A	4
Hanwoori	Korean/Japanese	Moderate	95	A	4
La Tavola Trattaoria	Italian	Expensive	95	B	5
Little Szechuan	Chinese	Inexpensive	95	A+	4
Mumbo Jumbo	American/ Continental	Expensive	95	C	7
Penang	Malaysian	Moderate	95	A	5
Rockin' Rob's B–B–Q	Barbecue	Inexpensive	95	A	5
Sa Tsu Ki	Japanese	Inexpensive	95	B	5
Soto Japanese Restaurant	Japanese	Expensive	95	C	3
Sotto Sotto	Italian	Moderate	95	A	5
Watershed	American/ Southern	Mod/Exp	95	C	5
Brasserie Le Coze	French Bistro	Mod/Exp	94	C	3
Horseradish Grill	American/ Southern	Mod/Exp	94	C	3
Pano's & Paul's	Continental	Very Exp	94	C	3
Tamarind	Thai	Moderate	94	C	8
Floataway Cafe	Mediterranean	Expensive	93	C	5

Name of Restaurant	Cuisine	Price Rating	Quality Rating	Value Rating	Zone
Four-Star Restaurants (continued)					
South City Kitchen	Southern	Expensive	93	C	8
Antica Posta	Italian	Expensive	92	C	3
Buckhead Diner	American	Moderate	92	C	3
dick and harry's	American	Expensive	92	C	4
Le Saint Amour	French	Expensive	92	C	5
Prime	Steak/Sushi	Expensive	92	C	3
Abruzzi	Italian	Mod/Exp	91	C	3
Annie's Thai Castle	Thai	Inexpensive	90	A	3
Biên Thùy	Vietnamese	Inexpensive	90	A	4
Canoe	American	Moderate	90	C	2
1848 House	Southern	Expensive	90	C	2
Hashiguchi Japanese Restaurant & Sushi Bar	Japanese	Moderate	90	B	3
Il Fornaio	Italian	Expensive	90	B	4
Imperial Fez	Moroccan	Expensive	90	B	3
Northlake Thai	Thai	Moderate	90	A	5
Park 75 Restaurant	American	Very Exp	90	B	8
Pricci	Italian	Expensive	90	C	3
Ruth's Chris Steak House	Steak	Expensive	90	C	3, 7
Thai Chili	Thai	Moderate	90	B	5
Tiburon Grille	American	Moderate	90	C	5
TomTom a Bistro and Sushi Bar	Mediterranean	Moderate	90	C	3
Vinny's on Windward	Italian	Expensive	90	C	4
McKendrick's	Steak	Very Expe	88	D	4
Queen of Sheba	Ethiopian	Inexpensive	88	A	5
Toulouse	American	Moderate	88	C	3
Three-Star Restaurants					
Zócalo	Mexican	Inexpensive	95	A	8
Hae Woon Dae	Korean	Moderate	93	A	4
Sundown Cafe	Southwestern	Mod/Exp	93	C	5
Tierra	Latin American	Expensive	93	B	8
Costa del Sol	Mexican/ Salvadoran	Inexpensive	92	B	4
Fonda San Carlos	Mexican	Moderate	92	B	4

Name of Restaurant	Cuisine	Price Rating	Quality Rating	Value Rating	Zone
Three-Star Restaurants (continued)					
Anthony's	Southern/ Continental	Very Exp	90	C	3
Asiana Garden	Korean/Japanese	Inexp/Mod	90	A	4
Canton House	Chinese	Moderate	90	B	4
Eno	Mediterranean	Expensive	90	C	8
The Food Studio	Contemporary	Moderate	90	C	2
Grazie, A Bistro	Italian/Continental	Mod/Exp	90	C	2
Greenwood's on Green Street	American/ Southern	Mod/Exp	90	C	3
Hal's	Creole/ Continental	Mod/Exp	90	B	3
Haveli Indian Restaurant	Indian	Inexpensive	90	C	2, 8
La Paz	Mexican/ Southwestern	Moderate	90	B	2, 3
Mirage	Persian/Vegetarian	Moderate	90	B	3
Murphy's	California American	Inexp/Mod	90	C	5
Nickiemoto's	Pan Asian	Inexp/Mod	90	A	8
Pacific Rim Bistro	Asian	Moderate	90	B	8
Poona	Indian	Moderate	90	A	5
Roman Lily Cafe	American	Moderate	90	A	5
Seoul Garden Restaurant	Korean/Japanese	Inexp/Mod	90	C	5
Sia's	Eclectic American	Expensive	90	B	3
Spiced Right	Barbecue	Inexpensive	90	B	5
Thomas Marketplace Restaurant	Southern	Inexpensive	90	A	6
Udipi Cafe	Indian	Inexpensive	90	B	5
Van Gogh's	Continental	Mod/Exp	90	C	3
Villa Christina	Italian	Mod/Exp	90	C	4
Violette	French	Mod/Exp	90	B	5
Zyka	Indian	Inexpensive	90	A	5
Le Giverny Bistro	French Bistro	Moderate	89	B+	5
SoHo	Southwestern	Expensive	89	C	2
Atlanta Fish Market	Seafood	Moderate	88	C	3
Babette's Cafe	European Country	Moderate	88	C	5
Basil's Mediter-ranean Cafe	Mediterranean	Moderate	88	C	3

Name of Restaurant	Cuisine	Price Rating	Quality Rating	Value Rating	Zone
Three-Star Restaurants (continued)					
Breezes	American	Expensive	88	C	Lake Lanier
Bridges	American	Expensive	88	B	3
Buckhead Bread Company and Corner Cafe	American	Inexpensive	88	B	3
The Cabin	American	Expensive	88	C	5
Circle Sushi	Japanese	Moderate	88	B	3
Chopstix	Chinese	Moderate	88	C	3
Dish	American	Expensive	88	C	5
Eclipse di Luna	Spanish/Tapas	Very Inexp	88	A	3
Fadó Irish Pub	Irish	Moderate	88	C	3
Ferrera's Bistro	Italian American	Moderate	88	C	3
Fishmonger	Seafood	Moderate	88	B	3
Fratelli di Napoli	Italian American	Moderate	88	C	3, 4
Georgia Grille	Southwestern	Moderate	88	C	3
Heaping Bowl & Brew	American	Inexpensive	88	B	6
Mambo Cuban Restaurant	Cuban	Moderate	88	C	5
Marra's Grill: Fresh Seafood and Great Steaks	Seafood/Steak	Moderate	88	C	5
McKinnon's Louisiane	Cajun/Creole	Moderate	88	B	3
Mi Spia	California Italian	Moderate	88	C	4
Nava	Southwestern	Expensive	88	D	3
Noche	Southwestern	Expensive	88	C	5
Pascal's Bistro	Eclectic	Moderate	88	B	P'tree City
Sage on Sycamore	American	Moderate	88	C	5
Savu	Asian	Expensive	88	C	4
Surin of Thailand	Thai	Inexp/Mod	88	A	5
Ten Degrees South	South African	Moderate	88	B	3
Vrney's Biergarten and German Grille	German	Inexp/Mod	88	B	4
Harvest	Mediterranean	Moderate	86	C	5
Hsu's Gourmet Chinese Restaurant	Chinese	Moderate	86	C	7

Name of Restaurant	Cuisine	Price Rating	Quality Rating	Value Rating	Zone
Three-Star Restaurants (continued)					
ACE Barbecue Barn	Barbecue/Southern	Inexpensive	85	B	8
Azteca Grill	Southwestern	Moderate	85	C	1
The Bread Market	American	Inexpensive	85	C	3
Café Lily	Mediterranean	Moderate	85	C	5
Food Business	American	Moderate	85	B	5
Frontera Mex-Mex Grill	Mexican	Inexpensive	85	B	4, 5
Kurt's	Continental	Moderate	85	C	4
R. Thomas Deluxe Grill	American	Inexpensive	85	C	3
The Rib Ranch	Barbecue	Inexpensive	85	A	2, 3
Stringer's Fish Camp	Southern/Seafood	Inexpensive	85	C	4
Sukothai	Thai	Inexpensive	85	C	2
Vinings Inn	American	Expensive	85	C	2
Vino!	Eclectic	Moderate	85	C	3
Two-Star Restaurants					
Dusty's	Barbecue	Inexpensive	90	A	5
Alameda	Latin American/ Mexican	Moderate	88	B	2
Anis Café and Bistro	French	Mod/Exp	88	C	3
Coco Loco Cuban & Caribbean Restaurant	Cuban	Inexp/Mod	88	B	3
Crazy Cuban	Cuban	Inexpensive	88	C	2
Crescent Moon	American	Inexp/Mod	88	A	5
Flying Biscuit Cafe	American	Inexpensive	88	B	5, 8
Gringos'	Mexican	Inexpensive	88	C	5
Loca Luna	Tapas	Inexpensive	88	A	8
Pastificcio Cameli	Italian	Moderate	88	B	6
Swallow at the Hollow	Southern/ Barbecue	Inexp/Mod	88	B	3
Thelma's Kitchen	Southern	Inexpensive	88	C	7
The Vortex Bar & Grill	American	Inexpensive	88	C	5, 8
Agnes & Muriel's	Southern	Inexp/Mod	86	C	5
Nuevo Laredo Cantina	Mexican	Inexpensive	86	A	2
Pattaya Seafood Restaurant	Thai/Seafood	Moderate	86	C	2

Restaurants by Star Rating (continued)

Name of Restaurant	Cuisine	Price Rating	Quality Rating	Value Rating	Zone
Two-Star Restaurants (continued)					
Aqua Terra	American	Moderate	85	B	4
Brooklyn Cafe	Italian	Moderate	85	C	3
Café Sunflower	Vegetarian	Inexpensive	85	C	3
Café Tu Tu Tango	Fusion	Inexpensive	85	C	3
Camille's	Italian American	Moderate	85	C	5
Fishbone & The Piranha Bar	Seafood	Moderate	85	C	3
Fuzzy's Place	Cajun/Creole	Inexpensive	85	A	5
Nona's Italian Kitchen	Italian	Moderate	85	B	3
Ten East Washington	Continental	Moderate	85	C	Newnan
Don Taco	Mexican	Inexpensive	83	B	4
Mary Mac's Tea Room	Southern	Inexpensive	83	B	8
American Roadhouse	American	Inexpensive	82	C	5
Basket Bakery & Cafe at the Village Corner	German	Inexpensive	82	C	5
Blue Ridge Grill	American	Expensive	82	C	3
Café Alsace	French	Inexpensive	82	B	5
Evans Fine Foods	Southern	Inexpensive	82	B	5
Food 101	American	Moderate	82	C	3
The Colonnade Restaurant	Southern	Inexpensive	80	B	5
Son's Place	Southern	Inexpensive	80	C	5
One-Star Restaurants					
Bajaritos	Southwestern	Inexpensive	85	A	3
Bobby & June's Kountry Kitchen	Southern/ Barbecue	Inexpensive	85	B	7
Fat Matt's Rib Shack/Fat Matt's Chicken Shack	Barbecue	Inexpensive	85	B	5
The Varsity	American	Inexpensive	80	A	2, 5, 8

Restaurants by Zone

Restaurant	Star Rating	Price Rating	Quality Rating	Value Rating
Zone 1: Southwest Atlanta				
◆ *Southwestern*				
Azteca Grill	★★★	Moderate	85	C
Zone 2: Northwest Atlanta				
◆ *American*				
Canoe	★★★★	Moderate	90	C
Vinings Inn	★★★	Expensive	85	C
The Varsity	★	Inexpensive	80	A
◆ *Barbecue*				
The Rib Ranch	★★★	Inexpensive	85	A
◆ *Contemporary*				
The Food Studio	★★★	Moderate	90	C
◆ *Cuban*				
Crazy Cuban	★★	Inexpensive	88	C
◆ *Indian*				
Haveli Indian Restaurant	★★★	Inexpensive	90	C
◆ *Italian/Continental*				
Grazie, A Bistro	★★★	Mod/Exp	90	C
◆ *Latin American/Mexican*				
Alameda	★★	Moderate	88	B
◆ *Mexican*				
Nuevo Laredo Cantina	★★	Inexpensive	86	A
◆ *Mexican/Southwestern*				
La Paz	★★★	Moderate	90	B
◆ *Southern*				
1848 House	★★★★	Expensive	90	C
◆ *Southwestern*				
SoHo	★★★	Expensive	89	C

Restaurant	Star Rating	Price Rating	Quality Rating	Value Rating
Zone 2: Northwest Atlanta (continued)				
◆ *Thai*				
Sukothai	★★★	Inexpensive	85	C
◆ *Thai/Seafood*				
Pattaya Seafood Restaurant	★★	Moderate	86	C
Zone 3: Buckhead/Sandy Springs				
◆ *American*				
Buckhead Diner	★★★★	Moderate	92	C
Toulouse	★★★★	Moderate	88	C
Sia's	★★★	Expensive	90	B
Bridges	★★★	Expensive	88	B
Buckhead Bread Company and Corner Cafe	★★★	Inexpensive	88	B
The Bread Market	★★★	Inexpensive	85	C
R. Thomas Deluxe Grill	★★★	Inexpensive	85	C
Blue Ridge Grill	★★	Expensive	82	C
Food 101	★★	Moderate	82	C
◆ *American/Asian*				
BluePointe	★★★★★	Expensive	90	C
◆ *American/Southern*				
Horseradish Grill	★★★★	Mod/Exp	94	C
Greenwood's on Green Street	★★★	Mod/Exp	90	C
◆ *Barbecue*				
The Rib Ranch	★★★	Inexpensive	85	A
◆ *Cajun/Creole*				
McKinnon's Louisiane	★★★	Moderate	88	B
◆ *Chinese*				
Chopstix	★★★	Moderate	88	C
◆ *Contemporary*				
Seeger's	★★★★★	Very Expensive	98	C
Asher Restaurant	★★★★	Expensive	95	A

80

Restaurants by Zone (continued)

Restaurant	Star Rating	Price Rating	Quality Rating	Value Rating
Zone 3: Buckhead/Sandy Springs (continued)				
♦ *Continental*				
Pano's & Paul's	★★★★	Very Expensive	94	C
Van Gogh's	★★★	Mod/Exp	90	C
♦ *Continental/Creole*				
Hal's	★★★	Mod/Exp	90	B
♦ *Cuban*				
Coco Loco Cuban & Caribbean Restaurant	★★	Inexp/Mod	88	B
♦ *Eclectic*				
Aria	★★★★★	Mod/Exp	95	A
Vino!	★★★	Moderate	85	C
♦ *French*				
Bacchanalia	★★★★★	Mod/Exp	98	A
Brasserie Le Coze	★★★★	Mod/Exp	94	C
Anis Café and Bistro	★★	Mod/Exp	88	C
♦ *Fusion*				
Café Tu Tu Tango	★★	Inexpensive	85	C
♦ *Irish*				
Fadó Irish Pub	★★★	Moderate	88	C
♦ *Italian*				
La Grotta Ristorante	★★★★★	Very Expensive	98	C
Antica Posta	★★★★	Expensive	92	C
Abruzzi	★★★★	Mod/Exp	91	C
Pricci	★★★★	Expensive	90	C
Brooklyn Cafe	★★	Moderate	85	C
Nona's Italian Kitchen	★★	Moderate	85	B
♦ *Italian American*				
Ferrera's Bistro	★★★	Moderate	88	C
Fratelli di Napoli	★★★	Moderate	88	C

Restaurants by Zone (continued)

Restaurant	Star Rating	Price Rating	Quality Rating	Value Rating
Zone 3: Buckhead/Sandy Springs (continued)				
◆ *Japanese*				
Kamogawa	★★★★	Very Expensive	96	C
Soto Japanese Restaurant	★★★★	Expensive	95	C
Hashiguchi Japanese Restaurant & Sushi Bar	★★★★	Moderate	90	B
Circle Sushi	★★★	Moderate	88	B
◆ *Lebanese/Middle Eastern*				
Cedars	★★★	Moderate	91	B
◆ *Mediterranean*				
TomTom, a Bistro and Sushi Bar	★★★★	Moderate	90	C
Basil's Mediterranean Cafe	★★★	Moderate	88	C
◆ *Mexican*				
Oh. . . María!	★★★★★	Moderate	95	B
◆ *Mexican/Southwestern*				
La Paz	★★★	Moderate	90	B
◆ *Moroccan*				
Imperial Fez	★★★★	Expensive	90	B
◆ *Persian/Vegetarian*				
Mirage	★★★	Moderate	90	B
◆ *Seafood*				
Chops/The Lobster Bar	★★★★	Very Expensive	95	C
Atlanta Fish Market	★★★	Moderate	88	C
Fishmonger	★★★	Moderate	88	B
Fishbone & The Piranha Bar	★★	Moderate	85	C
◆ *South African*				
Ten Degrees South	★★★	Moderate	88	B
◆ *Southern/Barbecue*				
Swallow at the Hollow	★★	Inexp/Mod	88	B

Restaurant	Star Rating	Price Rating	Quality Rating	Value Rating
Zone 3: Buckhead/Sandy Springs (continued)				
◆ *Southern/Continental*				
Anthony's	★★★	Very Expensive	90	C
◆ *Southwestern*				
Georgia Grille	★★★	Moderate	88	C
Nava	★★★	Expensive	88	D
Bajaritos	★	Inexpensive	85	A
◆ *Spanish/Tapas*				
Eclipse di Luna	★★★	Very Inexpensive	88	A
◆ *Steak*				
Bone's	★★★★★	Very Expensive	98	C
Chops/The Lobster Bar	★★★★	Very Expensive	95	C
Ruth's Chris Steak House	★★★★	Expensive	90	C
◆ *Steak/Sushi*				
Prime	★★★★	Expensive	92	C
◆ *Thai*				
Annie's Thai Castle	★★★★	Inexpensive	90	A
◆ *Vegetarian*				
Café Sunflower	★★	Inexpensive	85	C
Zone 4: Lenox/Chamblee				
◆ *American*				
dick and harry's	★★★★	Expensive	92	C
Aqua Terra	★★	Moderate	85	B
◆ *Asian*				
Savu	★★★	Expensive	88	C
◆ *California Italian*				
Mi Spia	★★★	Moderate	88	C

Restaurant	Star Rating	Price Rating	Quality Rating	Value Rating
Zone 4: Lenox/Chamblee (continued)				
◆ *Chinese*				
Little Szechuan	★★★★	Inexpensive	95	A+
Canton House	★★★	Moderate	90	B
◆ *Continental*				
Kurt's	★★★	Moderate	85	C
◆ *German*				
Vrney's Biergarten and German Grille	★★★	Inexp/Mod	88	B
◆ *Italian*				
La Grotta Ristorante	★★★★★	Very Expensive	98	C
Il Fornaio	★★★★	Expensive	90	B
Vinny's on Windward	★★★★	Expensive	90	C
Villa Christina	★★★	Mod/Exp	90	C
◆ *Italian American*				
E. 48th Street Italian Market	★★★★	Inexpensive	95	A
Fratelli di Napoli	★★★	Moderate	88	C
◆ *Korean*				
Hae Woon Dae	★★★	Moderate	93	A
◆ *Korean/Japanese*				
Hanwoori	★★★★	Moderate	95	A
Asiana Garden	★★★	Inexp/Mod	90	A
◆ *Mexican*				
Costa del Sol	★★★	Inexpensive	92	B
Fonda San Carlos	★★★	Moderate	92	B
Frontera Mex–Mex Grill	★★★	Inexpensive	85	B
Don Taco	★★	Inexpensive	83	B
◆ *Southern/Seafood*				
Stringer's Fish Camp	★★★	Inexpensive	85	C

Restaurant	Star Rating	Price Rating	Quality Rating	Value Rating
Zone 4: Lenox/Chamblee (continued)				
◆ *Steak*				
McKendrick's	★★★★	Very Expensive	88	D
◆ *Vietnamese*				
Biên Thùy	★★★★	Inexpensive	90	A
Zone 5: Northeast Atlanta				
◆ *American*				
Tiburon Grille	★★★★	Moderate	90	C
Roman Lily Cafe	★★★	Moderate	90	A
The Cabin	★★★	Expensive	88	C
Dish	★★★	Expensive	88	C
Sage on Sycamore	★★★	Moderate	88	C
Food Business	★★★	Moderate	85	B
Crescent Moon	★★	Inexp/Mod	88	A
Flying Biscuit Cafe	★★	Inexpensive	88	B
The Vortex Bar & Grill	★★	Inexpensive	88	C
American Roadhouse	★★	Inexpensive	82	C
The Varsity	★	Inexpensive	80	A
◆ *American/Southern*				
Watershed	★★★★	Mod/Exp	95	C
◆ *Barbecue*				
Rockin' Rob's B-B-Q	★★★★	Inexpensive	95	A
Spiced Right	★★★	Inexpensive	90	B
Dusty's	★★	Inexpensive	90	A
Fat Matt's Rib Shack/ Fat Matt's Chicken Shack	★	Inexpensive	85	B
◆ *Cajun/Creole*				
Fuzzy's Place	★★	Inexpensive	85	A
◆ *California American*				
Murphy's	★★★	Inexp/Mod	90	C

Restaurants by Zone (continued)

Restaurant	Star Rating	Price Rating	Quality Rating	Value Rating
Zone 5: Northeast Atlanta (continued)				
◆ *Chinese / Korean*				
Yen Jing	★★★★★	Inexpensive	95	A
◆ *Cuban*				
Mambo Cuban Restaurant	★★★	Moderate	88	C
◆ *Ethiopian*				
Queen of Sheba	★★★★	Inexpensive	88	A
◆ *European Country*				
Babette's Cafe	★★★	Moderate	88	C
◆ *French*				
Le Saint Amour	★★★★	Expensive	92	C
Violette	★★★	Mod/Exp	90	B
Café Alsace	★★	Inexpensive	82	B
◆ *French Bistro*				
Le Giverny Bistro	★★★	Moderate	89	B+
◆ *German*				
Basket Bakery & Cafe at the Village Corner	★★	Inexpensive	82	C
◆ *Indian*				
Poona	★★★	Moderate	90	A
Udipi Cafe	★★★	Inexpensive	90	B
Zyka	★★★	Inexpensive	90	A
◆ *Italian*				
La Tavola Trattoria	★★★★	Expensive	95	B
Sotto Sotto	★★★★	Moderate	95	A
◆ *Italian American*				
Camille's	★★	Moderate	85	C
◆ *Japanese*				
Sa Tsu Ki	★★★★	Inexpensive	95	B

Restaurant	Star Rating	Price Rating	Quality Rating	Value Rating
Zone 5: Northeast Atlanta (continued)				
◆ *Korean/Japanese*				
Seoul Garden Restaurant	★★★	Inexp/Mod	90	C
◆ *Malaysian*				
Penang	★★★★	Moderate	95	A
◆ *Mediterranean*				
Floataway Cafe	★★★★	Expensive	93	C
Harvest	★★★	Moderate	86	C
Café Lily	★★★	Moderate	85	C
◆ *Mexican*				
Frontera Mex-Mex Grill	★★★	Inexpensive	85	B
Gringos'	★★	Inexpensive	88	C
◆ *Seafood/Steak*				
Marra's Grill: Fresh Seafood and Great Steaks	★★★	Moderate	88	C
◆ *Southern*				
Agnes & Muriel's	★★	Inexp/Mod	86	C
Evans Fine Foods	★★	Inexpensive	82	B
The Colonnade Restaurant	★★	Inexpensive	80	B
Son's Place	★★	Inexpensive	80	C
◆ *Southwestern*				
Sundown Cafe	★★★	Mod/Exp	93	C
Noche	★★★	Expensive	88	C
◆ *Thai*				
Northlake Thai	★★★★	Moderate	90	A
Thai Chili	★★★★	Moderate	90	B
Surin of Thailand	★★★	Inexp/Mod	88	A
Zone 6: Southeast Atlanta				
◆ *American*				
Heaping Bowl & Brew	★★★	Inexpensive	88	B

Restaurants by Zone (continued)

Restaurant	Star Rating	Price Rating	Quality Rating	Value Rating
Zone 6: Southeast Atlanta (continued)				
◆ *Italian*				
Pastificcio Cameli	★★	Moderate	88	B
◆ *Southern*				
Thomas Marketplace Restaurant	★★★	Inexpensive	90	A
Zone 7: Downtown West				
◆ *American/Continental*				
Mumbo Jumbo	★★★★	Expensive	95	C
◆ *Chinese*				
Hsu's Gourmet Chinese Restaurant	★★★	Moderate	86	C
◆ *Continental/French*				
Nikolai's Roof	★★★★★	Very Expensive	96	C
◆ *Southern*				
Thelma's Kitchen	★★	Inexpensive	88	C
◆ *Southern/Barbecue*				
Bobby & June's Kountry Kitchen	★	Inexpensive	85	B
◆ *Steak*				
Ruth's Chris Steak House	★★★★	Expensive	90	C
Zone 8: Downtown East				
◆ *American*				
Park 75 Restaurant	★★★★	Very Expensive	90	B
Flying Biscuit Cafe	★★	Inexpensive	88	B
The Vortex Bar & Grill	★★	Inexpensive	88	C
The Varsity	★	Inexpensive	80	A
◆ *Asian*				
Pacific Rim Bistro	★★★	Moderate	90	B
◆ *Barbecue/Southern*				
ACE Barbecue Barn	★★★	Inexpensive	85	B

88

Restaurant	Star Rating	Price Rating	Quality Rating	Value Rating
Zone 8: Downtown East (continued)				
◆ *Contemporary*				
The Abbey	★★★★	Very Expensive	95	C
◆ *Indian*				
Haveli Indian Restaurant	★★★	Inexpensive	90	C
◆ *Italian*				
Veni Vidi Vici	★★★★★	Mod/Exp	98	B
◆ *Latin American*				
Tierra	★★★	Expensive	93	B
◆ *Mediterranean*				
Eno	★★★	Expensive	90	C
◆ *Mexican*				
Zócalo	★★★	Inexpensive	95	A
◆ *Pan Asian*				
Nickiemoto's	★★★	Inexp/Mod	90	A
◆ *Southern*				
South City Kitchen	★★★★	Expensive	93	C
Mary Mac's Tea Room	★★	Inexpensive	83	B
◆ *Tapas*				
Loca Luna	★★	Inexpensive	88	A
◆ *Thai*				
Tamarind	★★★★	Moderate	94	C
Out of Area				
◆ *American*				
Breezes (Lake Lanier Islands)	★★★	Expensive	88	C

Restaurants by Zone (continued)

Restaurant	Star Rating	Price Rating	Quality Rating	Value Rating
◆ *Continental*				
Ten East Washington (Newnan)	★★	Moderate	85	C
◆ *Eclectic*				
Pascal's Bistro (Peachtree City)	★★★	Moderate	88	B

The Abbey

Zone 8   Downtown East
163 Ponce de Leon Avenue, NE
(404) 876-8532

Contemporary Classic
★★★★
Very expensive

Quality 95   Value C

Reservations:	Accepted and if conventions are in town, essential
When to go:	Weekends when conventioneers are gone
Entree range:	$20–25
Payment:	Major credit cards
Service rating:	★★★★
Friendliness rating:	★★★
Parking:	Valet
Bar:	Separate lounge, full service
Wine selection:	Fabulous, with many half-bottles and good selections by the glass; excellent prices on older vintages of outstanding labels
Dress:	Everything from nice tieless casual to glitter
Disabled access:	Difficult
Customers:	Conventioneers during the week, locals on the weekend
Open:	Every day from 5 P.M. for cocktails, with last seating at 10 P.M.
Dinner:	Every day from 6 P.M.

Atmosphere/setting: Breathtaking stained-glass windows lend a solemn note to the formal atmosphere in this church-turned-restaurant.

House specialties: Foie gras, rabbit, salmon, duck, and lamb are always prepared in interesting ways on a menu that changes seasonally.

Other recommendations: Desserts, such as whatever flavor cheesecake is on the menu, are fabulous.

Entertainment & amenities: A pianist harpist positioned in the church's choir loft plays light classics and popular tunes.

Summary & comments: This is a superior dining experience, made even more outstanding by the depth of the wine list. A must for anyone interested in fine wines, the restaurant is excellent for business as well as romantic dining.

Honors & awards: More than 12 annual awards for the wine list from *Wine Spectator;* Five Star Diamond Award from the Academy Awards of the Restaurant Industry; *Restaurants & Institutions* magazine, Ivy Award of Distinction; American Express Salute to Service, First Place SE Region, USA; DiRona Distinguished Restaurants of North America.

Abruzzi

Zone 3 Buckhead/Sandy Springs	Italian
Peachtree Battle Shopping Center	★★★★
2355 Peachtree Road, NE	Moderate/Expensive
(404) 261-8186	Quality 91 Value C

Reservations:	Accepted
When to go:	Weekends when conventioneers are gone
Entree range:	$15–27
Payment:	Major credit cards
Service rating:	★★★★
Friendliness rating:	★★★★
Parking:	Fairly adequate, depends on season and shopping center lot
Bar:	No separate bar, but full service
Wine selection:	Wide-ranging, not just Italian, fairly expensive, with limited selections by the glass
Dress:	Tieless acceptable, but jacket please
Disabled access:	Yes
Customers:	Local and visitors, chiefly an older crowd
Lunch:	Monday–Friday, 11:30 A.M–2 P.M.
Dinner:	Monday–Thursday, 5:30–10 P.M.; Friday and Saturday, 5:30–11 P.M.

Atmosphere/setting: Elegant and understated, the dining room is quiet and refined. If you hate the high noise level at many restaurants, you will savor the contemplative calm of Abruzzi. A recent re-do covered the walls in striped teal and peach fabric, lending a warm, attractive glow to the dining room. This is a classic, Old World–style restaurant, with an ambiance like many in New York. Waiters are consummately professional. The entire restaurant now is nonsmoking.

House specialties: Sweetbreads in Madeira; pappardelle (broad noodles) with game or oxtail sauce; lemon sole; veal dishes (may be prepared any style); tiramisu.

Other recommendations: Game dishes, the daily specials that take advantage of market availability.

Summary & comments: Count on the pasta to be excellent, no matter which you choose. The kitchen does classic Italian cooking, with no attempt to be nouvelle. Service is elegant and formal. Best seating is found in the banquettes that are arranged along the side of the spacious dining room. There usually is a long list of specials each night, and they're worth giving close attention

Honors & awards: Delta's international flights use Abruzzi recipes in first and business classes; DiRoNA Award 1996–2001. "The award to me is my customers," says owner Nico Petrucci, a native of Abruzzi in Italy.

ACE Barbecue Barn

	Barbecue/Southern
	★★★
	Inexpensive
	Quality 85 Value B

Zone 8   Downtown East
30 Bell Street, NE, off Auburn Avenue
(404) 659-6630

Reservations:	Not accepted
When to go:	Any time
Entree range:	$5–8
Payment:	Cash only
Service rating:	★★★
Friendliness rating:	★★★★
Parking:	Self, off site in nearby lots and on street, good security
Bar:	None
Wine selection:	None
Dress:	Scruffy casual
Disabled access:	Yes
Customers:	Blue-collar types and businesspeople from nearby Auburn Avenue
Breakfast:	Monday–Friday, 6–10 A.M.
Lunch/Dinner:	Thursday–Saturday, 11 A.M.–3 A.M.; Sunday, Monday, and Wednesday, 11 A.M.–2 A.M.; Tuesday, closed

Atmosphere/setting: This nondescript brick building offers no pretense to atmosphere. A few tables are covered in clean, if worn, cloths. The wood in the huge old brick oven is lit by burning cardboard; here the ribs will be smoked over slow-burning, aged wood. Working people hunch over paper plates filled with fine, well-seasoned food.

House specialties: Baked chicken and dressing that melt like custard; collards; macaroni and cheese; barbecue; rib tips. Breakfast: grits, fried fish, pork chops, salmon patties, eggs, homemade biscuits.

Other recommendations: Outstanding sliced pork barbecue sandwich; rich smoky ribs.

Summary & comments: The best Southern food is often found in restaurants that have nothing to recommend but the food. ACE Barbecue Barn is an outstanding example of the breed; the focus is on the food. Nothing else.

Agnes & Muriel's

Zone 5 Northeast Atlanta	Southern/American
1514 Monroe Drive, NE	★★
just past Piedmont Avenue	Inexpensive/Moderate
(404) 885-1000	Quality 86 Value C

Reservations:	Not accepted, but call ahead for priority guest list or if going in a large group
When to go:	Early or late in each meal service, or on weekdays at dinner
Entree range:	$7.95–16.95
Payment:	Major credit cards
Service rating:	★★★
Friendliness rating:	★★
Parking:	Valet (do *not* park in the adjacent business lots; towing is inevitable if you do)
Bar:	Beer and wine only
Wine selection:	Chiefly American, all available by the glass and moderately priced
Dress:	Nice casual
Disabled access:	Ramped at the front and better than most
Customers:	Neighbors, all ages, couples and theatergoers at dinner
Brunch:	Saturday and Sunday, 10 A.M.–3 P.M.
Lunch/Dinner:	Monday–Thursday, 11 A.M.–11 P.M.; Friday, 11 A.M.–midnight; Saturday, 10 A.M.–midnight; Sunday, 10 A.M.–11 P.M.

Atmosphere/setting: A charming, rehabbed bungalow with appealing interior spaces is packed with tables, putting patrons elbow-to-elbow. Funky color combinations of 1950s-era greens and turquoises dominate; porcelain critter bric-a-brac rests on a wall shelf. Check out the vintage hat boxes from now-defunct Atlanta department stores in the ladies' room. The noise level is up there, but you can still easily hear your table's conversation. In good weather, enjoy outdoor seating on a rear-facing deck with a good view of the Midtown skyline.

House specialties: Unconventional salmon pot pie; boneless buttermilk fried chicken; Carmen Miranda chicken salad; trout; Agnes's chicken club with grilled chicken and caramelized onions; shrimp corn chowder (a special); fried green tomatoes; lemon sesame collard greens; green bean casserole; french-fried sweet potatoes; and barbecue shrimp.

(continued)

94

Other recommendations: Chocolate chiffon pie; banana pudding.

Summary & comments: This is the kind of food mother prepared for bridge parties and teas, but it has been respectfully and knowledgeably updated by a well-trained pair who named the restaurant for their mothers. Take-out is a major part of the business, and the whole pies may be had for $16.95–24.95 ($5 deposit on the pie tin) with a 24-hour notice. Catering off premises is another service. Original owners Glenn Powell and Beth Baskin established the restaurant. Beth has since sold her interest to David Sneed, a former manager, making the transition to a new era relatively seamless. Glenn recently wrote the restaurant's cookbook *The Agnes & Muriel's Café Cook Book* (Longstreet Press, 2000; $15).

Honors & awards: Atlanta Journal & Constitution, One of 10 Best New Restaurants, 1996; numerous other "bests," including *Atlanta* magazine every year since its opening in 1995; Best Place to Revisit Your Childhood 2000.

Alameda

3599 Atlanta Road, Suite 11A
Smyrna
(770) 805-9343

Latin American/Mexican
★★
Moderate

Quality 88   Value B

Reservations:	Not accepted
When to go:	Any time
Entree range:	$6.25–17.95
Payment:	Major credit cards
Service rating:	★★★
Friendliness rating:	★★★★★
Parking:	On site
Bar:	Beer and wine only
Wine selection:	Limited but decent
Dress:	Casual
Disabled access:	Easy
Customers:	Neighbors, both Anglo and Hispanic
Lunch:	Monday–Friday, 11 A.M.–3 P.M.
Lunch/Dinner:	Saturday, noon–10 P.M.; Sunday, 2–9 P.M.
Dinner:	Monday–Friday, 5–10 P.M.

Atmosphere/setting: Brick-outlined faux archways and stucco-like wall finishes craft a Latin setting that could be anywhere in Hispanic land. Large tables fill quickly with families who obviously are regulars. Staff and guests inquire about each other's circumstances, indicating easy familiarity. This is a neighborhood fixture.

House specialties: Seafood soup; fried yucca; chimichurri sauce (Argentine); seafood.

Other recommendations: Fresh-baked pork marinated in spicy sauce.

Summary & comments: In a world awash with silly approaches to Latin cooking, this straightforward, home-style fare seems singularly authentic. Home-style rules, with easy presentations and flavors.

Honors & awards: Taste of Smyrna, Best Entry, 2000, for grilled pork with yucca; *Atlanta Journal & Constitution,* Best Dish, Parilla Mar Caribe (grilled seafood), 2000; *Atlanta* magazine Best Taste of South America, 2000. Good local press.

AMERICAN ROADHOUSE

Zone 5   Northeast Atlanta
842 N. Highland Avenue, NE
(404) 872-2822

American
★★
Inexpensive
Quality 82   Value C

Reservations: Not accepted
When to go: Early or late in each meal's service, as it gets busy
                      in a hurry
Entree range: $8.95–12.95
Payment: Major credit cards
Service rating: ★★★
Friendliness rating: ★★★★
Parking: On site
Bar: Beer and wine only
Wine selection: Basic stuff
Dress: Very casual
Disabled access: Yes
Customers: Neighbors, families with children for weekend
                      breakfast, businesspeople at lunch
Breakast: Monday–Friday, 7–11:30 A.M.
Brunch: Saturday and Sunday, 10 A.M.–4 P.M.
Lunch: Monday–Friday, 11:30 A.M.–5 P.M.
Dinner: Sunday–Thursday, 5–10 P.M.; Friday–Saturday,
                      5 P.M.–midnight

Atmosphere/setting: The bustling diner ambiance of this popular neighborhood spot makes for a busy place at all meal times. Counter seating is a good place for solo patrons, providing the opportunity to talk with personnel when the pace permits.

House specialties: Blue plate specials.

Other recommendations: Breakfast dishes, milk shakes, meat loaf, vegetables.

Summary & comments: There's a Southern twist to the vegetables here, although some Northern taste has compelled the chef to sweeten up the collard greens with honey—a distinctly non-Southern perspective.

Honors & awards: Creative Loafing, Best American Bistro, 1998-99; Taste of Atlanta (Kidney Foundation) Best Chili, 1998.

Anis Café and Bistro

	French Provençal
Zone 3 Buckhead/Sandy Springs	★★
2974 Grandview Avenue, NE	Moderate/Expensive
(404) 233-9889	Quality 88 Value C

Reservations:	Accepted
When to go:	Any time
Entree range:	$12.95–18.95
Payment:	Major credit cards
Service rating:	★★★
Friendliness rating:	★★
Parking:	Self, behind the building and on street
Bar:	Separate small bar, beer and wine only
Wine selection:	Mostly French (lots from the south of France) with some California; about 30 by the glass
Dress:	Very casual, but preferably nice
Disabled access:	Best on the patio, difficult inside
Customers:	Mostly locals from surrounding neighborhoods
Lunch:	Monday–Saturday, 11:30 A.M.–2:30 P.M.
Dinner:	Sunday–Thursday, 6–10 P.M.; Friday and Saturday, 6–10:30 P.M.

Atmosphere/setting: Bustling, somewhat crowded, fun, lively, and a bit tight between the tables, Anis also offers a lovely outdoor patio for dining. The patio is sheltered and climate controlled, making it suitable for year-round use. Housed in a modest former residence and nicely adapted to accommodate dining patrons.

House specialties: Classic French-style simple roast chicken with Provençal flavors (tomato, garlic); mussels; sea bass; vegetable risotto; grilled lamb chops; bouillabaisse (Wednesday).

Other recommendations: Daily and seasonal specials; classic créme brûlée.

Entertainment & amenities: Three-piece jazz band every Thursday in the patio area.

Summary & comments: This is the classic neighborhood French bistro transported to a posh Atlanta area. Dishes are the sort that one finds all over the south of France—casual, well prepared, not afraid of seasoning, served in good portions—so they're designed to remind the expatriate Frenchman of home. Three guys from the south of France keep the place on track: Arnaud Michel, Jean Fredéric, and Matthieu Jordan Gassin.

Honors & awards: Atlanta magazine, Best of Atlanta New Cuisine, 1994 and 1995; *Creative Loafing,* Best Patio, 2000, and numerous "bests" throughout the years (open since 1994); *New York Times,* a "best" recommendation, 1996.

ANNIE'S THAI CASTLE

Zone 3   Buckhead/Sandy Springs
3195 Roswell Road, NW
(404) 264-9546

Thai
★★★★
Inexpensive
Quality 90   Value A

Reservations:	Accepted
When to go:	Dinner (less rushed and a wider menu offered)
Entree range:	$10.95–16.95
Payment:	Major credit cards
Service rating:	★★★★ (at lunch), ★★★★★ (at dinner)
Friendliness rating:	★★ (at lunch), ★★★★★ (at dinner)
Parking:	Self, in the back
Bar:	Full service
Wine selection:	A fairly large selection, updated with frequent changes and additions, but few selections (Riesling) suitable for Asian fare
Dress:	Nice casual
Disabled access:	Easy via back door
Customers:	Business patrons at lunch; young couples on dates and locals at dinner
Lunch:	Tuesday–Friday, 11 A.M.–2:30 P.M.
Dinner:	Tuesday–Thursday, 5:30–10:30 P.M.; Friday and Saturday, 5:30–11:30 P.M.; Sunday, 4–10 P.M.

Atmosphere/setting: Fine pieces of Thai art enhance this nondescript space. A separate bar becomes a popular drop-in-for-drinks spot after work for the Buckhead crowd. The pace is hectic at lunch, which is fine if you're looking for something good in a hurry. Dinner is more leisurely.

House specialties: Red curry duck; chicken or shrimp Masaman with avocado; pad thai; whole fish dishes.

Other recommendations: Spicy Thai sausage salad; Yum Yai salad; glass noodle salad; outstanding specials available at dinner on the weekends.

Summary & comments: The friendliness factor suffers at lunch only because of the staff's sensitivity to patrons' need for quick service, so sometimes it seems a little too brisk. Just ask them to slow down. Dating couples really like this place.

Honors & awards: Atlanta magazine, Best of Atlanta, 1995. Lots of good local press.

ANTICA POSTA

Zone 3   Buckhead/Sandy Springs
519 E. Paces Ferry Road
(404) 262-7112

Italian	
★★★★	
Expensive	
Quality 92	Value C

Reservations:	Strongly recommended
When to go:	Any time
Entree range:	$19–25
Payment:	Major credit cards
Service rating:	★★★★★
Friendliness rating:	★★★★
Parking:	Valet
Bar:	Full service
Wine selection:	Excellent, almost all Italian and constantly being revised
Dress:	Casual dressy
Disabled access:	Yes
Customers:	Buckhead's well-heeled residents and out-of-towners
Dinner:	Every day, 5:30–10:30 P.M.

Atmosphere/setting: This small former residence has been reconfigured within to provide two spaciously set dining zones on the entrance level. Upstairs, a private dining space (or overflow as needed) offers an intimate space for special events. Downstairs, a bar for pre-dining gatherings enables a glimpse of some of the wine collection. In the main dining room, fairly quiet circumstances prevail, enabling table conversation. A small fireplace.

House specialties: Pan-seared scallops on chickpea purée; osso buco with roasted potatoes; gnocchetti with duck ragù; risotto with asparagus; bowtie pasta with fresh lobster (a special); strip steak on arugula; panna cotta.

Other recommendations: Filet mignon in balsamic vinegar sauce; warm salad of rabbit and arugula; game in season; house-made breads.

Summary & comments: This authentic Tuscan trattoria feels like a bit of Italy moved to Atlanta. It's a comfortable place to dine, and the food—rustic and simple with clean flavors and no fussy presentation—represents the best of Tuscany. This wine list is a solid piece of work, with some American wines (but why do this?) and a gorgeous raft of fine Italian selections, all priced quite fairly.

Honors & awards: Atlanta Journal & Constitution three stars and Top 50 2000; *Atlanta* magazine, Best Italian, 2000.

Anthony's

Zone 3 Buckhead/Sandy Springs	Southern/Continental
3109 Piedmont Road, NE	★★★
near Peachtree Road	Very Expensive
(404) 262-7379	Quality 90 Value C

Reservations:	Recommended
When to go:	Any time
Entree range:	$18.95–32
Payment:	Major credit cards
Service rating:	★★★
Friendliness rating:	★★★
Parking:	Valet and self on site
Bar:	Full service
Wine selection:	Extensive wine list, with many French and California wines, a few Italians, and several modest selections by the glass
Dress:	Business suits and dresses
Disabled access:	No, although yes for the downstairs private-party area
Customers:	Out-of-towners, conventioneers
Dinner:	Monday–Saturday, 6–10 P.M.

Atmosphere/setting: The Pope-Walton House was begun in the late 18th century near Washington, Georgia, more than 100 miles east of Atlanta. The authentic antebellum mansion was moved over a three-year period to its present site on an urban tract, opening as a restaurant in 1967. Portraits of stylish 19th-century dowagers adorn one dining room; romantic landscapes repose in others.

House specialties: Southern elements give character to an otherwise continental menu: carpaccio of country ham with mustard-seed oil, golden pear chutney, and house-made crackers; Vidalia onion fritters on fresh mustard greens; peanut soup (an old Colonial Southern dish); Low-Country osso buco made with pork hock; game (done in a mixed grill). Chocolate bread pudding.

Summary & comments: Peter Alexander seems well established as the venerable restaurant's guiding chef. Vegetarians get respectful treatment here, and many dishes are cheerfully adapted to their needs.

Honors & awards: American Academy of Restaurant and Hospitality Sciences, Five Star Diamond Award, 1990-1996; *Mobil Travel Guide,* Three Stars; *Wine Spectator* Award of Excellence, 1998-2000.

AQUA TERRA

Zone 4   Lenox/Chamblee
55 E. Main Street (north of the city
via I-85 to Buford exit)
(770) 271-3000

American Bistro
★★
Moderate
Quality 85   Value B

Reservations:	Not accepted
When to go:	Any time
Entree range:	$15–22
Payment:	Major credit cards
Service rating:	★★★
Friendliness rating:	★★★
Parking:	On street
Bar:	There's a bar, but beer and wine only are served
Wine selection:	Limited but very good, with some thought given to variety and to the food being offered
Dress:	Casual dressy
Disabled access:	Yes
Customers:	Folks visiting the nearby art galleries and locals
Lunch:	Tuesday–Friday, 11:30 A.M.–2:30 P.M.
Dinner:	Tuesday–Thursday, 5–10 P.M.; Friday and Saturday, 5–11 P.M.; Sunday, 5–10 P.M.

Atmosphere/setting: A brick-lined segment of an early 20th-century commercial space holds a surprising Herencia Remondo mural, touting a fine Spanish wine. The place is lively, but noise levels are restrained. Buford is a small town in the northern' burbs that has become known for its art galleries. Couples walk hand-in-hand to visit them, then wind up for dinner at this little suburban bistro.

House specialties: Dishes change frequently; some recent ones: crab cakes; calamari; crisped halibut with truffled mashed potatoes (seasonal); lamb; osso buco; chocolate soup.

Other recommendations: House-cured salmon with potato-chive pie and crème fraiche; seared Georgia rainbow trout; vanilla tuile cookie with mixed berries; homemade pastas as specials at dinner.

Entertainment & amenities: Live music on occasional Sundays.

Summary & comments: Chef Brian Legault has jazzed up the menu, changing dishes with passion and regularity. There's a five-course wine dinner ($50) every third Monday of the month; reservations are required and must be guaranteed by credit card at least by the prior weekend. First Sunday of every month is Customer Appreciation day, with half-price wine by the bottle. This restaurant is becoming a serious dining destination in the north metro area.

ARiA

Zone 3 Buckhead/Sandy Springs	Eclectic
490 E. Paces Ferry Road, NE	★★★★★
at Maple Drive	Moderate/Expensive
(404) 233-7673	Quality 95 Value A

Reservations:	Recommended
When to go:	Any time
Entree range:	$20–32
Payment:	Major credit cards
Service rating:	★★★★
Friendliness rating:	★★★★★
Parking:	Valet
Bar:	Full service
Wine selection:	Excellent, with lots of superior choices by the glass and many unusual wines from all over the planet
Dress:	Casual dressy
Disabled access:	Excellent
Customers:	The upper end of Generation X plus hold-over regulars from Hedgerose
Dinner:	Monday–Saturday, 6–10 P.M.

Atmosphere/setting: This former residence in the old Hedgerose Heights section of Buckhead once housed the vaunted Hedgerose Heights Inn, which, when sold following the death of its founder, evolved into Hedgerose. But in that incarnation, it seemed to struggle, never quite finding a niche or an identity. Recognizing the problem and moving swiftly to fix it, the owners, including partner/chef Jerry Klaskala, tossed out the staid and moved in the lively. Now patrons enter a totally contemporary space through a silver beaded curtain, designed, says Klaskala, to represent a total rupture with Hedgerose. Boy, does it ever! A fine, handcrafted, contemporary Michael Gilmartin piece serves as the hostess stand. The anemone-shaped central light fixture by Atlanta designer Chris Moulder is hard to ignore. Walls and pilasters are painted gleaming white, serving as a background for contemporary art. The energy level has been raised substantially, yet it's not exactly noisy. Table conversation is, in fact, easy and not intruded on by neighbors' chatter.

House specialties: Braised dishes, such as Zinfandel-braised beef short ribs; Port and balsamic roasted pork; any of Pastry Chef Kathryn King's magnificent desserts.

(continued)

Other recommendations: Foie gras; seafood dishes, especially when they have slight Asian touches; warm chocolate cheesecake.

Summary & comments: When you've quit giggling over the beaded entryway and have had a chance to peruse the menu and wine list, you'll soon see how completely serious this kitchen is. Beautifully appointed with its decor now simplified, Aria has zoomed to the head of its class after being metamorphosed from staid, classical Hedgerose.

Honors & awards: *Atlanta Journal & Constitution,* three stars, Top 50, 2000; kudos from *Creative Loafing; Esquire* magazine, Top 22 New Restaurants, 2000, *Bon Appétit* Best New Restaurant, 2000; *Atlanta* magazine Best New Place for Lovers, 2000; reams of good local and national press.

Asher Restaurant

Zone 3   Buckhead/Sandy Springs
1085 Canton Street, Roswell
(770) 650-9838

<table>
<tr><td>Contemporary</td></tr>
<tr><td>★★★★</td></tr>
<tr><td>Expensive</td></tr>
<tr><td>Quality 95   Value A</td></tr>
</table>

Reservations:	Essential
When to go:	Any time
Entree range:	$45 fixed-price four courses without wines; $74 with wines
Payment:	Major credit cards
Service rating:	★★★★★
Friendliness rating:	★★★★★
Parking:	Self, on site
Bar:	No
Wine selection:	Excellent choices, from a wide range of sources
Dress:	Casual dressy
Disabled access:	Easy
Customers:	Neighbors and others seeking adventurous fare
Dinner:	Tuesday–Thursday, 6–10 P.M.; Friday and Saturday, two seatings, 5:45–6:45 P.M. and 8–9:30 P.M.

Atmosphere/setting: This modest, vernacular Victorian residence makes a fine setting for intimate, romantic dining. It sits on a busy main street in Historic Roswell, taking advantage of the village feeling one gets in this early 19th-century town, founded the same year as Atlanta (1837). The downstairs spaces constitute the restaurant's dining rooms. Tables are well spaced, and the soft noise and music levels mean conversation is never strained.

House specialties: This menu changes daily, depending on the market and the season. That said, look for delicious seafood, soups, game, and fruit-based desserts. Some samples: roasted sweet potato soup with lobster and vanilla oil; potato gnocchi with braised rabbit, mustard greens and Dijon mustard sauce; grilled venison with butternut squash purée and dried cherry sauce; red-wine poached pear stuffed with mascarpone cream and scattered dried currants.

Other recommendations: Don't pass up the cheese course, an $8 supplement that's plenty for two.

Summary & comments: These portions are not huge, but with four of them, plus a shared cheese course ($8) and an amuse bouche to start, it's plenty for most folks. What matters are the flavors.

Honors & awards: Atlanta Journal & Constitution three stars and Top 50, 2000; *Knife & Fork; Atlanta* magazine, Best New Restaurant outside I-285, 2000.

Asiana Garden

Zone 4   Lenox/Chamblee
Asian Square Shopping Center
5150 Buford Highway, NE, Doraville
(770) 452-1677 or (770) 452-0012

Korean/Japanese
★★★
Inexpensive/Moderate
Quality 90   Value A

Reservations:	Accepted
When to go:	Any time
Entree range:	$9–23
Payment:	Major credit cards
Service rating:	★★★
Friendliness rating:	★★★
Parking:	Self, on site
Bar:	No, but full service is available.
Wine selection:	Extremely limited—have beer or tea
Dress:	Nice casual
Disabled access:	Yes
Customers:	Korean families and knowledgeable locals of Occidental origin
Lunch/Dinner:	Every day, 11 A.M.–2 A.M.

Atmosphere/setting: Unfussy, plain, simple, and comfortable, this is your basic neighborhood Korean restaurant. Staff smiles easily and gleefully explains what to do with mysterious morsels. Children are especially warmly welcomed. This is a favorite spot for young Koreans out in groups.

House specialties: Bulgogi (Korean barbecued marinated strips of beef), chicken, shrimp, beef ribs, and salmon are given the same basic treatment and grilled tabletop in the traditional manner; hae naeng myun (glass noodles with vegetables and minced seafood).

Other recommendations: The classic Korean seafood pancake (hae mul pa jun); wonderful cheap lunch-box specials; supremely delicious eel; excellent sushi.

Summary & comments: Delve deeply into the ethnic diversity of Atlanta's Buford Highway corridor at this bright, lively restaurant. The restaurant supports Warren T. Jackson Elementary School with gift cards to encourage children and parents to come explore Korean food and culture.

Atlanta Fish Market

	Seafood
	★★★
	Moderate
	Quality 88 Value C

Zone 3   Buckhead/Sandy Springs
265 Pharr Road, NE
near Peachtree Road
(404) 262-3165

Reservations:	Limited, but essential for weekends
When to go:	Early is best for lunch and dinner
Entree range:	$16.50–35.95
Payment:	Major credit cards
Service rating:	★★★
Friendliness rating:	★★
Parking:	Valet
Bar:	Separate, full service
Wine selection:	Mostly California, some French and Italian, several excellent choices by the glass
Dress:	Casual but nice
Disabled access:	Easy, ramped entrance, elevator to second level banquet room
Customers:	An older crowd, many locals, with some out-of-town clientele
Lunch:	Monday–Friday, 11 A.M.–2:30 P.M.; Saturday, 11:30 A.M.–3 P.M.
Dinner:	Monday–Thursday, 5:30 P.M.–11 P.M.; Friday, 5 P.M.–midnight; Saturday, 3 P.M.–midnight; Sunday, 4–10 P.M.

Atmosphere/setting: Busy, high-energy, designed to resemble a train station, the restaurant is now distinguished by its huge and controversial 65-foot copper fish, perched as if leaping from the water at the entrance. The more sedate, separate Geechee Porch, adjacent to the dining room, is a relatively quiet space.

House specialties: Crab cakes; cashew-crusted swordfish; gumbo; New England clam chowder, Hong-style Chilean sea bass.

Other recommendations: Rum-raisin bread pudding with vanilla crème anglaise.

Summary & comments: Reportedly the only Hazard Analysis Critical Control Point–certified restaurant in the country, the Atlanta Fish Market was recognized for its special handling of seafood and the chefs' and managers' training in seafood safety. The attached Pano's Food Shop sells fresh fish to take home, and the staff can cook it for you to take home.

(continued)

Honors & awards: *Esquire* magazine's Top 25 Restaurants, 1994; *Atlanta* magazine, Best Seafood Restaurant, 1994-2000; *Creative Loafing,* Best Seafood Restaurant, Readers' and Critics' Choice, 1994-2000; *Jezebel* magazine, Top 12 Restaurants, 2000; *Food & Wine* magazine, Atlanta's Best Seafood, 1998; John Mariani, *Virtual Gourmet Newsletter,* Top 10 Seafood Restaurants, Sixth Place, 1996; *Esquire* magazine, Top 25 U.S. Restaurants, 1994; *Atlanta Business Chronicle,* Best Seafood, 2001.

AzTECA GRILL

Zone 1 Southwest Atlanta	Southwestern/Mexican
1140 Mt. Zion Road, off Jonesboro	★★★
Road, near Southlake Mall, Morrow	Moderate
(770) 968-0907	Quality 85 Value C

Reservations:	Not accepted
When to go:	Any time
Entree range:	$8.25–14.95
Payment:	Major credit cards
Service rating:	★★★
Friendliness rating:	★★★
Parking:	Self, on site
Bar:	Full service
Wine selection:	Limited, really quite perfunctory
Dress:	Casual
Disabled access:	Yes
Customers:	Locals, visitors zooming through on I-75, folks shopping at nearby Southlake Mall
Lunch/Dinner:	Monday–Thursday, 11 A.M.–10 P.M.; Friday, 11 A.M.–11 P.M.; Saturday, noon–11 P.M.; Sunday, noon–8 P.M.

Atmosphere/setting: Once a pizza operation, the building is divided into separate dining spaces, and an outside patio makes appealing summer seating. Noise levels are toned down by canopies.

House specialties: Posole (December only) made with authentic seasonings, although minus boiled pig head; fish tacos; green chile stew; poblano corn chowder; chocolate chimichanga (also available at Sundown but launched here); specials can be most interesting, such as different moles and tamales or grilled flank steak on a potato cake with a zippy cream sauce.

Other recommendations: Spicy turnip greens and ancho mashed potatoes, created by Eddie Hernandez, are legendary staples of this small operation; excellent enchiladas (especially spinach); tasty refried beans; Tejano meat loaf; famous Azuni Salad, which was served at the now-closed Azuni Grill.

Summary & comments: Almost a decade ago, this operation started in association with a locally owned Tex-Mex outfit. Each store (see Sundown Café, page 270) has its own ambiance and following, a core menu, and individual items and specials. But Azteca Grill continues to serve the dishes that made its original reputation.

Honors & awards: *Atlanta* magazine, Best Mexican, 1992.

Babette's Cafe

Zone 5   Northeast Atlanta
573 N. Highland Avenue NE
Poncey-Highland
(404) 523-9121

European Country
★★★
Moderate
Quality 88   Value C

Reservations:	Accepted and highly recommended for weekends
When to go:	Any time
Entree range:	$11.50–21.50
Payment:	Major credit cards
Service rating:	★★★
Friendliness rating:	★★★★
Parking:	Valet only
Bar:	Full service
Wine selection:	Modest (50 wines), with equal parts French and California, almost all served by the glass
Dress:	Nice casual
Disabled Access:	Excellent, via ramp
Customers:	Neighbors, but also locals from other areas
Brunch:	Sunday, 10:30 A.M.–2 P.M.
Dinner:	Tuesday–Thursday, 6–10 P.M.; Friday and Saturday, 6–11 P.M.; Sunday, 5–9 P.M.; Monday, closed

Atmosphere/setting: The classic neighborhood restaurant, with warm lighting and moderate noise, Babette's relocated in 2001 to a renovated c. 1916 house just down the street. A single main dining room, an outside deck overlooking Freedom Park, and warming fireplaces make the new digs a welcoming operation.

House specialties: Steamed mussels with strawberries and serrano peppers; fried oyster biscuits with cucumber sauce; grilled salmon with grapefruit; cassoulet (seasonal); veal; Babette's Benedict (brunch); vegetarian dishes.

Other recommendations: Espresso flan (seasonal); home-fried potatoes at brunch; chocolate bread pudding; homemade banana ice cream.

Summary & comments: Buckhead types and patrons from all parts of town pull on their nicest jeans to amble on down for a hearty dish of this substantial fare. My own favorite time to be here is brunch.

Honors & awards: Creative Loafing, Best Continental Restaurant, 1999; *Zagats,* Top 200 Restaurants in United States and rated no. 13 in Atlanta, 2001.

BACChANALIA

	French/American
Zone 3 Buckhead/Sandy Springs	★★★★★
3125 Howell Mill Road	Moderate/Expensive
(404) 365-0410	Quality 98 Value A

Reservations:	Essential
When to go:	Any time
Entree range:	$35 fixed price at lunch for three courses; $58 fixed price at dinner for four courses; chefs' tasting of six courses at lunch $48 without wines, $68 with wines (not offered at dinner); á la carte available at the bar only, entrees from $20 at lunch and from $25 at dinner
Payment:	Major credit cards
Service rating:	★★★★
Friendliness rating:	★★★★
Parking:	On site, ample
Bar:	Full service
Wine selection:	Excellent, fairly priced choices, a few by the glass, but a very good selection of fine half-bottles
Dress:	Casual
Disabled access:	Yes, ramp at parking lot
Customers:	Locals and out-of-towners, couples celebrating anniversaries, business dining
Lunch:	Tuesday–Saturday, 11:30 A.M.–1:30 P.M.
Dinner:	Tuesday–Saturday, 6–10 P.M.; Sunday and Monday, closed

Atmosphere/setting: Atlanta restaurant designer Dominick Coyne has crafted a stunning yet simple interior out of what once was a meat-packing plant. Retaining the industrial elements that contribute to the sleek interior, he has arranged a dining space that is both sharp and edgy yet welcoming and warm.

House specialties: Foie gras; crab fritters; especially fine greens from a local producer; risotto in cool weather; fish; lamb; squab; warm Valrhona chocolate cake; vegetarian specialties available on request.

Other recommendations: Homemade ice creams and sorbets; soups of any kind; cheese course.

(continued)

BACCHANALIA *(continued)*

Summary & comments: One is hard-pressed to dine better anywhere on the planet. Chef-owners Anne Quatrano and Clifford Harrison deserve every accolade one could attribute to them. It's Harrison who chiefly directs this operation, while Quatrano oversees Floataway Café, the recent addition to this little restaurant family. Bacchanalia's successful move to its new location took place in February 2000. The new surroundings are located in a former meat-packing plant, Star Provisions, which has become the name for the pair's additional enterprise here: a market purveying fine gourmet foods, ranging from cheeses and wines to breads and foie gras to take home.

Honors & awards: James Beard Foundation Benefit Dinner, 1996; *Food and Wine* magazine, Best Chefs of 1995; Aspen Food and Wine Classic, 1995; Bon Appétit, 10 Best New Restaurants of 1993; James Beard Award, Best Chef 1999; #1 Restaurant for *Zagat* in Atlanta; Gourmet magazine top five restaurants, 1999-2000; *Atlanta Journal & Constitution* four stars and Top 50 restaurants, 2000; nominated Best Chef James Beard Southeast region 2000; *Atlanta* magazine Best Romantic Lunch/Dinner, 2000.

BAJARITOS

Zone 3   Buckhead/Sandy Springs
Cherokee Plaza, 3877 Peachtree Road
NE, Brookhaven
(404) 239-WRAP

Southwestern Eclectic
★
Inexpensive
Quality 85   Value A

Reservations:	Not accepted
When to go:	Any time
Entree range:	$4.75–6.75
Payment:	AMEX, VISA, MC
Service rating:	★★★
Friendliness rating:	★★★★
Parking:	On site
Bar:	Beer and wine only
Wine selection:	Limited
Dress:	Casual
Disabled access:	Easy
Customers:	Businesspeople at lunch and young couples on a budget, neighbors at night
Lunch/Dinner:	Every day, 11 A.M.–10 P.M.

Atmosphere/setting: Contemporary, lively, and cleanly designed, the restaurant is a service line with style. You select your type of tortilla, your fillings, and your house-made fresh salsas, and slide your tray on down the line to pick up a drink. Then amble on over to a table and savor an unusual twist on the wrap.

House specialties: Chicken and steak fajitas; blackened salmon burrito with mashed potatoes; Thai curry chicken.

Other recommendations: Fish and shrimp tacos; barbecued burritos; vegetarian eggplant burrito.

Summary & comments: This is some of the best inexpensive dining in the city, and a nice, quiet place to go if you're dating on a budget and want to impress with quality for the dollar. This are full-meal deals, filling and tasty for basic chump change.

Honors & awards: Insight magazine, Best Burrito, 1998-1999; Best Salsa, 1998.

Basil's Mediterranean Cafe

	Mediterranean/ Middle Eastern
	★★★
Zone 3 Buckhead/Sandy Springs	Moderate
2985 Grandview Avenue, NE	
(404) 233-9755	Quality 88 Value C

Reservations:	Accepted
When to go:	Any time
Entree range:	$9–15
Payment:	Major credit cards
Service rating:	★★★
Friendliness rating:	★★
Parking:	Self, on site
Bar:	Full service
Wine selection:	A mixture of California, French, and Italian wines, with more than 20 by the glass
Dress:	Nice casual
Disabled access:	Yes
Customers:	Out-of-towners, locals, folks from the 'burbs
Lunch:	Tuesday–Saturday, 11:30 A.M.–2:30 P.M.
Dinner:	Monday–Thursday, Sunday, 5:30 P.M.–10 P.M.
	Friday and Saturday, 5:30 P.M.–11 P.M.

Atmosphere/setting: One of Buckhead's many former residences-turned-restaurants, Basil's is a bit cramped inside, with low ceilings and tightly set tables. But the outdoor space on the front deck, carpeted and sheltered for year-round use, is a delightful breezy spot for enjoying this ever-improving bill of fare.

House specialties: Pasta paella (saffron angel hair pasta with chorizo sausage, seafood, and sweet peppers); stuffed grape leaves; marinated lamb tenderloin on rosemary mashed potatoes with asparagus and shallot red wine sauce; grilled salmon on roasted vegetable ratatouille with basil pesto sauce and steamed potatoes.

Other recommendations: Baklava; homemade flan with dried fruit compote.

Summary & comments: From the moment it was founded in 1989, this has been a popular Buckhead spot for drinks and dinner on the front deck. Family-style recipes rule.

Honors & awards: Much good local press coverage.

114

Basket Bakery & Cafe at the Village Corner

German/American	
★★	
Inexpensive	
Quality 82	Value C

Zone 5   Northeast Atlanta
6655 James Rivers Drive/
Memorial Drive, Stone Mountain
(770) 498-0329

Reservations:	Accepted
When to go:	Any time (dinner menu has more German specialties)
Entree range:	$10–13
Payment:	Major credit cards
Service rating:	★★
Friendliness rating:	★★★
Parking:	Self, on site
Bar:	Full service
Wine selection:	Modest number of very interesting choices, including two from Virginia, and a wide range of German selections, including spätlese, Müller-Thurgau, and Silvaner by the glass!
Dress:	Casual
Disabled access:	Yes
Customers:	Locals and visitors looking for Stone Mountain
Breakfast:	Tuesday–Saturday, 7–11:30 A.M.
Brunch:	Sunday, 10 A.M.–4 P.M.
Lunch:	Tuesday–Saturday, 11:30 A.M.–4 P.M.
Dinner:	Tuesday–Sunday, 5–10 P.M.; Monday, closed

Atmosphere/setting: Airy, bright, and full of good aromas from the day's baking, this one has been freshened up and expanded recently.

House specialties: House-baked breads of myriad kinds; bread pudding (occasional special); German specialties (frikadellen); sausages; schnitzels; sauerbraten; spaetzle.

Other recommendations: White-chocolate-chunk macadamia-nut cookies —awesome!

Entertainment & amenities: Jazz, golden oldies, and live performances, Friday and Saturday, 8–11 P.M., in the tavern space to the rear.

Summary & comments: Spruced up for the Olympics, this popular spot is a good place to begin a shopping trip to Stone Mountain Village.

Biên Thùy

Vietnamese
★★★★
Inexpensive

Quality 90   Value A

Zone 4   Lenox/Chamblee
Northwoods Plaza
5095 F Buford Highway, NE,
at Shallowford Road, Doraville
(770) 454-9046

Reservations:	Accepted
When to go:	Any time
Entree range:	$4.75–16.95
Payment:	AMEX, VISA, MC
Service rating:	★★★
Friendliness rating:	★★★★ (especially if owner Suzanne Bojtchewsky is in)
Parking:	Self, on site
Bar:	Beer only
Wine selection:	None
Dress:	Casual
Disabled Access:	Yes
Customers:	Vietnamese, locals, former servicemen who served in Vietnam
Open:	Wednesday–Monday, 10 A.M.–10 P.M.; Tuesday, closed

Atmosphere/setting: This is a no-frills atmosphere. Vietnamese music wails on the tape player while families feast on noodle soups and home-style specialties. Lattice work dresses up some of the booths. TVs may play golf matches. But nothing matters but the food.

House specialties: Grilled, stuffed jumbo shrimp (lemongrass, onion, beef stuffing); hu tieu (glass noodle soup with seafood); banh xeo (stuffed pancakes); cha gio (spring rolls).

Other recommendations: All kinds of noodle dishes, anything with shrimp.

Summary & comments: The authentic Vietnamese food gives the American palate no quarter, so be prepared to dine adventurously. Ask the owner's assistance in composing your meal; she is gracious and eager to explain dishes. Hotness levels may easily be adjusted to accommodate individual requirements.

Honors & awards: Creative Loafing, Best Vietnamese Cuisine, 1999 and Best Asian Noodle House, 1998; *Atlanta* magazine, Best Vietnamese, 1994-1997.

116

BluePointe

Zone 3   Buckhead/Sandy Springs
The Pinnacle Building
3455 Peachtree Road, Buckhead
(404) 237-9070

American/Asian
★★★★★
Expensive
Quality 90   Value C

Reservations:	Accepted, essential on weekends
When to go:	During the week for dinner, and early or late in service times on weekends
Entree range:	$18–29
Payment:	Major credit cards
Service rating:	★★★★
Friendliness rating:	★★★★
Parking:	Valet only
Bar:	Full
Wine selection:	Extensive, with a very pricey special-bottles list
Dress:	Casual dressy
Disabled access:	Yes
Customers:	Out-of-towners and neighbors, plus some suburbanites
Lunch:	Monday–Friday, 11:30 A.M.–2:30 P.M.
Dinner:	Monday–Thursday, 5:30–11 P.M.; Friday and Saturday, 5:30 P.M.–midnight; Sunday, 5:30–10 P.M.

Atmosphere/setting: This New York–sleek interior sweeps the view up with its high ceilings and expansive fenestration. A surprising red cylinder, its center cut away to reveal a glimpse of the dining space beyond, separates the lower level from the upper one. Comfortable seating sweeps around the bar, where groups gather until late for drinks and chatter. There's also seating at a separate sushi bar. This atmosphere is high energy, but one can still easily hear conversation at one's table.

House specialties: Duck steak with savoy cabbage and Penang curry; wok-fried calamari "pasta" with pencil asparagus and chile (appetizer and lunch entrée); salt-crusted prime rib for two at dinner; sushi; various raw oysters; peanut-crusted grouper with Massaman curry; seared yellow-fin tuna on crispy soba cake; molten chocolate soufflé cake.

Other recommendations: Imaginatively prepared fish dishes, such as ginger-crusted cod with pork cracklins and wok-seared mustard greens; shrimp-stuffed shumai-style dumplings; shrimp satay with oysters stew; caramelized apple tart with walnut brittle ice cream.

(continued)

BLUEPOINTE   *(continued)*

Summary & comments: One of the town's hottest new restaurants and an instant hit, BluePointe keeps a steady drumbeat of business. Some folks may be a bit put off by the stylish, ultrasophisticated atmosphere; this is not your basic, down-home restaurant.

Honors & awards: *Frommer's Guide,* Best Newcomer, 2000; *WHERE/ Atlanta* magazine, Most Delightful Restaurant Bar, 2000; *USA Today,* Best Elegant New Restaurant, 2000; *Esquire* magazine, Top 22, 2000; Zagat Top Newcomer, Top Room, 'I' Places, and Power Scene, 2001; *Atlanta Journal & Constitution* three stars and Top 50, 2000; *Atlanta* magazine, Best New Restaurant, 2000. *Atlanta Business Chronicle,* Best New Restaurant, 2001.

Blue Ridge Grill

Zone 3 Buckhead/Sandy Springs	American
1261 W. Paces Ferry Road, NW	★★
(404) 233-5030	Expensive
	Quality 82 Value C

Reservations:	Priority seating
When to go:	Any time
Entree range:	$17–27
Payment:	Major credit cards
Service rating:	★★★
Friendliness rating:	★★★
Parking:	Valet
Bar:	Full service
Wine selection:	Mostly California, a wide selection, with a few good choices by the glass
Dress:	Nice casual
Disabled access:	Yes
Customers:	Business patrons at lunch; neighbors and tourists at dinner
Lunch:	Sunday–Friday, 11:30 A.M.–2 P.M.
Dinner:	Sunday–Thursday, 5:30–10 P.M.; Friday and Saturday, 5:30–11 P.M.

Atmosphere/setting: Refined, rustic architecture takes its inspiration from rural, north Georgia structures. Well-spaced tables, pleasant lighting, moderate noise levels, and a comfortable bar for before- or after-dinner sipping have made this a very popular spot, sometimes requiring lengthy waits at dinnertime.

House specialties: Grilled trout (with hot cabbage and bacon hash is a special); horseradish-crusted grouper with orange beurre blanc; crab and smoked trout cakes; hickory grilled steaks; seasonal fish dishes. The menu changes seasonally.

Other recommendations: Soups, which vary daily, can be outstanding, especially Hoppiní John soup (a frequent special) and vegetarian black bean soup.

Summary & comments: Southern touches complement this hearty, regional American menu. Good old-fashioned squash casserole, collard greens, and sweet potato gratin make it easy to compose a vegetarian meal. While the quality of the kitchen has sometimes been unstable, recent staff changes seem to have smoothed out some of the rough spots.

Bobby & June's Kountry Kitchen

	Southern/Barbecue ★ Inexpensive Quality 85 Value B

Zone 7   Downtown West
375 14th Street, NW
(404) 876-3872

Reservations:	Accepted for large parties (six or more) only
When to go:	Breakfast and lunch
Entree range:	$5–7
Payment:	AMEX, VISA, MC
Service rating:	★★★★
Friendliness rating:	★★★★★
Parking:	Self, on site
Bar:	None
Wine selection:	None
Dress:	Completely casual
Disabled access:	Easy, ramped to entrance
Customers:	Locals, blue-collar types, Georgia Tech students
Breakfast/Lunch:	Monday–Friday, 5:30 A.M.–3 P.M.; Saturday, 5:30 A.M.–2 P.M.; Sunday, closed

Atmosphere/setting: This rustic, country-style establishment is a bit of the authentic old South in the middle of urban sophistication. At lunch, it's crowded with hard hats who favor basic, Southern-style comfort food.

House specialties: For breakfast, eggs, biscuits, grits, country ham, and all the trimmings; sliced pork barbecue sandwich and cole slaw; country-fried steak and gravy; fried chicken.

Other recommendations: Apple and peach cobbler.

Summary & comments: Don't tell your doctor you ate here. Everything's cooked authentic Southern style, and that means plenty of fried food. The breakfast alone could cause cardiac arrest, but once in a while it's good for the soul. And although many vegetables are frozen and the fruit for the cobblers is canned, the dishes come out tasting pretty good. This is a classic Southern barbecue joint.

BONE'S

	Steak
Zone 3 Buckhead/Sandy Springs	★★★★★
5130 Piedmont Road	Very expensive
near Peachtree Road	
(404) 237-2663	Quality 98 Value C

Reservations:	Strongly recommended
When to go:	Any time
Entree range:	$22.95–37.95, except Maine lobster at $19.95/pound
Payment:	Major credit cards
Service rating:	★★★★
Friendliness rating:	★★★
Parking:	Valet
Bar:	Separate, full service
Wine selection:	Extensive, fairly priced, and excellent California, French, and Italian, with about 15 by the glass
Dress:	Coat and tie recommended but not required
Disabled access:	Difficult, through a ramped side entrance
Customers:	Mostly male business types
Lunch:	Monday–Friday, 11:30 A.M.–2:30 P.M.
Dinner:	Sunday–Thursday, 5:30–10:30 P.M.; Friday and Saturday, 5:30–11 P.M.

Atmosphere/setting: Clubby and very masculine, with archival photographs from Atlanta's past and signed star photos lining the walls. Secluded dining spaces are especially nice for business dining.

House specialties: Excellent filet mignon; lamb; crab cakes; seafood dishes.

Other recommendations: Outstanding lobster bisque, world's best onion rings.

Summary & comments: A bastion of male power-game dining, the restaurant feels like a clubhouse for over-the-hill fraternity types. Despite all that, the food is worth anyone's attention.

Honors & awards: Wine Spectator, Award of Excellence for the wine list, 1990–2000; *Atlanta* magazine, Best Steakhouse, consistently, including 2000; *Wine Spectator,* Top 15 Steak Houses, 1996; DiRoNa 2001; *Zagat,* 2001; *WHERE/Atlanta* Memorable Meals Awards Service, 1999, Most Memorable Fine Dining, 2000; *Atlanta Journal & Constitution* three stars and Top 50, 2000; *Atlanta Business Chronicle,* Reader's Choice Power Lunch with a Client, Best Steak, 2001.

BRASSERIE LE COZE

Zone 3   Buckhead/Sandy Springs
Lenox Square Mall
3393 Peachtree Road, NE
ground level next to Neiman Marcus
(404) 266-1440

French
★★★★
Moderate/Expensive

Quality 94   Value C

Reservations:	Accepted
When to go:	Any time
Entree range:	$12–25
Payment:	AMEX, DC, MC, VISA
Service rating:	★★★★
Friendliness rating:	★★★
Parking:	Valet and self on site
Bar:	Separate, full service with bar menu
Wine selection:	Heavily French with some California and more than 30 by the glass
Dress:	Casual but nice
Disabled access:	Excellent
Customers:	Shoppers from Lenox Square, especially at lunch; families at lunch on weekends; business dining on weekdays; romantic dining on the weekends
Lunch:	Monday–Thursday, 11:30 A.M.–2:30 P.M.; Friday, 11:30 A.M.–3 P.M.; Saturday, 11:30 A.M.–3:30 P.M.
Light menu:	Monday–Thursday, 2:30–5:30 P.M.; Friday, 3–5:30 P.M.; Saturday, 3:30–5:30 P.M.
Dinner:	Monday–Thursday, 5:30–10 P.M.; Friday and Saturday, 5:30–11 P.M.; Sunday, closed

Atmosphere/setting: Warm, gaslight-era interior, with comfortable banquettes and some outside seating in good weather mark this spot as a special bistro for romantic dining and close-friends reuniting.

House specialties: White bean soup with truffle oil; creamy onion soup; coq au vin; mussels marinière; quiche; skate wing with brown butter; chocolate soufflé cake.

Other recommendations: Country-style pâté; salads; lamb dishes.

Summary & comments: Founded by New York French restaurateur Maguy Le Coze, who also owns Le Bernardin in Manhattan, the Brasserie is a great place to relax after a heavy-duty shopping spree. I actually like it better than Le Bernardin. Here, it's not impossible to spot stars, such as sometime Atlanta resident

(continued)

122

BRASSERIE LE COZE   *(continued)*

Elton John, lunching after shopping at adjacent Neiman-Marcus. But Atlantans always leave them alone to dine in peace. That's why they're here. One of my favorite things about this restaurant is the use of the flat sauce spoon, a most ingenious piece of dining equipment, and one that doesn't often appear any more, even in the most pretentious restaurants. With it, you scoop up every last drop of these magnificent sauces.

Honors & awards: *Atlanta Journal & Constitution,* Favorite 10 Restaurants, 1996; *Creative Loafing,* Best Overall Restaurant (Readers' Choice), Best French (Readers' and Critics' Choice), Best Restaurant for Romantic Night Out (Readers' Choice), Best Soup (Readers' Choice), 2000; *Atlanta* magazine, Best Brasserie, 2000, *Zagat,* Second Most Favorite Restaurant in Atlanta, 2001; DiRoNa, 2001.

The Bread Market

	American
Zone 3 Buckhead/Sandy Springs	★★★
Brookwood Village	Inexpensive
1937 Peachtree Road, NE	
(404) 352-5252	Quality 85 Value C

Reservations:	Not accepted
When to go:	Any time
Entree range:	$4–7
Payment:	Major credit cards
Service rating:	★★★★
Friendliness rating:	★★★
Parking:	On site
Bar:	None
Wine selection:	None
Dress:	Casual
Disabled access:	Excellent
Customers:	Shoppers, locals, business types, staff and visitors from Piedmont Hospital
Open:	Monday–Friday, 7 A.M.–5 P.M.; Saturday and Sunday, 8 A.M.–4 P.M.

Atmosphere/setting: Bright, brisk, and bustling, the store is attractive and warmly aromatic. Join the folks at the display case to place your order. Be careful, or you'll walk out with an armload of loaves after lingering over your weekend breakfast and newspaper.

House specialties: Specialty sandwiches, including curry chicken salad sandwich and portobello and shiitake mushrooms sandwich with fresh mozzarella cheese; desserts (yummy brownies, cookies, and cheesecake); main-course dishes, such as grilled veggie lasagna, available to go.

Other recommendations: Fat-free muffins; breakfast burrito; daily omelet menu to order; good espresso.

Summary & comments: Breads now come from the Buckhead Bread Company (see page 130).

Honors & awards: Creative Loafing, Best Bakery, 1993.

BREEZES

North of the city via I-85 and I-985
9000 Holiday Road
Lake Lanier Islands
(770) 945-8921

American
★★★
Expensive
Quality 88   Value C

Reservations:	Accepted; required Friday for lobster boils
When to go:	Any time
Entree range:	$17.50–27
Payment:	Major credit cards
Service rating:	★★★
Friendliness rating:	★★★
Parking:	Valet or self, on site
Bar:	Separate with lounge, with good selections of distilled spirits
Wine selection:	The list has been reduced but still offers a sampling of Californian, French, Australian, and Italian wines, with about a dozen by the glass; many good Champagnes and sparkling wines
Dress:	Nice casual
Disabled access:	Easy, at the front door then continuing on the entrance level to the restaurant
Customers:	Atlantans seeking a weekend away
Breakfast/Lunch:	Every day, 7 A.M.–3 P.M.
Dinner:	Every day, 6–11 P.M. (out of season 6–10 P.M.)

Atmosphere/setting: Tables are arranged around the long perimeter of the dining space, giving patrons visual contact with the outdoors while dining.

House specialties: All fish dishes, especially grilled tuna; seafood gumbo; apple onion cider soup; signature dishes such as crab-stuffed, pan-fried chicken breast.

Other recommendations: All-you-can-eat lobster boil feasts on Friday nights April through September. Breakfast dishes, including house-made muësli and sausage-cream gravy on grits with biscuits.

Entertainment & amenities: Live entertainment Tuesday through Saturday evenings in the lounge in the resort season (February through November).

Summary & comments: This is a complete getaway resort, tucked into the shores of man-made Lake Lanier, about 45 minutes north of Atlanta. Chef Leslie Peat, from England, has elevated the cooking standards, adding inventive signature dishes to the menu. A new restaurant, called Fairway Steakhouse, opened in 2001

(continued)

in the golf club. It features Black Angus steaks, large portions of fresh fish (swordfish with truffle oil, for instance), fried green tomatoes with Gorgonzola drizzle, and strawberry shortcake in a giant margarita glass. For holidays, there's a "Knee-High" buffet for the children, a special treat that Chef Peat is particularly proud to have started. Kids' prices for the regular buffet are excellent, and kids ages five and under enjoy free buffets at each meal when accompanying dining adults.

   Honors & awards: Chef Peat brings personal numerous awards to this operation, such as the Chef's Award of Excellence, Renaissance Hotels worldwide, 1999.

Bridges

Zone 3 Buckhead/Sandy Springs	American Eclectic
Abbotts Village Shopping Center	★★★
11585 Jones Bridge Road, Suite 100	Expensive
at Abbotts Bridge Road, Alpharetta	
(678) 366-8852	Quality 88 Value B

Reservations:	Accepted; almost required for weekends
When to go:	Any time
Entree range:	$13.95–22.95
Payment:	Major credit cards
Service rating:	★★★★
Friendliness rating:	★★★★★
Parking:	Self, on site
Bar:	Full service
Wine selection:	With around 150 brands, mostly Californian, this is a big suburban wine list; more than 30 by the glass
Dress:	Casual sporty
Disabled access:	Easy, street level
Customers:	Neighbors, with lots of regulars
Brunch:	Sunday, 10:30 A.M.–2:30 P.M.
Dinner:	Monday–Thursday, 5:30–9:30 P.M.; Friday and Saturday, 5:30–10:30 P.M.; Sunday 5–9 P.M.

Atmosphere/setting: Collins Caruso, an architectural firm known more for its high schools than its restaurants, has crafted three of the four restaurants that Carson Restaurant Group owns, including 10th & Myrtle (see page 18) and the River Room. Warm but contemporary with a nice fireplace, the dining room is broken up into dining areas by curved walls. Intimacy is achieved, and the large space never overwhelms.

House specialties: Plantain-crusted mahi-mahi; halibut; rack of lamb (the finishes change, but the Thai peanut sauce is a good one); salmon.

Other recommendations: Pastas (the flavors change often); butterscotch crème brûlée and pecan pie from pastry chef Pam Shallow. Rattlesnake anyone? I don't know if I'd consider it a recommendation, but it's a sure sign the 'burbs are getting adventurous. Here it's a sausage.

Entertainment & amenities: Piano player Tuesday–Thursday and a vocalist Friday and Saturday. Sometimes, folks even get up and dance. Sometimes a blues or jazz duo might rule.

(continued)

127

Bridges *(continued)*

Summary & comments: Open in 1999, Bridges has caught the neighbors' fancy and never let go. Chef Ted Lescher likes to change things, but regulars often come in and ask for their favorite dishes, such as the ginger-dusted salmon with a tomato/mango salsa that was on the opening menu. Wine dinners are held the last Monday of every month, and wine-focused events are frequent, including Friday Night wine flights—four reds or whites or a combination—for $15. Sometimes more. It's a good deal.

Honors & awards: *Hudspeth Report,* Favorite Restaurant, 2000; *Access Atlanta,* Five Stars, 2000.

Brooklyn Cafe

Zone 3   Buckhead/Sandy Springs
Springs Landing Shopping Center
220 Sandy Springs Circle, NW
(404) 843-8377

Italian Continental
★★
Moderate

Quality 85   Value C

Reservations:	Not accepted, but call about an hour ahead to put your name on the waiting list
When to go:	Before noon and after 2 P.M., and before 7 P.M. and after 9:30 P.M., especially on weekends
Entree range:	$8.95–21.95
Payment:	Major credit cards
Service rating:	★★★
Friendliness rating:	★★★★
Parking:	Self, on site, ample
Bar:	Separate, with TV; beer and wine only
Wine selection:	Decent, leaning to California, fairly priced, with a few good selections by the glass; a newly developed half-bottle section focuses on high-end selections
Dress:	Casual
Disabled access:	Yes
Customers:	Neighbors from the surrounding suburbs
Lunch:	Monday–Friday, 11:30 A.M.–2:30 P.M.
Dinner:	Sunday–Thursday, 5:30–10 P.M.; Friday and Saturday, 5:30–10:30 P.M.

Atmosphere/setting: A neighborhood restaurant prominently positioned in a typical suburban strip center, the cafe is relaxed, comforting, and casual. An open kitchen invites patrons' inspection, as the young chefs go about their business.

House specialties: Mussels; calamari; vegetarian cannelloni; shrimp fra diavolo on angel hair pasta; veal medallions in Chianti sauce; Alaskan halibut on rock shrimp risotto; yellow tomato broth with ruby beet chips as a garnish; sauteed chicken breast with Italian sausage, rosemary potatoes, pepperoncini and calamata olives with Balsamic demi-glace on spaghetti.

Other recommendations: White chocolate bread pudding; good bread to be dipped in the olive oil provided at table.

Summary & comments: Substantial portions are provided for all dishes, but, happily, pastas may be ordered in half orders—and even these are huge.

Honors & awards: Atlanta magazine, Best of Sandy Springs, 1995–1999; *Zagat,* 2001.

129

Buckhead Bread
Company and
Corner Cafe

American
★★★
Inexpensive
Quality 88   Value B

Zone 3   Buckhead/Sandy Springs
3070 Piedmont Road, NE
(404) 240-1978

Reservations:	Not accepted
When to go:	Any time
Entree range:	$6.95–10.95
Payment:	Major credit cards
Service rating:	★★★★
Friendliness rating:	★★★
Parking:	Self
Bar:	None
Wine selection:	Limited but decent, plus a few good beers
Dress:	Casual
Disabled access:	Yes
Customers:	Mostly locals, all ages
Breakfast:	Every day, 6:30–11 A.M.
Brunch:	Saturday–Sunday, 8 A.M.–3 P.M.
Limited Lunch:	Saturday and Sunday, 3–5 P.M.
Bakery:	Monday–Friday, 6:30 A.M.–6 P.M.; Saturday and Sunday, 8 A.M.– 6:30 P.M.
Cafe:	Every day, 11 A.M.–2 P.M.; limited menu, 2–5 P.M.

Atmosphere/setting: Bright, busy, divided into several service areas, including sit down, to go, and coffee bar, the bakery became a necessity after so many people wanted to buy the bread that Buckhead Life produced for its restaurants. Comfortable tables and banquettes are filled with happy, conversing people at breakfast on the weekends, taking their leisure or, solo, reading the paper.

House specialties: Egg dishes (portobello eggs, frittata, and fried green tomato BLT Benedict at brunch); breads; soups.

Other recommendations: Pancakes and waffles; marble chocolate and momma's toast French toast; stone-ground grits; sandwiches and salads at lunch.

Summary & comments: Absolutely everything you ever wanted to have for breakfast is on the menu here. No foolin'. Great coffee and real butter. Chef Jeff Gomez cut his teeth over at the sister restaurant, Buckhead Diner, and as sous chef at Pano's & Paul's.

Honors & awards: *Atlanta* magazine, Best Bakery, 1996, 1998–2000; NBC's Today Show 1997; *Creative Loafing,* Top 10 American Restaurants, 2000.

BuckHead Diner

Zone 3   Buckhead/Sandy Springs
3073 Piedmont Road, NE
(404) 262-3336

American
★★★★
Moderate

Quality 92   Value C

Reservations:	Priority seating
When to go:	Early in each service period because the place is always packed; an hour wait is not uncommon; midafternoon is good, especially for snacks, desserts, and coffee or late lunch
Entree range:	$14–22
Payment:	Major credit cards
Service rating:	★★★★
Friendliness rating:	★★★★
Parking:	Valet
Bar:	Separate, full service
Wine selection:	Extensive and well selected, mostly California, but most major wine-growing regions are represented, and more than 30 available by the glass
Dress:	Dressy casual to black tie
Disabled access:	Excellent
Customers:	Locals, tourists, movie stars—just about everybody
Brunch:	Sunday, 10 A.M.–2 P.M.
Lunch/Dinner:	Monday–Saturday, 11 A.M.–midnight; Sunday, 10 A.M.–10 P.M.

Atmosphere/setting: Sumptuously designed and appointed, this neon-wrapped upscale take on the traditional American roadhouse has little in common with the original item. Neither does the menu, except in one or two instances. But the place is magical, attracting glitterati and ordinary folk alike. The high noise level bothers some folks, but table conversation is pretty easy no matter how busy the place gets.

House specialties: Veal and wild-mushroom meat loaf with celery mashed potatoes; spicy sweet-and-sour calamari; salmon BLT; rock shrimp; P.K. Lee salad (Asian-influenced ginger-lemon-poached chicken salad with Indonesian soy vinaigrette); homemade potato chips with Maytag blue cheese; white chocolate banana cream pie.

(continued)

Other recommendations: Malteds and homemade ice cream; peach bread pudding; soups.

Summary & comments: A great place to top off a fine evening at the theater or a concert, take a load off after shopping at nearby malls, or wow a date with fine food and wine. This is one of the six U.S. restaurants prototyped at EuroDisney in Paris (1992). Visiting Hollywood glitterati frequently stop in.

Honors & awards: *Nation's* Restaurant News, World's Best New Designed Restaurant for Patrick Kuleto's knock-out design, 1987; *Restaurants & Institutions,* Ivy Award, 1994; James Beard Foundation, Best Dessert, 1994 (white chocolate banana cream pie); *Atlanta* magazine, Best Casual, Best Hot Dogs, 1996; *Atlanta Homes & Lifestyles,* Best Value Wine List and Best Wines by the Glass, 1999; *Jezebel* magazine, Top 20 and Best Place for Celebrity Spotting, 2000; *Zagat.* And many, many more.

THE CABIN

Zone 5   Northeast Atlanta
2678 Buford Highway, NE
(404) 315-7676

American
★★★
Expensive
Quality 88   Value C

Reservations:	Accepted
When to go:	Any time
Entree range:	$18.95–32.95
Payment:	Major credit cards
Service rating:	★★★
Friendliness rating:	★★
Parking:	Valet at dinner, self, on site
Bar:	Full service
Wine selection:	Well-selected wine list of modest length, with 80 really good choices by the glass
Dress:	Nice casual
Disabled access:	Yes
Customers:	Locals and out-of-towners
Lunch:	Monday–Friday, 11:30 A.M.–2.30 P.M.
Dinner:	Monday–Thursday, 5:30–10 P.M.; Friday and Saturday, 5:30–11 P.M.; Sunday, closed

Atmosphere/setting: A rustic structure with warm, dim lighting and hunting motifs. A thoroughly guy-comfortable ambiance offers moderate noise levels for a soothing atmosphere. Downstairs is a fine bar with more seating for dining.

House specialties: What makes this restaurant distinctive is game—usually grilled, cooked rare to medium-rare to order, and appropriately garnished. Venison, buffalo, and elk rotate as nightly specials; casseroles, fish, soups, and sides all vary from day to day.

Other recommendations: House-made desserts, most especially Black Bottom Pie; crab cakes; duck sausage with horseradish raspberry sauce; quail with Pinot Noir sauce on cheese grits; horseradish-crusted grouper.

Summary & comments: Oddly enough, this is a popular spot for Mother's Day celebrations, despite the decidedly masculine atmosphere.

Honors & awards: Wine Spectator recognition for the California wines on the list, 1999; *Atlanta* magazine for service and romantic dining, 1999; *Zagat,* 2001.

Café Alsace

Zone 5   Northeast Atlanta
121 E. Ponce de Leon Avenue
at Church Street, Decatur
(404) 373-5622

Alsatian French
★★
Inexpensive

Quality 82   Value B

Reservations:	For parties of six or more only
When to go:	Any time
Entree range:	$9.95–15.95
Payment:	D, MC, VISA
Service rating:	★★★★
Friendliness rating:	★★★★★
Parking:	On street or parking deck with entrance on Church Street
Bar:	Beer and wine only
Wine selection:	A small, well-chosen selection emphasizing beers and wines from Alsace
Dress:	Casual nice
Disabled access:	Easy
Customers:	Neighbors
Brunch:	Sunday, 10 A.M.–2 P.M.
Lunch:	Tuesday–Friday, 11:30 A.M.–2:30 P.M.
Dinner:	Tuesday–Saturday, 6–10 P.M.

Atmosphere/setting: Tiny and cozy, with all the sweet atmosphere two lovely young French ladies, Benedicte Cooper from Alsace and Cecile Mignotte from Burgundy, could possibly muster, Café Alsace is intimate and warm. The neighbors—from older couples looking for an inexpensive but nice meal out to young couples with kids or bent on romance—fill its few tables.

House specialties: Spaetzle; chicken liver pâté; quiche Lorraine; onion tarte; profiteroles.

Other recommendations: Salads, soups, specials (sometimes frogs legs, magret de canard, delectables like that). Cecile is from Burgundy, so boeuf bourguignon and oeufs meurette may appear from time to time. Brunch dishes, especially stuffed crepes.

Summary & comments: When you want a taste of classic, simple, neighborhood bistro cooking that's perfect, make time for Café Alsace.

Honors & awards: Taste of Decatur, Garden of Eating, second prize for the pâté, 2000.

Café Lily

Zone 5   Northeast Atlanta
308B W. Ponce de Leon Avenue
Decatur
(404) 371-9119

Mediterranean	
★★★	
Moderate	
Quality 85	Value C

Reservations:	Not accepted
When to go:	Any time
Entree range:	$9.95–17.95
Payment:	Major credit cards
Service rating:	★★★
Friendliness rating:	★★★★★
Parking:	Limited, off street; nearby parking decks
Bar:	Full service
Wine selection:	Short but interesting, frequent wine dinners and events
Dress:	Casual but nice
Disabled access:	Easy
Customers:	Neighbors, Emory-area folks
Brunch:	Sunday, 10:30 A.M.–2:30 P.M.
Lunch:	Monday–Friday, 11:30 A.M.–2:30 P.M.; Sunday, 10:30 A.M.–4:30 P.M. (same menu as brunch, but egg dishes are no longer served after 2:30 P.M.)
Dinner:	Monday–Thursday, 5:30–10 P.M.; Friday and Saturday, 5:30–11 P.M.; Sunday, 4:30–9:30 P.M.

Atmosphere/setting: Sitting on a corner of this renovated Decatur strip center, the restaurant seems removed from the urban rush. An intimate bistro, it's an oasis where regulars are warmly greeted.

House specialties: Salmon steak; filet mignon; rum-cured salmon; onion rings.

Other recommendations: Rack of lamb (occasional special); bife acebollado (Portuguese steak); panna cotta; lemon custard sponge; tiramisu.

Entertainment & amenities: On special occasions, a solo live performer.

Summary & comments: Angelo and Elizabeth Pitillo opened this neighborhood trattoria in 1999 to showcase the skills of their son Anthony. Anthony graduated from the Culinary Institute of Atlanta in 1998. Pop's proud. "He's worked and grown up in this business," he says, "and boy he has really blossomed." Ask about wine dinners and wine-focused events.

Café Sunflower

<table>
<tr><td>Vegetarian</td></tr>
<tr><td>★★</td></tr>
<tr><td>Inexpensive</td></tr>
<tr><td>Quality 85   Value C</td></tr>
</table>

Zone 3   Buckhead/Sandy Springs
Brookwood Square
2410 Peachtree Road, NE, Buckhead
(404) 352-8859

Zone 3   Buckhead/Sandy Springs
Hammond Springs Shopping Center, 5975 Roswell Road
Suite 353, NE at Hammond Drive, Sandy Springs
(404) 256-1675

Reservations:	Accepted, highly advised on weekends
When to go:	Any time
Entree range:	$8.95–16.95 (Buckhead); $8.95–13.95 (Sandy Springs)
Payment:	Major credit cards
Service rating:	★★★
Friendliness rating:	★★★★
Parking:	On site
Bar:	Beer and wine (Buckhead only)
Wine selection:	Very limited, but they're good selections, and two are organics
Dress:	Casual
Disabled access:	Easy
Customers:	Vegetarians from all over the metro area and even out of state at Buckhead; neighboring residents and business folk at Sandy Springs
Lunch:	Monday–Friday, 11:30 A.M.–2:30 P.M.; Saturday, noon–2:30 P.M.
Dinner:	Buckhead: Monday–Thursday, 5–9:30 P.M.; Friday and Saturday, 5–10 P.M.;
	Sandy Springs: Monday–Thursday, 5–9 P.M.; Friday and Saturday, 5–9:30 P.M.; Sunday, closed

Atmosphere/setting: The Buckhead location has a bright, cheery, contemporary interior with high ceilings and lots of light; Sandy Springs is more enclosed, seeming smaller and more intimate.

House specialties: Buckhead: Napoleon polenta; fajitas; moo shu vegetables;

(continued)

burritos; veggie burgers. Sandy Springs: stir-fry vegetables with tofu; quesadillas; vegetable soup.

Other recommendations: Chocolate peanut butter tofu pie (nobody would ever know it was made from tofu); carrot cake; original chocolate cake (dairy free).

Summary & comments: Husband/wife team Edward and Lin Sun and Amy Head jointly own these two restaurants, but they differ widely in style and even in food. There's a decided Asian touch to many of the dishes in both locations, but while the food is similar at lunch, it differs completely at dinner. Occasionally, the Sandy Springs location offers cooking classes. These vegetarian folks even have a pastry chef on staff.

Honors & awards: Atlanta Journal & Constitution, Readers' Select Best Vegetarian, 2000; CitySearch Best Vegetarian, 2000 nomination; *Insight,* Best Vegetarian, 2000.

Café Tu Tu Tango

Fusion
★★
Inexpensive
Quality 85   Value C

Zone 3   Buckhead/Sandy Springs
East Village Square
220 Pharr Road, NE
(404) 841-6222

Reservations:	Not accepted, but there's a pager system for wait-listed patrons and priority seating
When to go:	Off hours to avoid the crowds, before 7 P.M., especially on the weekends; early Sunday afternoon is nearly ideal
Entree range:	$3.95–8.95
Payment:	Major credit cards
Service rating:	★★★
Friendliness rating:	★★★
Parking:	Valet, in front (do not park within the square on Bolling Way)
Bar:	Two, one on each level, full service
Wine selection:	Modest but well selected, with all (32) available by the glass
Dress:	Casual but nice
Disabled access:	Yes, but not to the second level
Customers:	A young, hip crowd, the heart of Generation X, usually for romantic evenings
Lunch/Dinner:	Sunday–Tuesday, 11:30 A.M.–11 P.M.; Wednesday, 11:30 A.M.–midnight; Thursday–Saturday, 11:30 A.M.–2 A.M.

Atmosphere/setting: A re-creation of an artist's attic studio, with pieces by local artists strategically positioned to enforce the point. Dimly lit, high energy, attractive to the young and the young at heart.

House specialties: Pizzas; cajun chicken egg rolls; hummus with pita bread; empanadas; pot stickers; skewers; croquetas.

Other recommendations: House-made sangría (red and white); Mediterranean spinach dip (a vegetarian dish); Barcelona stir-fry.

Entertainment & amenities: The wacky interior is designed to suggest a starving artist's garret, and, indeed, two to three artists are on site daily painting. There's nightly entertainment—anything from tango dancers to puppeters—on the main level and moving throughout the space, including upstairs if there's not

(continued)

138

a private party up there. More than 300 pieces of art are for sale at any time, done by the artists who work there.

Summary & comments: Plates are designed to be shared, unless you have a gargantuan appetite. The idea is to order a couple of items, so bring friends. This is a spot to be enjoyed with a group. The children's menu is an art palette with watercolors (it won design award Best in the Nation from Nation's Restaurant News). The kids' party program lets them design their own pizzas, so the place is wildly popular for kids' parties.

Honors & awards: *Hispanic* magazine, Best Hispanic Restaurant in Georgia, 1994; *Creative Loafing,* Best Appetizers, 1995–2000; Nation's Restaurant News, Best New Concept, 1996.

CAMILLE'S

Zone 5   Northeast Atlanta
1186 N. Highland Avenue, NE
(404) 872-7203

Italian American
★★
Moderate
Quality 85   Value C

Reservations:	Parties of ten or more only
When to go:	Any time
Entree range:	$12.95–15.95
Payment:	Major credit cards
Service rating:	★★★
Friendliness rating:	★★
Parking:	Self, on site
Bar:	Full service
Wine selection:	Good Italian and California wines, all good ones by the glass
Dress:	Nice casual
Disabled access:	Yes
Customers:	Neighbors from the Virginia-Highland area, both families and couples
Dinner:	Every day, 5:30–11 P.M.

Atmosphere/setting: The epitome of the neighborhood trattoria, Camille's (named for the late Camille Sotis, owner with her husband, Bob) is a snapshot of old Brooklyn. Family recipes guide much of the cooking. Outdoor seating is comfortable even in cooler weather, with the heavy plastic protection in place.

House specialties: Deep-fried calamari with tangy marinara sauce for dipping; rice balls; individual pizzas; pastas. It's red sauce all the way, and, hey, that's Italian!

Other recommendations: The mussels—oh, the mussels! Vegetarian dishes are hits in this neighborhood.

Summary & comments: The neighbors really love this one, keeping it packed even on weeknights during prime hours. Go early, especially if feeding the wee ones, or prepare to wait. Children love the individual pizzas, and if you're going to get them to try calamari, this is the place to do it. Some families love Camille's so much they come with kids in huge strollers, but that's a real menace, so leave those things in the car and carry the kids into the restaurant.

Honors & awards: Numerous "bests" from sundry publications over the 17-year history of this well-loved neighborhood establishment. The *New York Times, National Geographic's Traveler* magazine, and *USA Today* are among the national presses that have lauded the restaurant. *Atlanta Journal & Constitution* featured the aroncini (rice balls) in the Food Section, November 2000.

CANOE

Zone 2   Northwest Atlanta
4199 Paces Ferry Road, NW
(770) 432-2663

American
★★★★
Moderate

Quality 90   Value C

Reservations:	Recommended
When to go:	Before 6:30 P.M. and after 10 P.M. on weekends
Entree range:	$14–20
Payment:	Major credit cards
Service rating:	★★★★
Friendliness rating:	★★★
Parking:	Valet
Bar:	Elegant space with full service and bar menu
Wine selection:	Heavy on California, with some French and Italian, and many good ones by the glass
Dress:	Nice casual to business attire
Disabled access:	Excellent
Customers:	Business types and leisure ladies at lunch; couples celebrating special events and business patrons at dinner; both locals and out-of-towners
Brunch:	Saturday and Sunday, 10:30 A.M.–2:30 P.M.
Lunch:	Monday–Friday, 11:30 A.M.–2:30 P.M.
Dinner:	Monday–Thursday, 5:30–10:30 P.M.; Friday and Saturday, 5:30–11:30 P.M.; Sunday, 5:30–9:30 P.M.

Atmosphere/setting: Other restaurateurs would kill for this setting, along the banks of the Chattahoochee River, where Civil War troops massed. A charming garden setting with imposing sculpture invites weddings and special events. The noise level inside can make dining uncomfortable for some people; if that's a concern, ask about a table on the porch or, in nice weather, outside.

House specialties: House-smoked salmon; rock shrimp cakes; almond-studded catfish strips with green curry sauce; Chinese-style duck; grilled vegetable plate (changes seasonally); pappardelle and other fresh pastas.

Other recommendations: Chocolate hazelnut praline cake; lamb sandwich; squash soup.

Summary & comments: Nowhere does one find a better combination of food and view than at Canoe.

Honors & awards: Nominated for James Beard Foundation's Best New Restaurant, 1996, one of only five chosen nationwide; numerous kudos from the *Zagat;* Trend/Wire, Best American Bistro, 1996; *Esquire* magazine, Best New Restaurant, 1996; *Atlanta* magazine, Best Restaurant, 1999 and Best Location, 2000.

141

Canton House

Zone 4   Lenox/Chamblee
4825 Buford Highway, Chamblee
(770) 936-9030

Chinese/Cantonese	
★★★	
Moderate	
Quality 90	Value B

Reservations:	Accepted (but not on Saturday and Sunday)
When to go:	Any time
Entree range:	$5.50–24; $65 for abalone
Payment:	Major credit cards
Service rating:	★★★
Friendliness rating:	★★★
Parking:	Self, on site
Bar:	Beer and wine only
Wine selection:	Limited
Dress:	Nice casual
Disabled access:	Access at side door
Customers:	Chinese families with small children; neighbors, including Occidentals with adventurous palates
Lunch/Dinner:	Saturday, 10:30 A.M.–11 P.M.; Sunday, 10:30 A.M.–10:30 P.M.
Lunch:	Monday–Friday, 11 A.M.–3 P.M.
Dinner:	Monday–Thursday, 5–10:30 P.M.; Friday, 5–11 P.M.

Atmosphere/setting: Busy and lively on Saturday and Sunday mornings, as smiling young girls deftly wheel huge carts loaded with dim sum, maneuvering them skillfully among the tables. Conversation is lively and obviously happy families enjoy late breakfast, Chinese style.

House specialties: Dim sum; lobster and crab with ginger and scallion; whole steamed or braised fish; abalone.

Other recommendations: Barbecued pork buns; Chinese broccoli (galan) with garlic sauce.

Summary & comments: One of the most authentic Chinese restaurants in town, it eagerly welcomes Occidental patrons. It's so popular that sometimes you have to wait for a table, or agree to sit in the smoking section (it's not really awful).

Honors & awards: A favorite of local critics and publications. *Creative Loafing,* Best Dim Sum 1997–1999; Citysearch, Best Chinese Restaurant in Atlanta, 2000.

Cedars

Zone 3   Buckhead/Sandy Springs
2770 Lenox Road, NE
(404) 261-1826

| Lebanese/ |
| Middle Eastern/American |
| ★★★ |
| Moderate |
| Quality 91   Value B |

Reservations:	Accepted
When to go:	Any time, but buffet lunch is a value ($7.75), while dinner is more adventurous
Entree range:	$12.95–17.95
Payment:	Major credit cards
Service rating:	★★★★
Friendliness rating:	★★★★
Parking:	Self, on site
Bar:	Full service
Wine selection:	Limited but decent, with maybe a dozen by the glass
Dress:	Casual
Disabled access:	Yes
Customers:	Neighbors and visitors, a wide range of all types and ages
Lunch:	Monday–Friday, 11:30 A.M.–2:30 P.M.; Sunday, noon–3 P.M.
Dinner:	Sunday–Thursday, 6–9:30 P.M.; Friday, 6–10:30 P.M.; Saturday, 5:30–10:30 P.M.

Atmosphere/setting: Contemporary, bright, cheerful spaces form a noncaricatured setting for Lebanese and Middle Eastern fare, resisting the temptation to overexpress this region's art and culture.

House specialties: The special for two, a selection of two grilled items—shrimp and lamb are excellent choices—on rice; good hummus and tahini; kibbeh.

Other recommendations: Lentil soup; excellent tabbouleh (cracked wheat salad).

Summary & comments: It's difficult to find this restaurant, even though it is very close to Lenox Road. Look for a pair of unnamed shopping strips facing each other and running perpendicular to Lenox Road. The restaurant is in the corner of the left-hand strip. Once you find it, you're rewarded with intimate atmosphere and very fine service.

Honors & awards: U.S. Chefs Open, three gold medals for lentil soup, tabbouleh salad, and raw kibbeh, 1989, 1990, 1991. Nothing more recent.

Chops/The Lobster Bar

	Steak/Seafood
Zone 3 Buckhead/Sandy Springs	★★★★
70 W. Paces Ferry Road, NW	Very expensive
(404) 262-2675	
	Quality 95 Value C

Reservations:	Strongly recommended
When to go:	Any time
Entree range:	$16.95–38.50
Payment:	Major credit cards
Service rating:	★★★★
Friendliness rating:	★★
Parking:	Valet
Bar:	Full service
Wine selection:	Extensive and excellent
Dress:	Business attire to casual
Disabled access:	Yes
Customers:	Buckhead business types
Lunch:	Monday–Friday, 11:30 A.M.–2:30 P.M.
Dinner:	Monday–Thursday, 5:30–11 P.M.; Friday and Saturday, 5:30 P.M.–midnight; Sunday, 5:30–10 P.M.

Atmosphere/setting: The very masculine atmosphere attracts entire tables of businesspeople. A false ceiling in dark, warm wood is lit with brass-and-glass fixtures. Black leather banquettes provide comfortable seating. The place is clearly inspired by New York or Chicago steakhouses. Downstairs has been developed as a supremely posh lobster bar, worth checking out for its own merits.

House specialties: Steak, steak, and more steak. But also excellent veal chops; terrific fish (especially the swordfish lightly dusted with coarsely ground peppercorns and ground almonds); crab cakes.

Other recommendations: Any and all soups, which change daily, and the vegetable side dishes, especially the mashed potatoes. Vegetarian guests will have no problem composing a delectable plate.

Summary & comments: A place for business dining more than for romantic purposes, Chops gets high marks from the steak-loving set for the size of the cuts (veal chop weighs in at 14 ounces) and the quality. The bar staff knows what to do when pouring a bourbon, but don't trust it with more subtle matters, such as chilling sherry correctly or pouring a decent one to start with.

Honors & awards: *Wine Spectator,* Award of Excellence, 1998; *Gourmet* magazine Top 10 Restaurants in Atlanta, 1999; *Jezebel* magazine No. 1 Restaurant, 2000; *Zagat; Creative Loafing,* Best Steaks, 2000; DiRoNa, 1997–2000.

144

Chopstix

Hong Kong Chinese
★★★
Moderate

Quality 88   Value C

Zone 3   Buckhead/Sandy Springs
Chastain Square
4279 Roswell Road, NE
(404) 255-4868

Reservations:	Accepted
When to go:	Any time
Entree range:	$15.95–29.95; $39.95 Peking duck
Payment:	Major credit cards
Service rating:	★★★
Friendliness rating:	★★★★ (owner), ★★ (staff)
Parking:	Self, on site
Bar:	Full service
Wine selection:	Moderate-priced California selections, with a few by the glass; only a few selections by the bottle (and none by the glass) appropriately complement this food; list needs to be rethought with the food in mind
Dress:	Nice casual
Disabled access:	Yes
Customers:	Neighbors, businesspeople, families, and couples on romantic missions
Lunch:	Monday–Friday, 11:30 A.M.–2 P.M.
Dinner:	Every day, 6–11 P.M.

Atmosphere/setting: It takes a minute to get used to the warm, dim lighting (a bit too low perhaps), but at dinner the lighting serves to invite intimate couple chatter. Tux-garbed waiters are a bit stiff and distant, but they are efficient.

House specialties: Assorted dumplings: seafood pot stickers, roast duck ravioli, spicy dumplings; black pepper oysters; pine nut chicken; moo shu beef; pork tenderloin stir fried with ginger and garlic; steamed sea bass; roast duck breast with mango.

Other recommendations: All forms of soft-shell crab, served only in season; pan-seared foie gras with scallions; nori and a touch of Cointreau.

Entertainment & amenities: Piano music nightly.

Summary & comments: Appetizers are large enough to do duty as light entrees for late-night dining. The only problem is, if you order two of them, they will come simultaneously instead of sequentially, no matter what you say. This food is really continental with Asian touches, a most delicious intersection of traditions.

(continued)

145

Chopstix *(continued)*

One of the city's most inventive Chinese restaurants, it's casual white tablecloth, making it suitable for business dining and romance.

Honors & awards: *Atlanta* magazine, Best Gourmet Chinese Restaurant, since 1986; Executive Chefs of America, Chef of the Year for chef-owner Philip Chan, 1994; DiRoNA award, 1994–2000; *Gourmet* magazine, Top 20, November 1996; *Atlanta Journal & Constitution,* Best in Fulton County, 2000; *Atlanta Business Chronicle,* Readers' Choice Best Chinese, 2001; *Zagat,* Best Chinese, 2001.

Circle Sushi

Zone 3   Buckhead/Sandy Springs
Dunwoody Plaza II, Suites 7/8
8725 Roswell Road
(770) 998-7880

Japanese	
★★★	
Moderate	
Quality 88	Value B

Reservations:	Accepted, and required for parties of six or more
When to go:	Any time
Entree range:	$9.50–22
Payment:	Major credit cards
Service rating:	★★★★★
Friendliness rating:	★★★★
Parking:	Self, on site
Bar:	Beer and wine only
Wine selection:	Limited, but about eight premium sakes
Dress:	Casual dressy
Disabled access:	Easy
Customers:	Locals, many Japanese
Lunch:	Monday–Friday, 11:30 A.M.–2:30 P.M
Dinner:	Sunday–Thursday, 5:30–10 P.M.;
	Friday and Saturday, 5:30–10:30 P.M.

Atmosphere/setting: This cleanly designed, contemporary space feels like the handiwork of a modern Japanese architect. Tables are well spaced, and the staff flits easily among them without disturbing diners. Noise levels are subdued, and the atmosphere is quiet without being temple-like. Children and adults alike feel comfortable in this ambiance.

House specialties: Sushi and sashimi; katsu dishes (fried Japanese style); traditional soups and noodle dishes; traditional and special rolls; Bento boxes.

Other recommendations: Shumai and gyoza (dumplings); teriyaki.

Summary & comments: This restaurant likes to emphasize the positive and healthful aspects of Japanese food, enhanced by a glass of chilled premium sake. Guests are encouraged to ask for special items and to discuss with staff any food allergies they may have. The adventurous will find everything from sea urchin to eel, while there are plenty of choices for those who prefer more familiar sushi material. Vegetarians will love the large section of vegetarian rolls.

Honors & awards: Knife & Fork; and other positive local press.

Coco Loco Cuban & Caribbean Restaurant

Cuban/Caribbean	
★★	
Inexpensive/Moderate	
Quality 88	Value B

Zone 3   Buckhead/Sandy Springs
Crossing Mall, Suite G-40
2625 Piedmont Road, NE
Buckhead
(404) 364-0212

Reservations:	Accepted for parties of four or more; essential on weekends
When to go:	Any time
Entree range:	$8.50–16.95
Payment:	Major credit cards
Service rating:	★★★★
Friendliness rating:	★★★★★
Parking:	Self, on site
Bar:	Separate bar with full service, with tapas from main menu
Wine selection:	A few Chilean, Spanish, and Californian wines, with some by the glass
Dress:	Casual
Disabled access:	Easy, street level
Customers:	A total melting pot; baseball players of Hispanic background make weekends here during the season if they're not playing
Lunch:	Monday–Thursday, 11 A.M.–2:30 P.M.
Lunch/Dinner:	Friday, 11 A.M.–10:30 P.M.; Saturday, noon–11 P.M.; Sunday, 1–9 P.M.
Dinner:	Monday–Thursday, 6–10 P.M.

Atmosphere/setting: A bright, lively cafe with plenty of atmospheric decor, the place packs with friends and families enjoying the home-style fare. The colors are pure Caribbean, with brilliant greens and turquoises vying for attention. The wall mural on the entrance-space wall sports a bas relief executed by Ana Guzmán, wife of owner Julio Guzmán.

House specialties: Pork chunks and roast pork; Argentinian-style steak (churrasca with chimichurri sauce—available in two portion sizes); jerked shrimp or chicken; black beans; shrimp Creole; paella ($36.95 for two); lobster (market price). A quick-version Paella Coco Loco is available nightly without prior order ($9.95).

(continued)

Coco Loco Cuban &
Caribbean Restaurant *(continued)*

Other recommendations: All tapas; croquetas; tostones rellenos; empanadas; conch fritters; super Cuban sandwiches; house-made sangría; coconut flan.

Entertainment & amenities: Saturday salsa.

Summary & comments: Start your visit off right with a glass of chilled sangría. You will relax here from the moment you step in the door. If ordering paella for a crowd, call ahead for the big one. When ordering main dishes, which are consistently delicious, choose a side of yucca, plaintain, or black beans, which are well seasoned and quite tasty. The side-dish rice—and this has nothing whatsoever to do with the paella or arroz con pollo—is colorful but lacks any character. Skip it. The Cuban coffee, too, is a bit lame, thin, and Americanized. Celebrities love this place, which has hosted such stars as Tito Puentes, Marc Anthony, Carlos Santana, and Julia Roberts.

Honors & awards: *Hispanic* magazine, One of 15 Best Hispanic Restaurants in the Country, 1995–1999; *Creative Loafing,* Gwinnett Best Cuban, 1999, and Topside Best Cuban, 2000. Lots of positive local press.

THE COLONNADE
RESTAURANT

Zone 5   Northeast Atlanta
1879 Cheshire Bridge Road, NE
near Piedmont Road
(404) 874-5642

Southern	
★★	
Inexpensive	
Quality 80	Value B

Reservations:	Not accepted
When to go:	Any time
Entree range:	$6–20
Payment:	Cash and check (out-of-town check okay with ID)
Service rating:	★★★
Friendliness rating:	★★★★
Parking:	Self, on site
Bar:	Separate bar with lounge and full service
Wine selection:	Limited but good selections, with some by the glass
Dress:	Casual
Disabled access:	Yes
Customers:	Locals, restaurateurs on their days off
Lunch:	Wednesday–Saturday, 11:30 A.M.–2:30 P.M.
Dinner:	Monday–Thursday, 5–9 P.M.; Friday and Saturday, 5–10 P.M.
Lunch/Dinner:	Sunday, 11:30 A.M.–9 P.M.

Atmosphere/setting: An ample dining room, brightly lit, with well-spaced tables and a sort of contemporary country decor, The Colonnade is where the iced-tea set mingles for lunch.

House specialties: Fried chicken; fried shrimp; prime rib; oyster stew; coconut cream pie.

Other recommendations: Chicken pot pie; salmon patties; bone-in, center-cut ham steak; trout; vegetables; chicken-fried steak.

Summary & comments: After a fire nearly destroyed this landmark establishment, it came back to life in better shape than ever. It's not glossy, and shouldn't be, but the comfortable interior decor makes a perfect scene for this food.

Honors & awards: Best testimony? The long lines of waiting, hungry, patrons that show up every day. There's been lots of positive press, so much that nobody at the restaurant keeps any records of specific kudos.

Costa del Sol

Zone 4   Lenox/Chamblee
Cedar Village Shopping Center
5265 Jimmy Carter Boulevard
Suite 6228, Norcross
(770) 840-6040

Mexican/Salvadoran	
★★★	
Inexpensive	
Quality 92	Value B

Reservations:	Not accepted
When to go:	Any time
Entree range:	$6.50–25
Payment:	Major credit cards
Service rating:	★★★
Friendliness rating:	★★★★
Parking:	Self, on site
Bar:	Beer only
Wine selection:	None
Dress:	Casual
Disabled access:	Easy
Customers:	Local Hispanics, mostly from Mexico and El Salvador
Lunch/Dinner:	Every day, 11 A.M.–11 P.M.

Atmosphere/setting: This simply decorated restaurant has lively colors to suggest the feeling of home, which for most of the customers is somewhere in the Hispanic world.

House specialties: Papusas (stuffed corn cakes); pozole (pork stew with chiles); fried yuca with chicharrón (pork rinds); tamales; menudo (tripe soup); atol de elote (sweet corn soup—weekends only).

Other recommendations: All kinds of shrimp dishes, especially shrimp a la diabla (jalapeno-wrapped shrimp with bacon); chicken mole; grilled steak; traditional breakfast dishes.

Summary & comments: Practice your Spanish and have fun at this popular restaurant, because here is authenticity at its finest. Traditional breakfast dishes are served throughout the day.

Honors & awards: Knife & Fork; other good local press.

CRAZY CUBAN

Zone 2 Northwest Atlanta	Cuban
Terrell Mill Junction Shopping Center	★★
1475 Terrell Mill Road, Suite 103	Inexpensive
Marietta	Quality 88 Value C
(770) 226-0021	

Reservations:	Not accepted
When to go	Any time
Entree range:	$8.99–12.99
Payment:	Major credit cards
Service rating:	★★★
Friendliness rating:	★★★
Parking:	On site
Bar:	Beer and wine only
Wine selection:	Limited, with recognizable labels from good wineries; a few by the glass
Dress:	Casual
Disabled access:	Easy
Customers	From the neighborhood and all over the metro area; most are Anglo
Lunch:	Monday–Saturday, 11:30 A.M.–3 P.M.
Dinner:	Monday–Thursday, 5:30–9:30 P.M.; Friday and Saturday, 6–10 P.M.

Atmosphere/setting: A lively Hispanic ambiance permeates this high-energy newcomer, decorated with memorabilia designed to make the place feel like home for any Latinos who might drop in for some home cooking.

House specialties: Ropa vieja (shredded beef brisket); vaca frita (fried beef brisket steak); Cuban sandwiches; Three Milks Cake.

Other recommendations: Empanadas; steak empanizado.

Entertainment & amenities: Traditional live salsa music on the weekends.

Summary & comments: This is a family-style Cuban restaurant, with dishes that reflect the widely diverse sources of Cuban food, from Spanish to African.

Honors & awards: Some good local press coverage.

CRESCENT MOON

Zone 5 Northeast Atlanta	American
174 W. Ponce de Leon Avenue	★★
Parking Deck at One West	Inexpensive/Moderate
Court Square, Decatur	Quality 88 Value A
(404) 377-5623	

Reservations:	Not accepted
When to go:	Any time
Entree range:	$6.50–12.99
Payment:	Major credit cards
Service rating:	★★★★★
Friendliness rating:	★★★★★
Parking:	On street or the ground level of the One West Court Square Parking Deck (off Swanton Way) near the MARTA pick-up
Bar:	Beer and wine only
Wine selection:	Limited
Dress:	Casual
Disabled access:	Excellent, at front door on street
Customers:	Decaturites
Breakfast/Lunch:	Sunday–Thursday, 7:30 A.M.– 3 P.M.; Friday and Saturday, 7:30 A.M.–10:30 P.M.
Dinner:	Tuesday–Thursday, 5:30–9:30 P.M.; Friday and Saturday, 5:30–10:30 P.M.

Atmosphere/setting: Crescent Moon recently discarded its down-at-the-heel diner style for a new look. Since picking up and moving to a new location just a few steps away from the original, it's been transformed into a spiffy designer diner with a down-home feel. Now, there's even a place to park!

House specialties: Omelets and breakfast skillets; hotcakes; roasted tofu; homemade chili (occasionally done as soup of the day); house-smoked barbecue pork sandwich; blue plate specials.

Other recommendations: Buttermilk-battered fried chicken; meat loaf; roasted chicken pot pie; huge stuffed baked potatoes.

Summary & comments: Rob Atherholt launched the original Crescent Moon in 1995. It grew and grew until he moved it in late 2000, when he took the opportunity to add space and some nifty design features, making the transition to a dining location. Families gather at Formica-topped tables and booths, and there's lovely counter seating for singles. The entire restaurant is nonsmoking.

Honors & awards: *Creative Loafing,* Best Diner, 1999–2000; *Zagat,* 1998–2001, for food and service; lots of positive local press.

dick and Harry's

Zone 4   Lenox/Chamblee
Holcomb Woods Village Shopping
Center, 1570 Holcomb Bridge Road
Roswell
(770) 641-8757

American
★★★★
Expensive
Quality 92   Value C

Reservations	Highly advised
When to go:	Monday–Thursday for dinner; lunch is OK, but dinner is when the place shines; weekends are jammed
Entree range:	$12.95–30.40
Payment:	Major credit cards
Service rating:	★★
Friendliness rating:	★★★
Parking:	On site
Bar:	Full service
Wine selection:	Short, but with some very good choices, some good ones by the glass, and a fine half-bottle list. Customers seem to prefer the expensive selections, so the prices have notched up some.
Dress:	Casual dressy
Disabled access:	Yes
Customers:	Eager patrons from all over town
Lunch:	Monday–Friday, 11:30 A.M.–2:30 P.M.
Dinner:	Monday–Thursday, 5:30–10 P.M.; Friday and Saturday, 5:30–11 P.M.

Atmosphere/setting: Located in a busy suburban shopping center, this is one of the northside 'burb's best restaurants. A sleek, contemporary ambiance insulates the place from its surroundings. It's bit on the noisy side, especially in the evening, but that doesn't seem to interfere with its persistent popularity.

House specialties: Game; emu; crab cakes; crème brûlée.

Other recommendations: Oysters; veal chop; side dishes.

Summary & comments: To savor the glories of this cooking, be sure your first visit is at dinner. Some friends report being rushed when the place is full with patrons waiting for tables, but most report good service, and my own service experiences over three visits have been good.

Honors & awards: Lots of positive local press from day one. *Atlanta* magazine, Best New Restaurant, 1996, Best of the Burbs, 2000; *Gourmet* magazine, America's Top Tables, 1999; *Wine Spectator* Award of Excellence, 2000.

Dish

Zone 5   Northeast Atlanta
870 N. Highland Avenue, NE
Virginia-Highland
(404) 897-3463

American Eclectic
★★★
Expensive

Quality 88   Value C

Reservations:	Reservations accepted for parties of five or more
When to go:	Sunday–Tuesday is easier to access, and before 7 P.M.
Entree range:	$14–22
Payment:	Major credit cards
Service rating:	★★★★
Friendliness rating:	★★★★
Parking:	On site, but very limited
Bar:	Full service, with a large, central U-shaped bar that gathers friendly folks
Wine selection:	Long, with many by the glass; mostly American; good reserve list
Dress:	Casual
Disabled access:	Yes, easy
Customers:	Neighbors, lots of Generation Xers
Dinner:	Sunday–Thursday, 5:30–10 P.M.; Friday and Saturday, 5:30–11 P.M.

Atmosphere/setting: Once this was a gas station; then it became a very popular wine bar (R.J.'s, featured in the last edition). Then it was sold and became Dish. The popular place to dine remains the sheltered, tented patio, but there is table seating indoors. The atmosphere is light, uncomplicated, and youthful, as neighbors gather to share drinks and dine.

House specialties: Rosemary-scented popcorn; endive, Gorgonzola, grilled pear salad; free-form lobster lasagna with shrimp and scallops, lobster cream sauce, and arugula coulis (when available); fish dishes (skate wing, red snapper).

Other recommendations: Crab beignets on mango.

Summary & comments: Early on, some dishes made no culinary sense, such as a too-hot (spicy) treatment of crab cakes. But the menu today, and the kitchen's execution, are first rate.

Honors & awards: Very positive local press. *Atlanta* magazine, Best Reason to go to Virginia-Highland, 1998–2000.

Don Taco

Mexican
★★
Inexpensive
Quality 83   Value B

Zone 4   Lenox/Chamblee
4997 Buford Highway, Chamblee
(770) 458-8735

Zone 4   Lenox/Chamblee
Perimeter Mall, 4400 Ashford Dunwoody Road, Dunwoody
(770) 394-0084

Zone 4   Lenox/Chamblee
5884 Buford Highway, Doraville
(770) 457-6103

Reservations:	Not accepted
When to go:	Any time
Entree range:	$3.95–5.99
Payment:	Major credit cards
Service rating:	★★★
Friendliness rating:	★★★
Parking:	Self, on site, or drive-through
Bar:	None
Wine selection:	Beer only (Buford Highway)
Dress:	Super casual
Disabled access:	Yes
Customers:	Local Mexicans, Central Americans, Anglos
Lunch/Dinner:	Doraville and Chamblee: Monday–Thursday, 11 A.M.–11 P.M.; Friday–Sunday, 11 A.M.– midnight
	Dunwoody: Monday–Friday, 10 A.M.–9 P.M.; Saturday, 11 A.M.–9 P.M.; Sunday, noon–6 P.M.

Atmosphere/setting: At Buford Highway, a fast-food joint has been transformed into a fast-paced operation with a drive-through and comfortable seating. A sign in Spanish on the front door advises the inebriated that they're not welcome.

House specialties: Grilled steak plate; rib-eye tacos; shrimp fajita quesadilla.

Other recommendations: Vegetarian burritos; queso fundido.

Summary & comments: A unit of the successful company that also launched Frontera Mex-Mex Grill (see page 183), this charming crew deserves more attention than it has gotten to date. As for the food, some friends sent me over here to get supper one night. Their evaluation? "Como en casa" (just like home).

Honors & awards: Positive press coverage from local and industry press.

Dusty's

Reservations:	Not accepted
When to go:	Any time
Entree range:	$7.22–15
Payment:	Major credit cards and checks
Service rating:	★★★★
Friendliness rating:	★★★
Parking:	Self, on site
Bar:	Beer and wine
Wine selection:	Limited
Dress:	Very casual
Disabled access:	Yes
Customers:	Students, business types, locals of all kinds
Lunch/Dinner:	Sunday–Thursday, noon–9 P.M.;
	Friday and Saturday, noon–10 P.M.

Atmosphere/setting: Rustic, stylized, "about-to-fall down" charm.

House specialties: North Carolina–style barbecue with vinegar-pepper sauce and house-made cole slaw to put on top. All sauces house-made; spice levels range from mild to sizzlin' hot.

Other recommendations: Hush puppies, which North Carolinians consider essential with barbecue.

Summary & comments: Drive-through convenience means you can grab a 'cue-and-slaw sandwich on the run. You'll probably have it snarfed before leaving the parking lot, however.

Honors & awards: Creative Loafing, Best Barbecue Sandwich and Side Dish, 1995, and Readers' Poll nine times; Guest Quarters Best of Atlanta for parties; WSB Viewers' Poll, Georgia's Top 10 Barbecue.

E. 48TH STREET ITALIAN MARKET

Italian-American Deli	
★★★★	
Inexpensive	
Quality 95	Value A

Zone 4   Lenox/Chamblee
Williamsburg at Dunwoody
Shopping Center, 2462 Jett Ferry Road
at Mt. Vernon Road, Dunwoody
(770) 392-1499

Reservations:	Not accepted
When to go:	Any time, but avoid busy Saturday
Entree range:	$4.25–5.95 (sandwiches); $2.25 (per manicotti)–$5.75 (pasta and meatballs); salads $.99–$4.99
Payment:	Cash or check (out-of-town checks with ID)
Service rating:	★★★★
Friendliness rating:	★★★★★
Parking:	Self, on site
Bar:	Beer and wine by the glass
Wine selection:	Mostly Italian
Dress:	Casual
Disabled access:	Tight, but outdoor dining available
Customers:	Locals, visiting expatriate New Yorkers, businesspeople at lunch
Open:	Monday–Friday, 10 A.M.–7 P.M.; Saturday, 10 A.M.–6 P.M.; Sunday, closed

Atmosphere/setting: A small, shopping-center space, the market would be nondescript were it not for the center shelves piled with imported dried pastas and other staples of Italian cooking. On Saturday, the place gets jammed with expatriate New Yorkers of Italian descent looking for dishes from the homeland (Brooklyn and da Bronx).

House specialties: Italian beef sandwich; stoffato (Italian deli meats with house sauce on house-made bread); muffuletta; prosciutto with fresh mozzarella.

Other recommendations: House-made biscotti; anginetti (lemon cookies); specialty seasonal treats, such as torta rustica and baccalá salad (holidays).

Summary & comments: No other deli in Atlanta supplies this kind of quality, from the deli meats to the homemade mozzarella and other cheeses to the freshly baked breads. Breads are stored unwrapped on a shelf so the crusts stay fresh and crisp. Owners Charlie and Anita Augello opened their dream shop about a decade ago, and Atlantans have responded with enthusiasm.

Honors & awards: Numerous Best of Atlanta awards from local press.

Eclipse di Luna

Zone 3   Buckhead/Sandy Springs
764 Miami Circle
(404) 846-0449

Spanish/Tapas	
★★★	
Very inexpensive	
Quality 88	Value A

Reservations:	Accepted for six or more, and highly recommended at night
When to go:	Lunch or early in the dinner service
Entree range:	$3.25–18
Payment:	Major credit cards
Service rating:	★★★
Friendliness rating:	★★★★
Parking:	On site
Bar:	Full service
Wine selection:	Extensive; everything is available by the glass; good prices, starting at $5.50, with bottles costing just $20
Dress:	Dressy casual to resort casual
Disabled access:	Yes
Customers:	At lunch, the business folks of Miami Circle, a curving road threading together art galleries, design studios, and furniture businesses, find their way to the end of the line and lunch at this cleverly constructed emporium. At night, a whole different crowd comes out: Generation X dolls up and spends the entire evening sipping wines, nibbling tapas, and yakking it up with friends
Lunch:	Tuesday–Saturday, 11:30 A.M.–2:30 P.M.
Dinner:	Tuesday–Thursday, 5:30–10 P.M.; Friday and Saturday, 5:30–11 P.M.; Sunday, 6–10 P.M.

Atmosphere/setting: Funky, origami-like cloud shapes and chairs dangle suspended from the metal ceiling. Bullfight posters line the back of the bar, over which hangs an ornately framed, shapely female nude. Colorful contemporary art perks up the walls. The furniture is pure potluck at the flea market, with brightly painted tables and mismatched chairs.

House specialties: Spanish serrano ham; patatas bravas (with Romesco sauce); Manchego cheese with grapes; Catalan bread with tomatoes; chicken cooked in garlic; paella for two or more.

(continued)

Other recommendations: Crab salad in curry oil; barbecued Spanish-style ribs.

Entertainment & amenities: Live jazz is featured Wednesday–Saturday.

Summary & comments: Now-closed Luna Sí's founding chef Paul Luna established this tapas and wine bar after leaving Atlanta and coming back. Now partner James Ehrliche has bought the place. Nothing much has changed from the kitchen, however. Even when it's packed like a book of matches in the evenings, it's delightful to sit at the bar, make new friends, and know this is one outfit that keeps the fino sherry chilled instead of tossing it on the rocks.

1848 House

<table>
<tr><td></td><td>Southern/American
★★★★
Expensive</td></tr>
</table>

Zone 2   Northwest Atlanta
780 S. Cobb Drive, SE
with entrance on Pearl Street
(770) 428-1848

Southern/American
★★★★
Expensive

Quality 90   Value C

Reservations:	Required
When to go:	Any time
Entree range:	$17.95–25.95
Payment:	Major credit cards
Service rating:	★★★★
Friendliness rating:	★★★★
Parking:	Valet and self, on site
Bar:	Separate, full service
Wine selection:	Chiefly California, with a moderate by-the-glass selection
Dress:	Dressy to business casual
Disabled access:	Excellent, via elevator from the rear of the house; first floor only
Customers:	A well-heeled set
Brunch:	Sunday, 10:30 A.M.–2:30 P.M.
Dinner:	Tuesday–Saturday, 6–9:30 P.M.; Sunday, 5:30–8 P.M.; Monday, closed

Atmosphere/setting: Housed in an elegant Greek Revival antebellum home built in 1848 and listed on the National Register, the restaurant is on the site of a Civil War skirmish. The 13-acre site is dramatically lit at night. A most romantic ambiance, quiet and tranquil. Recent restoration efforts have focused on the old kitchen, with its stone floor and huge hearth.

House specialties: She-crab soup; grilled shrimp wrapped in country ham with fried green tomatoes on organic arugula; passion fruit vinaigrette; sweet Georgia brown (a chocolate dessert, but the exact nature varies).

Other recommendations: Venison (specials).

Entertainment & amenities: Jazz on Sunday at brunch.

Summary & comments: This is an excellent choice for quiet romantic dining. Perfect for Mother's Day, ideal for popping the question (perhaps after an intimate stroll of the grounds), and especially wonderful in the spring.

Honors & awards: Atlanta magazine, Best Reason to go to Marietta, 2000; *Wine Spectator,* Award of Excellence, 1996–2000; AAA Four Diamond Award, 1997–2000, DiRoNa 1997–2000.

Eno

Zone 8   Downtown East
800 Peachtree Street, NW
at 5th Street, Midtown
(404) 685-3191

Mediterranean/Italian	
★★★	
Expensive	
Quality 90	Value C

Reservations:	Accepted
When to go:	Any time
Entree range:	$15–25
Payment:	Major credit cards
Service rating:	★★★★
Friendliness rating:	★★★★
Parking:	Lot
Bar:	Full service
Wine selection:	Excellent, with lots by the glass and very adventurous selections
Dress:	Casual
Disabled access:	Easy
Customers:	Neighbors and locals from all over the metro area
Brunch:	Sunday, 11:30 A.M.–3 P.M.
Lunch:	Tuesday–Friday, 11:30 A.M.–2:30 P.M.
Dinner:	Tuesday–Thursday, 5:30–10 P.M.; Friday and Saturday, 5:30–11 P.M.
Wine bar:	Tuesday–Thursday, 2:30–11 P.M.; Friday and Saturday, 2:30 P.M.–midnight

Atmosphere/setting: This is a wine bar, as Italians mean when they say "enoteca," serving lots of adventurous wines by the glass. The bar and enclosed sidewalk dining area are the patron's first introduction to this warmly lit restaurant, which feels like it might be in Tuscany itself. Antiques and fine rugs are scattered throughout—an exquisite antique tapestry is in the private dining room—but the décor doesn't come across as stuffy.

House specialties: Handmade pastas; fried olives and chickpeas; whole-roasted fish; house-hickory smoked grilled oysters; bistecca for two.

Other recommendations: Mussels Cataplana; free-range poussin; seafood stew Provençal; seasonal fresh fruit tarts; panna cotta.

Entertainment & amenities: Nothing musical, but the wine bar is an ideal place for exploring new wines and learning what pleases your palate.

Summary & comments: Some table seating in the bar area makes a perfect

(continued)

spot to grab a bite before or after a performance at the nearby Fox Theatre. Pairing food and wine is a passion for owners Doug Strickland and Jamie Adams. Both are trained as culinary professionals, but Doug watches the front of the house, and Jamie keeps his eye on the pots.

Honors & awards: *Gourmet* magazine, Best Atlanta Wine List, 2000; *Atlanta Journal & Constitution,* two stars and Top 50 restaurants, 2000; *Wine Spectator,* Award of Excellence, 2000; *Food and Wine* magazine, Best Wines by the Glass, 2000; *Creative Loafing, Jezebel* magazine, Top Restaurants, 2000; *Knife & Fork* 2000; *Atlanta* magazine, Best New Near Atlanta Theaters, 2000; *Atlanta Business Chronicle,* Readers' Choice Best Wine Selection, 2001.

Evans Fine Foods

<table>
<tr><td></td><td>Southern</td></tr>
<tr><td>Zone 5   Northeast Atlanta</td><td>★★</td></tr>
<tr><td>2125 N. Decatur Road, Decatur</td><td>Inexpensive</td></tr>
<tr><td>(404) 634-6294</td><td>Quality 82   Value B</td></tr>
</table>

Reservations:	Not accepted
When to go:	Any time
Entree range:	$3–9
Payment:	Personal checks, no credit cards
Service rating:	★★★
Friendliness rating:	★★★★
Parking:	Self, on site
Bar:	None
Wine selection:	None
Dress:	Casual
Disabled access:	Yes
Customers:	Neighbors, locals, fans from all walks of life
Open:	Monday–Saturday, 5:30 A.M.–9 P.M.; Sunday, closed

Atmosphere / setting: Bright, busy, full of booths and waitresses that "honey" and "sugar" you while they briskly take orders and deliver dishes. This is the fundamental Southern diner, offering people-watching opportunities at least as good as the food. Friends greet each other; regulars have been coming for years; the staff knows their favorite dishes. It doesn't get more authentic Southern than this.

House specialties: Country-fried steak; fried chicken; chicken livers; meat loaf; vegetables.

Other recommendations: Cobbler with a big scoop of ice cream.

Entertainment & amenities: None, unless you count the customers.

Summary & comments: This stalwart of Southern cooking typifies what one finds throughout the South: Greeks who took to Southern food with major enthusiasm.

Honors & awards: "There've been so many, I really can't remember them all," says co-owner Mike Kontoes. Among them, *Georgia Journal,* Best Chicken Livers, 1996.

Fadó Irish Pub

Zone 3   Buckhead/Sandy Springs
3035 Peachtree Road, NE
(404) 841-0066

Irish	
★★★	
Moderate	
Quality 88	Value C

Reservations:	Weekdays only, parties of six or more
When to go:	Any time
Entree range:	$9.50–11.95
Payment:	Major credit cards
Service rating:	★★★
Friendliness rating:	★★★
Parking:	Self, off site, difficult on weekends and in evenings
Bar:	Full service
Wine selection:	Limited, but one comes for the Irish beers on tap
Dress:	Nice casual
Disabled access:	Yes
Customers:	Denizens of Buckhead pouring out of offices after work and celebrating the weekend
Brunch:	Saturday and Sunday, 11:30 A.M.–3 P.M.
Lunch:	Monday–Friday, 11:30 A.M.–3 P.M.
Dinner:	Sunday–Thursday, 3–11 P.M.; Friday and Saturday 3–10 P.M.; appetizer menu until midnight

Atmosphere/setting: Rich, dark-paneled wood walls and intimate seating coves line up opposite a huge and inviting bar. The place jams, and has from the moment it opened, attracting patrons as much for its food as for its fun. It feels like a bit of Galway in the heart of Buckhead, and the Irish accents that greet you from the bar are as authentic as the boxty.

House specialties: Fish and chips; boxty (Irish potato pancakes with varied fillings); Asian salmon; corned beef sandwich; house-made soda bread.

Other recommendations: Bread pudding; soda bread ice cream.

Entertainment & amenities: On Monday (traditional music) and Wednesday nights (Irish rock); Gaelic football games (soccer and rugby) are shown on the big-screen TV almost daily, but especially on the weekends.

Summary & comments: Just when it seems that Buckhead can't possibly fill another nightspot, along comes something unique that surprises and delights with its authenticity and charm. An Irish pub could have come off like a piece of an amusement park, but this one has all the allure of the real thing. Amazingly, it's still here, in a part of Atlanta where nightspots come and go with startling frequency.

Honors & awards: Citysearch, Best Pub, 2001.

Fat Matt's Rib Shack/ Fat Matt's Chicken Shack

Barbecue
★
Inexpensive
Quality 85   Value B

Zone 5   Northeast Atlanta
1811 Piedmont Road, NE (Rib Shack)
(404) 607-1622

Zone 5   Northeast Atlanta
1821 Piedmont Road, NE (Chicken Shack)
(404) 875-2722

Reservations:	Not accepted
When to go:	Any time
Entree range:	$3.75–16 (Rib Shack); $5.50–6.50 (Chicken Shack)
Payment:	No credit cards
Service rating:	★★★
Friendliness rating:	★★
Parking:	Self, on site
Bar:	None
Wine selection:	Beer only
Dress:	Grunge casual
Disabled access:	Yes
Customers:	Locals who know their 'cue
Lunch/Dinner:	Chicken Shack: Monday–Saturday, 11:30 A.M.–1:30 P.M.; Sunday, 2–9 P.M. Rib Shack: Sunday, 2–11:30 P.M.; Monday–Thursday, 11:30 A.M.–11:30 P.M.; Friday and Saturday, 11:30 A.M.–12:30 A.M.

Atmosphere/setting: Walls are lined with black-and-white publicity stills of famous blues performers who have strummed or sung at the small performance space.

House specialties: Splendid chopped-pork sandwiches; quite good barbecued chicken; fair ribs at the Rib Shack. Fried chicken (some of the city's best); terrific, wicked cheap whiting and catfish dinners at the Chicken Shack, where they make their own tartar sauce and cole slaw.

Other recommendations: Cole slaw and baked beans.

(continued)

Entertainment & amenities: Fat Matt's Rib Shack is the site of hot blues performances, but the quality varies, so check who's performing before going.

Summary & comments: Some days, nothing picks up the spirits quite like one of these chopped-pork sandwiches. The outdoor deck is a lovely spot in summer for listening to the music, chatting, sipping suds, and nibbling. Inconsistency has dogged the kitchen lately. Ribs can be wonderful one day or overcooked and dry the next; Brunswick stew can be just perfect one day and then tasting of canned ingredients the next.

Honors & awards: Creative Loafing, Best Ribs, Readers' Choice, 1992–2000; *Atlanta* magazine, panel's choice, Best Ribs, 1996; *Atlanta Business Chronicle,* Readers' Choice Best Barbecue, 2001. Too many to keep track of.

FERRERA'S BISTRO

Zone 3 Buckhead/Sandy Springs	Italian/American
635 Atlanta Street	★★★
(770) 640-5345	Moderate
	Quality 88 Value C

Reservations:	Accepted; a good idea on weekends
When to go:	Any time
Entree range:	$10–17
Payment:	Major credit cards
Service rating:	★★★★
Friendliness rating:	★★★★★
Parking:	Self, on site
Bar:	Full service
Wine selection:	Limited, but with a range of choices, and about 15 by the glass
Dress:	Casual sporty
Disabled access:	Easy, street level
Customers:	Lots of loyal neighbors
Dinner:	Tuesday–Thursday, 5–10 P.M.; Friday and Saturday, 5–11 P.M.

Atmosphere/setting: This is a neighborhood spot, with casually garbed local residents gathered around the bar until the owners finally declare the place shuttered for the night. It's a back-slapping kind of place. Black-and-white stills of Frank Sinatra, Lauren Bacall with Humprhey Bogart, Marilyn Monroe, Elvis Presley, and George Burns, among others, dot the walls. Dean Martin's photo is there, too, and at 9 P.M. on Friday and Saturday nights, the lyrics to his hit song "That's Amore" are handed out, and everybody croons the tune.

House specialties: White pizza; potato-crusted sole; roasted garlic scampi; veal Nicholas (pounded medallions, pesto sauce, prosciutto, sliced roma tomatoes, garlic, spinach, fresh mozzarella) over spaghetti.

Other recommendations: Salmon stuffed with lump crabmeat; lobster quesadilla (special).

Summary & comments: New Jersey natives Michael and Donna Petrucci ditched the North and his promising medical career to come to the South and cook. Ferrera's Bistro, open in 1998, and the new steakhouse Stetson's (see New Places, page 17) across Sloan Street from Ferrera's, are sister operations.

Honors & awards: Atlanta Journal & Constitution, Top 10 New Italian Restaurants (North Fulton), 1999.

Fishbone &
The Piranha Bar

Zone 3 Buckhead/Sandy Springs	Seafood
1874 Peachtree Street, NW	★★
(404) 367-4772	Moderate
	Quality 85 Value C

Reservations:	Accepted, usually for parties of four or more, especially on weekends
When to go:	Any time
Entree range:	$14–20 (except lobster at market, $36–38)
Payment:	Major credit cards
Service rating:	★★★
Friendliness rating:	★★★★
Parking:	Valet and self, on site
Bar:	Full service
Wine selection:	More than 100, mostly California selections, with about 20 by the glass
Dress:	Casual
Disabled access:	Main entrance
Customers:	Local folks from the immediate neighborhood
Lunch:	Monday–Friday, 11:30 A.M.–4:30 P.M.
Dinner:	Monday–Thursday, 4:30–10 P.M.; Friday, 4:30–11 P.M.; Saturday, 5–11 P.M.; Sunday, 5–10 P.M.

Atmosphere/setting: Fish swim everywhere in tanks and in icons. Tropical-Caribbean-icthyic imagery swarms—from the big welcoming bar that makes a fine place for after-work alliances to the large dining room and the dining porch that's perfect for large parties. The atmosphere is lively without being noise-ridden. Tables and booths are well spaced for comfort and privacy. The lighting is warm, but you can still find your date and read your menu.

House specialties: Wild striped bass; swordfish; grilled tuna; filet mignon; calamari; mussels; salmon.

Other recommendations: French toast with caramelized fruit, the only dessert made on the premises.

Summary & comments: Steak and chicken also are on this menu in case the fish fiends bring meat-eating friends. Chef Richard Blais, from New York, has re-jiggered this menu to simplify the presentations and point up the reason for coming: FISH! The branda de morue was initially made with salted cod, but the clientele wouldn't buy it, so it's now made with fresh cod. The change leaves us purists puzzled, and the flavors untrue, but the crowds seem to prefer it.

Honors & awards: *Atlanta* magazine, Best Seafood, 2000.

FishMONGER

Belle Isle Square Shopping Center
4969 Roswell Road, Suite 160
(404) 459-9003

	Seafood
	★★★
	Moderate
	Quality 88 Value B

Reservations:	Accepted
When to go:	Any time
Entree range:	$13–22
Payment:	Major credit cards
Service rating:	★★★★
Friendliness rating:	★★★★
Parking:	Self, on site
Bar:	Full service
Wine selection:	Excellent, with half coming from California and other half from South Africa, New Zealand, and Australia. Some 30 are offered by the glass
Dress:	Casual sporty
Disabled access:	Easy, street level
Customers:	Neighbors from Sandy Springs, and some Buckhead
Dinner:	Sunday–Thursday, 5:30–10 P.M.; Friday and Saturday, 5:30–11 P.M.

Atmosphere/setting: A mite hard to find, this warm and inviting neighborhood bistro swims with fish all the way around. The patio is shaped by rebar, painted black, that forms fish frames around its perimeter.

House specialties: Shrimp and crab cake; Mediterranean mussels; scallops; calamari; sauteed Portuguese-style prawns; lobster fettuccine.

Other recommendations: Seafood soup; paella; Argentine filet with three peppercorn cream Cognac sauce or chimichurri sauce for the non-fish eaters; blondie brownie with ice cream and chocolate fudge caramel sauce.

Summary & comments: Nik Panagopaulos, of Greek descent but from South Africa, opened this comfortable neighborhood bistro in 1999, and focuses on fish and seafood with flavors of the Mediterranean world.

Honors & awards: Atlanta magazine, Menu Guide, 2001, one of ten best new seafood restaurants; *Creative Loafing,* best for the seafood soup, 2001.

170

Floataway Cafe

	Eclectic/Mediterranean/American
Zone 5 Northeast Atlanta	★★★★
1123 Zonolite Road, Suite 15	Expensive
(404) 892-1414	Quality 93 Value C

Reservations:	Accepted and highly recommended
When to go:	Early
Entree range:	$13–24
Payment:	Major credit cards
Service rating:	★★★★
Friendliness rating:	★★★
Parking:	On site
Bar:	Full service
Wine selection:	Excellent, with lots of choices by the glass that go with the food
Dress:	Casual
Disabled access:	Yes, ramp at parking lot
Customers:	Mostly locals, from all over town
Dinner:	Tuesday–Saturday, 5–10 P.M.

Atmosphere/setting: An industrial warehouse area now chock full of artists and even containing a theater and a gay newspaper publisher is home to one of the city's most exciting restaurants. From the same couple that gave us top-rated Bacchanalia (see page 111)—Anne Quatrano and Clifford Harrison—comes this casual, high-energy, industrial-chic restaurant that attracts a hip crowd of Generation Xers. Whimsy rules in cloud-like ceiling treatments and soft gauzy hangings that lend some measure of privacy to dining spaces. The space is small and very narrow, and can get a bit noisy because of hard surfaces, but that hasn't deterred Atlantans from flocking to it, often waiting long times to secure a seat.

House specialties: Piccolo fritto (baby squid, red onions, and fried lemon slices); organic produce, such as ruby queen beets in season; chicken livers on rosemary skewers with red onion jam; roast chicken with oven-roasted bread salad; flourless chocolate cake (gateau victoire with chantilly cream).

Other recommendations: Medjool dates with shaved Rocca Parmesan cheese; farmstead handcrafted cheeses (both domestic and imported); fish; individual pizzas.

Summary & comments: This is one of the most inventive kitchens in town, with imagination and taste running all over the place. Sourcing ingredients from local suppliers and small national purveyors means Quatrano and company must

(continued)

171

FLOATAWAY CAFE   *(continued)*

change this menu frequently, so dishes do come and go. Still, the juxtaposition of flavors usually is intriguing without ever crossing over into the "weird" zone. Wines by the glass that pair well with the food, good imported and domestic beers, freshly made lime and lemonades, even a twist on iced tea (here flavored with vanilla) all indicate the level of quality and care that defines dining at Floataway.

Honors & awards: *Food and Wine* magazine, Best New Restaurant Atlanta, 1998; *Gourmet* magazine, Top Five, 1999; *Atlanta Journal & Constitution,* three stars and Top 50, 2000; *Atlanta* magazine, Best Escape from Reality, 2000.

Flying Biscuit Cafe

	American
Zone 5 Northeast Atlanta	★★
1655 McClendon Avenue, NE	Inexpensive
Candler Park	
(404) 687-8888	Quality 88 Value B

Zone 8   Downtown East
1001 Piedmont Avenue, Suite 103, Midtown
(404) 874-8887

Reservations:	Not accepted
When to go:	Any time
Entree range:	$4.95–8.50
Payment:	AMEX, VISA, MC
Service rating:	★★★
Friendliness rating:	★★★
Parking:	None for Candler Park, Lot beside and behind the Midtown location
Bar:	Beer and wine only
Wine selection:	Nice but limited, with everything by the glass
Dress:	Casual
Disabled access:	Easy at both locations
Customers:	Locals mostly, but the occasional wandering out-of-towner has been sighted
Open:	Every day, 8:30 A.M.–10 P.M. (Candler Park); Every day, 7 A.M.–10 P.M. (Midtown)

Atmosphere/setting: The Candler Park location is tucked inside an early 20th-century commercial space. Narrow and tight, it makes efficient use of every inch. Tables are close together, but no one seems to mind. This is a funky, super-casual spot, where nobody checks to see whether your jeans are designer or not. The newer Midtown location is more upscale, perched right on a busy corner and seemingly eager to be a part of the Midtown scene.

House specialties: Biscuits; organic oatmeal pancakes with warm peach compote and maple syrup; Flying Biscuit Breakfast; turkey sage sausage made especially for the Flying Biscuit by former Braves' catcher, Biff Pocaroba; in cold weather, chicken and dumplings, made with a poached biscuit; turkey meat loaf; fresh-baked muffins and cookies from the bakery at Candler Park (also available at Midtown).

Other recommendations: Frittata; goat cheese omelet; grits.

(continued)

FlyiNG BiscuiT CAfE   (continued)

Summary & comments: Well-established and highly regarded, the Biscuit turns out a big, fluffy biscuit that may not suit everybody's taste. No argument about the muffins, though. And the cookies—mega yummers. The bakery next door to the Candler Park location produces them to take home.

Honors & awards: *Bon Appétit; Gourmet* magazine, Top 10 Family Favorites, 1999; *Atlanta* magazine, Best All-Day Breakfast, 2000.

Fonda San Carlos

Zone 4   Lenox/Chamblee
Maxim Shopping Center
2077 Beaver Ruin Road, Suite 170
(I-85 north of the city to Beaver
Ruin Road exit), Norcross
(770) 797-2828

Mexican	
★★★	
Moderate	
Quality 92	Value B

Reservations:	Accepted
When to go:	Any time
Entree range:	$6.99–18.99
Payment:	Major credit cards
Service rating:	★★★★
Friendliness rating:	★★★★★
Parking:	On site
Bar:	Beer and wine only
Wine selection:	Limited
Dress:	Casual
Disabled access:	Yes
Customers:	Folks from north of the border in the early service, and Mexicans take up the spaces in the later-service hours, as they tend to eat both lunch and dinner later
Breakfast:	Every day, 8–11 A.M.
Lunch/Dinner:	Sunday–Thursday, 11 A.M.–10 P.M., Friday and Saturday, 11 A.M.–4 A.M.

Atmosphere/setting: The sheltered patio, centered by a fountain, is the place to dine, although the dining room certainly is fine, with its attached bar and little fish market display case off to the side. Late at night, the clientele shows up to relax, dine on homestyle food, and watch TV. The private room is a good choice for parties.

House specialties: Menudo (tripe soup) for breakfast; posole; seafood soup; almohada marina (seafood pillow); molcajete pesado (grilled steak, onions, queso fresco, paddle cactus, guacamole, and sauces in a tripod stone bowl); asada de la Zamora (spicy!); ceviche (marinated raw fish); chile relleno; shrimp a la diabla (spicy!).

Other recommendations: Soups; queso fundido; excellent raw oysters; really good freshly made guacamole; garlic shrimp; homemade flan with cream cheese and rompope (egg nog sauce).

(continued)

FONDA SAN CARLOS   *(continued)*

Entertainment & amenities: Good private rooms for parties, and a market that sells fresh fish a couple of days a week. Live mariachi music plays Fridays, Saturdays, and Sundays in the evenings.

Summary & comments: This is one of the most successful reflections of Mexican culture and cuisine in the Atlanta area. The food is outrageously good, and the people are supremely friendly. Young owner Carlos Chávez has future plans that will position him as a stellar member of the Atlanta restaurant community. In the fall of 2000 he opened Puras Tortas (see New Places, page 16) across the street to introduce locals to the authentic Mexican sandwich.

Food Business

Zone 5 Northeast Atlanta	Contemporary American
115 Sycamore Street, Decatur	★★★
(404) 371-9121	Moderate
	Quality 85 Value B

Reservations:	For parties of ten or more, during the week only
When to go:	Any time
Entree range:	$9.95–16.95
Payment:	AMEX, VISA, MC
Service rating:	★★★★
Friendliness rating:	★★★★
Parking:	On street only
Bar:	Full service
Wine selection:	Short but decent, good choices by the glass
Dress:	Casual
Disabled access:	At the front door, but seating is on the lower level in the bar/entry area; no elevator going upstairs
Customers:	Decaturites during the week, but a wide range of metro patrons on the weekend
Lunch:	Monday–Friday, 11 A.M.–3 P.M.
Dinner:	Monday–Saturday, 6–10 P.M.

Atmosphere/setting: This historic commercial space near the Decatur MARTA station houses one of the small town's most popular restaurants. Two dining levels sit atop the entrance level, which houses the bar and a few tables for guests with physical disabilities. Fabric banners soften the industrial-looking ceiling, and rich colors (pumpkin and aquamarine) play well against the brick walls.

House specialties: Lake trout with pumpkin-seed butter and fresh corn succotash; pork tenderloin with Szechwan peppercorn crust; beet and avocado salad; imaginative vegetarian dishes; specialty sandwiches at lunch (a few also at dinner).

Other recommendations: Fried tomatoes (green, yellow, or red depending on the season); house-made pizzas; calamari with lemon aioli; fresh fruit cobblers.

Entertainment & amenities: Guitar player on Friday nights.

Summary & comments: Owner Deena Duval opened the Food Business in a small Decatur location on Church Street, then popularity propelled her to relocate to this historic storefront spot in 1997. In 2000 she opened the Metromart, a slick downtown Decatur gourmet market. . An excellent kids' menu ranges from the Jiff peanut butter and raspberry jelly sandwich on good white bread to house-grilled pizza. The under-12 set gets complimentary goldfish. Nice touch.

Honors & awards: Atlanta Journal & Constitution, review and rated B+, 1998.

Food 101

American
★★
Moderate

Quality 82   Value C

Zone 3   Buckhead/Sandy Springs
Belle Isle Square Shopping Center
4969 Roswell Road, Suite 2000
(404) 497-9700

Reservations:	For parties of six or more; otherwise call ahead for wait list
When to go:	Any time
Entree range:	$13–24
Payment:	Major credit cards
Service rating:	★★★★
Friendliness rating:	★★★★★
Parking:	Self, on site
Bar:	Full service
Wine selection:	Very good, mostly Californian, with some unusual choices by the glass (Arneis and Petite Sirah, for instance)
Dress:	Casual sporty
Disabled access:	Easy, street level
Customers:	The neighbors
Lunch:	Sunday–Friday, 11:30 A.M.–2:30 P.M.
Dinner:	Sunday–Wednesday, 5:30–10 P.M.; Thursday–Saturday, 5:30–11 P.M.

Atmosphere/setting: A basic shopping-center space has been dressed to the nines with lovely wood finishes, dark hardwood floors, strategically placed lighting illuminating each table, and a wood/glass wall that in nice weather opens from the bar to the patio. The place is white tablecloth, but still kid-friendly, and the neighbors show up with their wee ones in tow during the early dinner hours. Dating couples and groups of couples tend to take over later. The place buzzes, but the noise level is temperate.

House specialties: Homemade potato chips with French onion dip; onion rings battered with Pabst Blue Ribbon batter and served with goat cheese and spicy rémoulade; crab and rock shrimp cakes; pork chop with red Zinfandel gravy and Yukon Gold mashed potatoes; pan-seared sea bass with red orange vinaigrette and black lentil risotto.

Other recommendations: Butternut squash soup; waffle with almond toffee crunch ice cream; peanut butter chocolate pie with milk chocolate.

(continued)

178

Summary & comments: After three visits, I'm still not convinced the food here is as good as it could be. The butternut squash risotto comes with crisply cooked vegetables, but the rice is way overcooked to anyone with a taste for classical, al dente Italian risotto. Yet, it tastes good. I think the way to maneuver this restaurant into your corner is to be firm about how dishes are cooked: Ask for the risotto to be done to the al dente stage. The first time I had the pork chop, it was way overcooked. So the next time I asked for it medium, and the kitchen delivered. Green beans don't come crisply cooked; they're hot but raw, so tell the kitchen you want them cooked to the crisp stage if that's your preference. And stick to dishes that have to be cooked to order; the braised ones, in my experience, lack flavor. But don't go away without dessert; these are really good. This is a very popular family spot, dating spot, and good for kids, too. At 9:30 P.M. on weekends, they're often still seating new arrivals.

Honors & awards: *Atlanta* magazine, Best Reason to go to Sandy Springs, 2000; Community Profiles, Our Favorite 52 Restaurants, 2000; *Jezebel* magazine, Top 100, 2000.

The Food Studio

Zone 2 Northwest Atlanta	Contemporary American
King Plow Arts Center	★★★
887 W. Marietta Street, Studio K-102	Moderate
(404) 815-6677	Quality 90 Value C

Reservations:	Strongly recommended, even for weekdays
When to go:	Any time
Entree range:	$18–29
Payment:	Major credit cards
Service rating:	★★★★
Friendliness rating:	★★★★
Parking:	Valet
Bar:	Separate lounge, full service
Wine selection:	Very strong, American, with many by the glass
Dress:	Casual
Disabled access:	Yes
Customers:	Customers from the company's other restaurants
Lunch:	Takeout only
Dinner:	Sunday–Thursday, 5:30–11 P.M.; Friday and Saturday, 5:30 P.M.–midnight

Atmosphere/setting: Hip, restored King Plow Arts Center provides a textured backdrop for this innovative restaurant from the same group that produced South City Kitchen (see page 266). A former warehouse district, King Plow boasts many sophisticated amenities, including a theater. The restaurant operates on two levels, with tolerable noise, comfortably spaced tables, and a handsome, comfortable bar. Well-selected CDs offer blues, jazz, and popular music.

House specialties: Ahi tuna tartare; tequila salmon; American farmhouse cheese course; game; lemon bombe. Seasonal menu changes at least quarterly.

Other recommendations: Rabbit (when available); cold-smoked salmon; locally grown organic vegetables.

Summary & comments: Despite being a bit hard to find, The Food Studio, aptly named for its location among artists' studios, is packed to the rafters. Some might prefer their vegetables a bit more cooked than the very al dente style offered but there's no arguing with the delicious treats centering the plates. Founding chef Christopher Brandt has been with the operation since its founding in the summer of 1996. Pastry Chef Gary Scarborough makes all the breads and pastries for the entire company, including South City Kitchen (see page 266) and La Tavola Trattoria (see page 211). His chocolate truffles are legendary.

Honors & awards: AAA, four diamonds, 2000; *Atlanta* magazine, Best Romantic Date, 2000. Chef Chris Brandt did a James Beard Dinner in 2000.

Fratelli di Napoli

<table>
<tr><td>

Zone 3   Buckhead/Sandy Springs
2101-B Tula Street off Peachtree Street
next to Brookwood Square
(404) 351-1533

</td><td>

Italian American
★★★
Moderate

Quality 88   Value C

</td></tr>
</table>

Zone 3   Buckhead/Sandy Springs
928 Canton Street, Roswell
(770) 642-9917

Zone 4   Lenox/Chamblee
5980 North Point Parkway, Alpharetta
(678) 879-5404

Reservations:	Only for parties of more than six persons
When to go:	Before 7 P.M., especially on weekends
Entree range:	$10–26
Payment:	Major credit cards
Service rating:	★★★★
Friendliness rating:	★★★★
Parking:	Valet and self, on site
Bar:	Separate, full service
Wine selection:	Lots of California and Italian wines, with 50 or more by the glass
Dress:	Nice casual
Disabled access:	Ramp around back
Customers:	Families, especially on Sunday, groups of young people
Lunch/Dinner:	North Point: Saturday–Sunday, noon–midnight
Dinner:	Bennett Street: Monday–Thursday, 5–11 P.M.; Friday and Saturday, 5 P.M.–midnight; Sunday, 4–10 P.M.
	Roswell: Monday–Thursday, 5–10 P.M., Friday and Saturday, 5–11 P.M., Sunday, 4–10 P.M.
	North Point: Monday–Thursday, 4–11 P.M.

Atmosphere/setting: A high-energy place with a somewhat elevated noise level, this popular new spot has been crafted out of a warehouse-style space near a frequently running railroad line (Tula Street). The Roswell location is similarly styled in a 19th-century commercial space. In both locations, lighting is warm,

(continued)

the place is friendly, and the ambiance welcomes a wide diversity of patrons. The third location, built in 2001, was not ready to be viewed at press time.

House specialties: All pastas (rigatoni with vodka); excellent salads; snapper in basil sauce; chicken Marsala; and chicken cacciatore.

Other recommendations: Dessert platter.

Summary & comments: Family-style service on all entrees means that a single entree will serve two to four persons, depending on appetites. So bring a gang. New owners Jimmy Prince and Jerry Heilpern purchased the restaurants in late 1999 and immediately made plans to expand. The result is a new location open in 2001. Monday is martini and cigar night at all locations.

Frontera Mex-Mex Grill

Zone 4 Lenox/Chamblee	Mexican
Smoke Tree Shopping Center	★★★
4606 Jimmy Carter Boulevard	Inexpensive
Norcross	
(770) 493-8341	Quality 85 Value B

Zone 5   Northeast Atlanta
5070 Stone Mountain Highway, SW (U.S. 78), Stone Mountain
(770) 972-3366

Zone 4   Lenox/Chamblee
3466 Holcomb Bridge Road, Norcross
(770) 441-3488

Reservations:	Not accepted
When to go:	Any time
Entree range:	$6.99–11.95
Payment:	Major credit cards
Service rating:	★★★★
Friendliness rating:	★★★★
Parking:	Self, on site
Bar:	Small but with full service
Wine selection:	Limited, with a few by the glass, and sangría
Dress:	Casual
Disabled access:	Yes
Customers:	A mix of local Mexican residents, especially at Sunday brunch after Mass, and Anglos
Brunch:	Stone Mountain and Norcross only: Sunday, 11 A.M.–3 P.M.
Lunch:	Monday–Saturday, 11 A.M.–3:30 P.M.
Dinner:	Every day, 3–10:30 P.M.

Atmosphere/setting: A bright, cheerful international Latino crew (name-plates indicate not only names but also country of origin) sets a happy, peppy mood in these attentively run operations. Walls and spaces are filled with traditional artifacts, such as textiles and pottery.

House specialties: At brunch, menudo (traditional tripe soup), carne asada en salsa roja (meat cooked in red sauce), mole poblano (chicken in dark mole

(continued)

sauce); at dinner, carnitas (deep-fried pork chunk), steak tampiqueño, Baja-style fish tacos.

Other recommendations: Hibiscus tea; ceviche; xochitl soup (chicken and avocado, Yucatecan style).

Entertainment & amenities: Mariachi music entertains at brunch and during dinner.

Summary & comments: This young Atlanta-based company (founded in 1987) has a total of seven locations, all in the Atlanta area, stretching from Duluth to Conyers. An eighth location is due in 2001 in Suwanee. For the best dishes, focus on those listed as the "Especialidades." This is a good spot for children of all ages. The brunch is served at Norcross and Stone Mountain locations only.

Honors & awards: *Creative Loafing,* Critics Choice Best Mexican Food in Atlanta, 2000.

Fuzzy's Place

<table>
<tr><td></td><td>Cajun/Creole</td></tr>
<tr><td></td><td>★★</td></tr>
<tr><td>Zone 5   Northeast Atlanta</td><td>Inexpensive</td></tr>
<tr><td>2015 N. Druid Hills Road, NE
at Buford Highway</td><td></td></tr>
<tr><td>(404) 321-6166</td><td>Quality 85   Value A</td></tr>
</table>

Reservations:	Not accepted
When to go:	Any time
Entree range:	$6–10
Payment:	Major credit cards
Service rating:	★★★
Friendliness rating:	★★★★
Parking:	Self, on site
Bar:	Full service
Wine selection:	Limited but decent; with most poured by the glass
Dress:	Anything from grunge casual to black tie
Disabled access:	Yes, but wheelchair difficult in performance space
Customers:	Locals, music lovers
Lunch:	Every day, 11 A.M.–5 P.M.
Dinner:	Every day, 5–10 P.M.

Atmosphere/setting: The quintessential neighborhood pub, Fuzzy's long bar separates a dining space from a performance space, where smoke curls and music plays into the wee hours. Televisions present sports events in both spaces. As grungy as it looks, solo women are not generally bothered, but should unwanted attentions surface, the staff stands ready to fend off the offender. Longtime Atlanta restaurateur Joe Dale, now somewhat retired, guides the menu.

House specialties: Seafood Patsy (seafood in a rich cream sauce); various quesadillas; veggie burrito; buffalo shrimp; carpetbagger steak (stuffed with oysters); étouffée.

Other recommendations: Bread pudding.

Entertainment & amenities: One of the best line-ups of local musical talent (blues and rock) holds court here almost every day of the week until 2 A.M. Small dance floor.

Summary & comments: Start off with an early dinner, and prepare to grab a seat by 9 P.M. if the headliners are really popular. Look for Cold Chills, Barry Richman, Francine Reed (recently nominated for a Handy award), King Johnson among many, many other fine performers.

Honors & awards: The loyal and devoted following gives it many accolades.

GEORGIA GRILLE

<table>
<tr><td></td><td>Southwestern</td></tr>
<tr><td>Zone 3   Buckhead/Sandy Springs</td><td>★★★</td></tr>
<tr><td>Peachtree Square Shopping Center</td><td>Moderate</td></tr>
<tr><td>2290 Peachtree Road</td><td></td></tr>
<tr><td>(404) 352-3517</td><td>Quality 88   Value C</td></tr>
</table>

Reservations:	Priority seating, and reservations for parties of six or more
When to go:	Any time, but early in the dinner service is best
Entree range:	$12–22
Payment:	Major credit cards
Service rating:	★★★
Friendliness rating:	★★★
Parking:	Self, on site
Bar:	Full service
Wine selection:	Eclectic, drawn chiefly from California, with some from Australia, but mostly from small-production wineries
Dress:	Nice casual
Disabled access:	Excellent
Customers:	A young, lively set of locals
Dinner:	Tuesday–Thursday, 6–10 P.M.; Friday and Saturday, 6–11 P.M.; Sunday, 5:30–9 P.M.

Atmosphere/setting: Colors and interior finishes reflect the warm, traditional tones of the American Southwest, more so after a recent renovation and renewal of the decor. The place packs quickly, so the noise level can be high. The restaurant was named for artist Georgia O'Keeffe, and work by Athens, Georgia–based artist Steve Penley enlivens the walls.

House specialties: Lobster enchilada (an award winner); beef tenderloin on mashed potatoes with roasted corn salsa; chicken corn chowder (seasonal); flan; gumbo; goat cheese quesadilla.

Other recommendations: Hot Shots (cheese-stuffed, deep-fried jalapeño peppers); black bean cumin pancake; potato-stuffed burritos with green chile sauce.

Summary & comments: When you want to light up your palate, savor Georgia Grille. Lively flavors, yet often classically simple preparations (such as the perfect flan), bring luster to the Southwestern culinary tradition. No wonder the place stays packed.

Honors & awards: Georgia Seafood Challenge, Governor's Cup, 1992, for the lobster enchilada; *Atlanta* magazine, Best Chocolate Dessert, 1992, for the triple chocolate mousse; *Gourmet* magazine, kudos for the chicken corn chowder, 1995; *Zagat* 2001.

GRAZIE, A BISTRO

	Northern Italian/ Continental
Zone 2 Northwest Atlanta	★★★
West Marietta Crossing Shopping Center, 1000 Whitlock Avenue	Moderate/Expensive
at Burnt Hickory Road, Marietta (770) 499-8585	Quality 90 Value C

Reservations:	Accepted, and recommended
When to go:	Any time
Entree range:	$15–26 ($30 for the lobster tail)
Payment:	Major credit cards
Service rating:	★★★
Friendliness rating:	★★★
Parking:	Self, on site
Bar:	Two; outside patio bar reserved for private parties
Wine selection:	Moderate-sized wine list, mostly California with some Italian; 45 by the glass; Grazie Stash Wine List features high-end, mostly California labels
Dress:	Nice casual
Disabled access:	Yes
Customers:	Neighbors and other folks from the northern 'burbs
Brunch:	Sunday, 11 A.M.–2 P.M.
Lunch:	Every day, 11 A.M.–2 P.M.
Dinner:	Sunday–Thursday, 5–10 P.M.; Friday and Saturday, 5–11 P.M. (bar stays open until about midnight)

Atmosphere/setting: The location does not prepare one for this opulent interior: a serious collection of antiques includes a 1,000-pound Italian marble fireplace surround. The wine cabinet gates were part of an old elevator from Italy. Entrance painting and the "Iron Lady" console table are from Italy, but the front doors are American (1896). For romantic dining, this is a popular destination.

House specialties: Crab cakes (all pure crab with a beurre blanc); tomato artichoke soup; calamari with roasted garlic aïoli and Italian salsa; lamb; and wild mushroom tart.

Other recommendations: Penne and sausage (lunch only); crème brûlée.

Entertainment & amenities: Darryl Adams tickles the keyboard on the weekends.

Summary & comments: Freshly made stocks are, literally, the fond de cuisine here. Chef Andrew Smith, a Culinary Institute of America graduate (1992), does things right.

Greenwood's on Green Street

	American/Southern
	★★★
Zone 3 Buckhead/Sandy Springs	Moderate/Expensive
1087 Green Street, Roswell	Quality 90 Value C
(770) 992-5383	

Reservations:	Not accepted
When to go:	Any time
Entree range:	$5.25–17.50
Payment:	Cash or check (out-of-town checks with ID)
Service rating:	★★★★
Friendliness rating:	★★★★★
Parking:	Self, on site
Bar:	Beer and wine
Wine selection:	Limited, with American wines and several by the glass
Dress:	Nice casual
Disabled access:	Excellent
Customers:	Everybody comes here, ordinary locals to glitterati, sometimes even visiting Hollywood stars; owner Bill Greenwood is having the menu translated into seven languages to accommodate the many international visitors
Lunch:	Sunday, 11:30 A.M.–2:30 P.M.
Dinner:	Wednesday–Saturday, 5–10 P.M.; Sunday, 5–9 P.M.; Monday and Tuesday, closed

Atmosphere/setting: A tiny house remodeled for restaurant purposes, it gets packed at night and is always bustling. The decor could be described as urban folksy.

House specialties: Fried chicken; duck; Georgia trout; mashed potatoes; crawfish tail cakes (in season). Known for deep-dish homemade fruit pies, but honestly we think they look better than they taste.

Other recommendations: Shrimp and grits; lemon meringue pie.

Summary & comments: Come hungry because the portions are huge. Seasonings can be peppery, so if that's a personal issue, inquire before ordering. This is food like mother used to make—only rarely did she make it this good. Entirely nonsmoking. Greenwood also is owner of a nifty barbecue joint, Swallow at the Hollow (see page 272).

Honors & awards: Figaro magazine, A Best Restaurant in Atlanta, 1996; *Gourmet* magazine, Top 10, 1999. Much positive press.

GRINGOS

Zone 5   Northeast Atlanta
1238 DeKalb Avenue, NE, between
Oakdale Road and Moreland Avenue
(404) 522-8666

Mexican	
★★	
Inexpensive	
Quality 88	Value C

Reservations:	Not accepted
When to go:	Any time
Entree range:	$8.95–14.95
Payment:	AMEX, VISA, MC
Service rating:	★★
Friendliness rating:	★★★
Parking:	Self, on site, fenced lot
Bar:	No, but full service
Wine selection:	Limited but decent; aged pure agave tequilas; Mexican beers
Dress:	Grunge/funky casual
Disabled access:	Yes
Customers:	Neighbors
Dinner:	February to November: Tuesday–Thursday, 5–10 P.M.; Friday and Saturday, 5–10:30 P.M.; Sunday, 5.–9: 30 P.M. December to January: Monday and Tuesday, closed

Atmosphere/setting: It takes a good bit of imagination to look at an abandoned two-bay, run-down garage and fancy putting in a restaurant. But that's what Gringos did. There's something special about this place, a delightful neighborhood spot. When the rain beats down on metal, it feels somehow especially comforting to sit beneath its shelter, the bay doors up, sipping a margarita or an aged agave tequila. In recent years, a sheltered patio has been added, brightly lit with colored lights and banners reflecting the Mexican national colors (green, white, and red).

House specialties: Budín azteca (a tortilla chips/chicken/chile pepper casserole); cochinata pibil (pork cooked in banana leaves—a Yucatecan specialty); three kinds of moles.

Other recommendations: Chile rellenos with your choice of fresh corn kernel stuffing or picadillo (ground pork and tomato).

Summary & comments: The menu features dishes never seen in the pseudo-Mexican restaurants dotting the Atlanta landscape, making the name just a touch ironic. This is a supremely popular spot, making it imperative to arrive early to avoid a lengthy wait on the deck.

Honors & awards: *Atlanta* magazine, Best Margarita, 1999.

189

HAE WOON DAE

Zone 4 Lenox/Chamblee	Korean
Treasure Village Shopping Center	★★★
5805 Buford Highway, Suite 5	Moderate
Doraville	Quality 93 Value A
(770) 451-7957	

Reservations:	Reservations accepted on weekends
When to go:	Any time
Entree range:	$7.95–14.94
Payment:	Major credit cards
Service rating:	★★★★★
Friendliness rating:	★★★★★
Parking:	On site
Bar:	Full service
Wine selection:	Practically nonexistent
Dress:	Casual
Disabled access:	Yes
Customers:	Area Koreans and admiring Occidentals
Lunch/Dinner:	Thursday–Tuesday, 10 A.M.–6 A.M.; Wednesday, 10 A.M.–midnight

Atmosphere/setting: A simple decor is set off by tables rigged with barbecue cooking pits. Korean language fills the air as most patrons are from the home country. Staff English is often limited, but they're willing to try, often giggling at their own attempts to express difficult concepts. There's little attempt to re-create any kind of Korean-looking ambiance here. All the effort goes into the food, which is first rate.

House specialties: Korean barbecue; spicy soups; noodle dishes.

Other recommendations: Seafood pancake; side dishes (especially potato salad).

Summary & comments: Opened in 1991, this temple of Korean cooking has in recent years bridged the divide between Korean and non-Asian patrons, attracting the latter to its wood-cooked barbecue.

Honors & awards: Atlanta Journal & Constitution, two stars and Top 50, 2000; *Atlanta* magazine, Best Korean, 2000.

HaL's

<table>
<tr><td colspan="2">Continental/Creole</td></tr>
<tr><td colspan="2">★★★</td></tr>
<tr><td colspan="2">Moderate/Expensive</td></tr>
<tr><td>Quality 90</td><td>Value B</td></tr>
</table>

Zone 3   Buckhead/Sandy Springs
30 Old Ivy Road
(404) 261-0025

Zone 3   Buckhead/Sandy Springs
Shops at St. Ives, 10305 Medlock Bridge Road, Duluth
(770) 418-0448

Reservations:	Recommended for weekends
When to go:	Anytime, but less crowded Monday and Tuesday
Entree range:	$16–31.95; pasta $11
Payment:	Major credit cards
Service rating:	★★★
Friendliness rating:	★★
Parking:	Valet or self, on site
Bar:	Full service
Wine selection:	Heavy on chardonnay and cabernet sauvignon, many by the glass, and many reserve bottles
Dress:	Nice casual, business, and evening
Disabled access:	Yes
Customers:	Locals and tourists
Open:	Monday–Saturday, 4–11 P.M.; Sunday, closed

Atmosphere/setting: Rough-textured brick walls softened by warm lighting, sconces with pleated glass shades, and comfortably spaced tables all make this a popular neighborhood spot. Regulars come and go and shout their greetings to other regulars. The generous bar is a popular watering hole for locals.

House specialties: Shrimp and crab rémoulade; trout fillet with crab meat; snapper française; duck à l'orange; bread pudding; stone crabs (in season).

Other recommendations: Soft-shell crab meunière; specials reflecting owner Hal Nowak's New Orleans origins. Recently, prime New York strip steaks and 22-ounce bone-in rib eyes have been added.

Entertainment & amenities: Piano and live band, usually four pieces, by Henry Parrilla and Friends Monday–Saturday.

Summary & comments: Now there is a separate nonsmoking section in the front of the dining room. Good ventilation systems draw the smoke off. A new location opened in Duluth, replacing the Tuscan Steak House, in late 2000. It replicates the menu, live music, and great bar of the Buckhead location.

Honors & awards: Hudspeth Report, Top 10; *Atlanta Business Chronicle,* Best Happy Hour 40-plus Crowd, 2001.

Hanwoori

<table>
<tr><td>Zone 4   Lenox/Chamblee</td><td>Korean/Japanese</td></tr>
</table>

Zone 4   Lenox/Chamblee
4251 N. Peachtree Road, Chamblee
(770) 458-9191

Korean/Japanese
★★★★
Moderate

Quality 95   Value A

Reservations:	Accepted
When to go:	Any time
Entree range:	$10–15
Payment:	Major credit cards
Service rating:	★★★★
Friendliness rating:	★★★★
Parking:	Self, on site
Bar:	Full service
Wine selection:	Decent, especially for an Asian restaurant
Dress:	Nice casual
Disabled access:	Yes
Customers:	Mostly Asians, a good sign
Lunch/Dinner:	Every day, 11 A.M.–11 P.M.

Atmosphere/setting: Posh, elegant with gleaming rich woods and formal in feeling (but friendly and accommodating in service), this is one of the best highlights of Atlanta's Asian dining scene. Enter through automatic glass doors and decide which country you will visit. Korea is to the left, set with barbecue tables for cooking bulgogi and other dishes at table. Japan abides to the right, with its sushi bar and tatami rooms.

House specialties: Korean specialties include barbecued marinated short ribs; bulgogi (marinated beef to be cooked tableside); plenty of pickled dishes (very good kimchee); gooksoojuhngol (noodles, vegetables, and beef cooked in a seasoned broth); spicy squid. Japanese dishes include myriad good sushi and sashimi; barbecued, meltingly tender eel; Mongolian stock pot.

Other recommendations: Bracing miso soup and good agedashi (deep-fried) tofu.

Summary & comments: Soothing, elegant, and special, this is one to save for special guests who can appreciate authentic cuisine. Despite formality, the staff knows how to make children feel welcome.

Honors & awards: Atlanta Journal & Constitution, One of 10 Best New Restaurants, 1996.

HARVEST

Zone 5 Northeast Atlanta	Eclectic/Mediterranean
853 N. Highland Avenue, NE	★★★
Virginia-Highland	Moderate
(404) 876-8244	Quality 86 Value C

Reservations:	Sunday–Thursday, accepted for anyone; Friday–Saturday and Sunday brunch, for parties of six or more only
When to go:	Early or late to avoid a long wait
Entree range:	$11.95–18.95
Payment:	Major credit cards
Service rating:	★★★★
Friendliness rating:	★★★★★
Parking:	Valet
Bar:	Full service
Wine selection:	Well-chosen list has good ones by the glass, and has broadened its range since our last edition, adding Riesling and Viognier, for instance
Dress:	All kinds of casual, but mostly nice
Disabled access:	Difficult (chairs have to be lifted)
Customers:	Neighbors
Brunch:	Sunday, 11 A.M.–2:30 P.M.
Lunch:	Monday–Friday, 11:30 A.M.–2:30 P.M.
Dinner:	Sunday–Thursday, 5:30–10 P.M.; Friday and Saturday, 5:30–11 P.M.

Atmosphere/setting: Another former Virginia-Highland residence turned restaurant, this one has a charming front porch with some seating and a wait space. Outdoors, several umbrella-sheltered tables line a small strip running down the length of the front yard toward the street. The interior has undergone a hefty renovation upstairs.

House specialties: House-smoked pork chops; soups; grilled loin lamb chops; sea bass; dishes with Asian touches, such as basil crab spring rolls; horseradish-crusted oysters.

Other recommendations: Creative vegetarian dishes, such spinach gnocchi.

Summary & comments: Keeping the prices down and the creativity level up is the goal of young chef Justin Ward and partner Tommy Mather. The neighborhood has responded with enthusiasm.

Honors & awards: Creative Loafing, Top 50, 2000.

Hashiguchi Japanese Restaurant & Sushi Bar

Japanese	
★★★★	
Moderate	
Quality 90	Value B

Zone 3   Buckhead/Sandy Springs
Terrace Shopping Center
3000 Windy Hill Road, NW
at Powers Ferry Road, near I-75
(770) 955-2337

Zone 3   Buckhead/Sandy Springs
Around Lenox Shoppping Center, 3400 Wooddale Drive, NE
(404) 841-9229

Reservations:	Accepted
When to go:	Any time
Entree range:	$12–20
Payment:	AMEX, MC, VISA
Service rating:	★★★
Friendliness rating:	★★★★★
Parking:	Self, on site
Bar:	Beer and wine (sake)
Wine selection:	Virtually nonexistent
Dress:	Nice casual
Disabled access:	Yes
Customers:	Local regulars, some Japanese at Windy Hill Road; visitors and conventioneers at the location on Wooddale Drive
Lunch:	Monday–Friday, 11:30 A.M.–2 P.M.
Dinner:	Windy Hill Road: Monday–Thursday, 5:30–10 P.M.; Friday and Saturday, 5:30–10:15 P.M.; Sunday, closed
	Wooddale Drive: Tuesday–Thursday, 5:30–10 P.M.; Friday and Saturday, 5:30–10:30 P.M.; Sunday, 5–9:30 P.M.; Monday, closed

Atmosphere/setting: Simple elegance defines this long-popular Japanese restaurant, a pace-setter in the genre. Long and narrow, both restaurants feature a long sushi bar on the right as you enter the space. Tasteful Japanese prints, the occasional small screen or piece of porcelain, a strategically placed piece of fabric, and waitresses in traditional garb announce the heritage.

(continued)

194

Hashiguchi Japanese Restaurant & Sushi Bar (continued)

House specialties: Perfectly pristine sushi and sashimi; agedashi (crisply fried) tofu; vegetable appetizers, such as Japanese eggplant; chawan mushi (a custard with seafood and veggies baked within); edamame (soy beans); codfish pâté; grilled cod with sake and miso sauce; Japanese mushroom/shrimp tempura (shrimp sandwiched between two shiitake mushroom caps) and tempura fried.

Other recommendations: Beef negima (beef filet wrapped around scallions); soft-shell crab appetizer; the long list of appetizers with unusual tidbits, such as grated Japanese yam with diced tuna or sea urchin paste if you're adventurous.

Summary & comments: Warm, bright, cheerful, and altogether inviting, both restaurants have their distinctive appeal. The one in Buckhead is smaller and seems more intimate, but the Marietta location is nicely sized and seems a bit more brightly lit. Both have busy sushi bars. For engaging sushi conversation with the chefs, sit at the sushi bars. Masato Hashiguchi met his wife, Aoi, when he was a young chef working at another Japanese restaurant more than 20 years ago.

Honors & awards: Atlanta Journal & Constitution, two stars and Top 50, 2000.

Haveli Indian Restaurant

Zone 2   Northwest Atlanta
490 Franklin Road
(770) 955-4525

Zone 8   Downtown East
Gift Mart Building, 225 Spring Street, NW
(404) 522-4545

<table>
<tr><td></td><td>Indian</td></tr>
<tr><td></td><td>★★★</td></tr>
<tr><td></td><td>Inexpensive</td></tr>
<tr><td></td><td>Quality 90   Value C</td></tr>
</table>

Reservations:	Not accepted
When to go:	Any time
Entree range:	$8–13; lunch buffet $6.95
Payment:	Major credit cards
Service rating:	★★
Friendliness rating:	★★
Parking:	Self, on site in Cobb; paid parking next door downtown
Bar:	Separate, full service
Wine selection:	Domestic and imported
Dress:	Nice casual
Disabled access:	Ramp
Customers:	Mostly locals, some Indians (Cobb); business-people and out-of-towners (downtown)
Lunch:	Monday–Friday, 11:30 A.M.–2:30 P.M.; Saturday-Sunday, noon–2:30 P.M. (Cobb); Saturday, noon–3 P.M. (downtown)
Dinner:	Every day, 5:30–10:30 P.M. (Cobb); Every day, 5:30–10 P.M. (downtown)

Atmosphere/setting: Quiet and serene, with light music in the air, the restaurant has become a community fixture, often participating in local restaurant charity events. Its focal point is the tandoor oven. The downtown location is more utilitarian, as it serves the busy crowds that attend trade shows.

House specialties: Tandoor dishes; curries; mango ice cream; saag paneer (sautéed creamy spinach with homemade cheese); chickpea dishes; stuffed breads.

Other recommendations: Vegetable dishes inspire vegetarians.

Summary & comments: The buffet lunch, a first-rate value, is a hit with businesspeople working in the area. The dishes are very approachable if you're unfamiliar with Indian food. The original location on Cobb Parkway was bulldozed last year, but the owners wasted no time relocating and re-opening on Franklin Road.

Honors & awards: *Atlanta* magazine, Best of Atlanta, for Best Indian Restaurant, 1993–present; *Atlanta Business Chronicle,* Readers' Choice Best Indian, 2001.

Heaping Bowl & Brew

Zone 6   Southeast Atlanta
469 Flat Shoals Avenue, SE
East Atlanta Village
(404) 523-8030

American
★★★
Inexpensive
Quality 88   Value B

Reservations:	For six or more only
When to go:	Any time
Entree range:	$6.95–8.95
Payment:	AMEX, MC, VISA
Service rating:	★★★★
Friendliness rating:	★★★★
Parking:	On street and behind the building
Bar:	Full service
Wine selection:	Limited, but with decent selections that serve this food fairly well
Dress:	As casual as you want
Disabled access:	Easy, street level
Customers:	Residents of this reviving neighborhood, and everything else from guys in dreds to suited threads
Brunch:	Saturday and Sunday, 10 A.M.–4 P.M.
Lunch/Dinner:	Monday–Saturday, 10 A.M.–11 P.M.; Sunday, 10 A.M.–10 P.M.

Atmosphere/setting: Music from the '70s and '80s creates a hip atmosphere that attracts a widely varied audience. If you're wearing your favorite jeans with the knees ripped out, and don't feel like changing to go out to dinner, c'mon. The store-front style space is funky and friendly, and invites gathering the gang for sharing these generously proportioned plates, and just hangin' out.

House specialties: Greens and beans; heaping salad bowl; Southwestern chicken stir fry. Brunch: Southwestern chicken hash; Polish eggs Benedict with pierogis; burritos; homemade biscuits; and pancakes. Brunch specials vary; some recent examples: salmon cakes on jalapeño yellow stone-ground grits; two eggs over easy on yellow stone-ground grits topped with Hollandaise.

Other recommendations: Pierogis with sour cream and onions; banana pudding (sufficient for a whole scout troop—the only dessert).

Entertainment & amenities: Trivia on Wednesday at 8 P.M.

Summary & comments: Here's how it works: You select a base (spaghetti, salad, greens and beans, whatever) and have it either solo or choose any one of a

(continued)

number of outstanding toppings for a few dollars more. Thus, the greens and beans may be enhanced with sausage. The "heaping bowl" concept is to be taken literally, and the portions are more than sufficient to share. Great cheap-date place. Tuesday and Thursday nights are $2 draught night, and Sunday and Wednesday are $3.50 margarita nights. Todd Semrau and Tricia Donegan opened this operation in 1997, and it rapidly became a linchpin enterprise in the revitalization process of this neighborhood, where both owners live.

    Honors & awards: Lots and lots of good local press. *Atlanta* magazine, Best of East Atlanta, 1998.

Horseradish Grill

Zone 3 Buckhead/Sandy Springs	American/Southern
4320 Powers Ferry Road, NW	★★★★
(404) 255-7277	Moderate/Expensive
	Quality 94 Value C

Zone 3   Buckhead/Sandy Springs
3070 Windward Plaza, Suite P, Alpharetta
(770) 442-3123

Reservations:	Accepted and highly recommended
When to go:	Early in any given service shift
Entree range:	$17–27
Payment:	Major credit cards
Service rating:	★★
Friendliness rating:	★★★
Parking:	Valet and self on-site
Bar:	Full service, with bar menu
Wine selection:	Extensive, chiefly California, and reasonably priced, with many good selections by the glass
Dress:	Casual but nice to glitter
Disabled access:	Excellent
Customers:	A young-at-heart crowd, families celebrating special events, locals, and out-of-towners
Brunch:	Sunday, 11 A.M.–2:30 P.M.
Lunch:	Monday–Friday, 11:30 A.M.–2:30 P.M.
Dinner:	Monday–Thursday, 5:30–10 P.M.; Friday and Saturday, 5–11 P.M.; Sunday, 5–9 P.M.

Atmosphere/setting: An old horse barn converted into a restaurant many years ago remained dark and forbidding until transformed by local restaurant architect Bill Johnson into a bright, dynamic dining room. Large windows admit light, and tables are comfortably spaced in both the front porch area and the main dining room. Near one of Atlanta's major parks and performance venues, the restaurant fills quickly for both meal services. Private affairs in the back are wonderful in nice weather. The noise level is high for some folks, but the place is so well designed, you can easily hear your table's conversation.

House specialties: Lowcountry shrimp paste on grits; rabbit pot pie; Carolina-style barbecue on corn cakes with slaw and Chef Berry's father's barbecue sauce; trout; fried chicken; catfish fingers; Kentucky oatmeal spice cake; barbecued duck.

Other recommendations: Chicken pot pie; pecan pie.

(continued)

Summary & comments: Chef David Berry cooked at the James Beard House in November 1999, and the foundation named him a Rising Star of American Cuisine.

Honors & awards: *Esquire* magazine, Best New Restaurant, 1994; *Bon Appétit,* Best New Restaurant, 1994; *Atlanta* magazine, Best Southern Cuisine, 1995, Best Alfresco Dining 1997, Best Place to Take Out-of-Town Guests, 1999, Best Place to Put a Feed Bag on a Yankee, 2000; *Atlanta Journal & Constitution,* Best Newcomer, 1994, Top 10 Desserts in Atlanta, 2000 for the oatmeal spice cake, and two stars and Top 50, 2000; Catfish Institute, Nation's Ten Best Catfish Restaurants, 1996.

Hsu's Gourmet
Chinese Restaurant

Zone 7 Downtown West	Hong Kong Chinese
192 Peachtree Center Avenue, NE	★★★
(404) 659-2788	Moderate

Hong Kong Chinese
★★★
Moderate

Quality 86   Value C

Reservations:	Recommended
When to go:	Any time
Entree range:	$12–20
Payment:	Major credit cards
Service rating:	★★★
Friendliness rating:	★★★
Parking:	Nearby parking deck (validated at dinner only)
Bar:	Separate, full service
Wine selection:	Respectable, with many imported and domestic choices
Dress:	Nice casual to business attire
Disabled access:	Yes
Customers:	Non-Asian locals, out-of-towners
Lunch/Dinner:	Monday–Thursday, 11:30 A.M.–10 P.M.; Friday 11:30 A.M.–11 P.M.; Saturday, 5–11 P.M.; Sunday, 5–10 P.M. (closing times depend on whether there's a convention in town)

Atmosphere/setting: Straight out of elegant, sophisticated Hong Kong, the restaurant is an oasis of calm and tranquility. Highly composed surroundings showcase art objects. Guests are warmly greeted by owners Raymond and Anna Hsu.

House specialties: Classic Chinese banquet fare and Hong Kong–style dishes, all elegantly conceived and executed, such as Peking duck in traditional two courses. Shrimp with black bean sauce; steamed sea bass Hong Kong style.

Other recommendations: Shrimp or chicken with mango; all shrimp dishes; iceberg lettuce wrapped around seasoned minced pork; ginger ice cream.

Summary & comments: This is a knife-and-fork kind of place, perfect for entertaining a business client who might enjoy the food but is not familiar with using chopsticks and would feel uncomfortable and put down by a host's showing off. Chopsticks are available—they recline on silver rests—but they can easily be ignored as all places are set with knife and fork.

Honors & awards: Mobil Travel Guide, Three Stars; Atlanta Convention & Visitors' Bureau Member of the Year award to Anna Hsu 2000, in recognition of the fine work the Hsus restaurants do. She also won GHTA Hospitality Leader of the Year, 1999. See also Pacific Rim Bistro (page 235).

Il Fornaio

Zone 4   Lenox/Chamblee
700 Ashford Parkway
(678) 579-0000

Italian
★★★★
Expensive

Quality 90   Value B

Reservations:	Accepted and highly recommended
When to go:	Any time
Entree range:	$9.95–24.95
Payment:	Major credit cards
Service rating:	★★★★
Friendliness rating:	★★★
Parking:	On site and valet
Bar:	Full service
Wine selection:	Excellent, with emphasis, naturally, on Italian wines
Dress:	Casual dressy
Disabled access:	Yes
Customers:	Neighbors from the Dunwoody residences and shoppers from nearby Perimeter Mall
Brunch:	Saturday and Sunday, 11 A.M.–3 P.M.
Lunch/Dinner:	Sunday–Thursday, 11 A.M.–10 P.M.; Friday and Saturday, 11 A.M.–11 P.M.

Atmosphere/setting: Taking design cues from Tuscany, the restaurant features textures shaped by tiles and stucco finishes. While the restaurant is large, intimacy for dating couples is secured in the booth seating, while large business parties dine happily at long tables.

House specialties: Lobster ravioli; pastas (which come out perfectly al dente); tenderloin with black peppercorn sauce; lamb chops.

Other recommendations: Assorted brunch pastries from the bakery; butter-nut squash–stuffed ravioli with butter; bruschetta.

Entertainment & amenities: There's a lovely enclosed patio by the entrance, enhanced by a subtle musical presence, and in cool weather a roaring fireplace adds to the warmth. The attached bakery offers to-go sandwiches, desserts, and breads. There's a bocce ball court with permanent seating to serve the bakery.

Summary & comments: As an Italian friend said, this is perhaps the most authentically Italian restaurant in Atlanta. There's just enough bustle to make it feel lively. Watch for special dinners that focus on the regional cooking of Italy.

Honors & awards: WHERE/Atlanta magazine, Italian wine list, 2000. Based on the West Coast, Il Fornaio's restaurants have taken numerous *Wine Spectator* awards for their wine lists, and this list is similar to the others.

Imperial Fez

Zone 3 Buckhead/Sandy Springs	Moroccan
Peachtree Battle Condominium	★★★★
2282 Peachtree Road, NE	Expensive
(404) 351-0870	Quality 90 Value B

Reservations:	Strongly recommended
When to go:	Any time
Entree range:	$45 per person for five courses
Payment:	Major credit cards
Service rating:	★★★★
Friendliness rating:	★★★★
Parking:	Self, on site
Bar:	Full service
Wine selection:	Wide ranging, including some from North Africa, with many by the glass
Dress:	Dressy casual to business attire
Disabled access:	Yes
Customers:	Locals and occasional out-of-towners
Dinner:	Every day, 6–11 P.M.

Atmosphere/setting: Inside the door, enter an exotic world filled with exciting aromas and sights. Park your shoes, and your business cares, at the front door. You'll recline on soft cushions and be presented with warm, scented water to wash your hands.

House specialties: Harrira (cumin-scented lentil soup); couscous, b'stella (cinnamon-flavored pastry wrapped around Cornish hen); tagine (slow-baked food done in a clay dish); vegetarian dishes available every day.

Other recommendations: The way this works is the patron chooses a meat to top the couscous; soup, appetizer, salad, and dessert are part of the dinner. Thus, you might choose lamb or chicken to top your couscous, or vegetables (a very Moroccan selection). Dietary requirements can be handled with advance notice, about 24-48 hours.

Entertainment & amenities: Traditional female Moroccan dancing every night.

Summary & comments: Women may want to wear long skirts or pants to make sitting on cushions more comfortable. Prepare to leave shoes on racks at the front door before entering the dining room. Owner Rafih Benjelloun is a committed advocate for Arabic culture, often lecturing in public schools and participating in community events to achieve his goal.

(continued)

IMPERIAL FEZ   *(continued)*

Honors & awards: Recognized by the Chaine des Rotisseurs; *Creative Loafing,* Best of Atlanta/Exotic Food Restaurant, five consecutive years. *Gourmet* magazine, America's Top Tables, 1999; National Restaurant Association Restaurant of the Millenium, Best International Restaurant in the USA, 2000; *WHERE/Atlanta* Memorable Meals, Most Memorable Meal, 1998; *Atlanta* magazine, Best Place to Unwind after a Harrowing Day, 2000. James Beard invited chef 2000.

KAMOGAWA

Zone 3   Buckhead/Sandy Springs
Grand Hyatt Atlanta
3300 Peachtree Road, NE
(404) 841-0314

Japanese	
★★★★	
Very Expensive	
Quality 96	Value C

Reservations:	Recommended
When to go:	Any time
Entree range:	$17–39; $50, $70, and $100 for multicourse gastronomic experiences
Payment:	Major credit cards
Service rating:	★★★★★
Friendliness rating:	★★★
Parking:	Valet (free with validation) or self, on site
Bar:	Full service
Wine selection:	Extensive and chiefly Californian, with about a dozen by the glass
Dress:	Business attire to very formal
Disabled access:	Yes
Customers:	Japanese clientele, internationals, knowledgeable locals
Lunch:	Monday–Friday, 11:30 A.M.–2 P.M.
Dinner:	Every night, 6–10 P.M.

Atmosphere/setting: Elegant, serene, formal, and exalted, Kamogawa is the place visiting Japanese businessmen choose when entertaining local guests. Guests' shoes wait patiently outside the tatami rooms until dinner is concluded.

House specialties: Keiseki banquet (with three days' advance notice preferred, starts at $70 per person); sushi and sashimi; sampling dinner (Omakase dinner/$50 per person) of assorted appetizer-sized dishes (must be ordered no later than 9 P.M., preferably earlier).

Other recommendations: Soft-shell crab appetizer; duck.

Summary & comments: No one could argue with the quality or the authenticity of Kamogawa. There's no steak ceremony here, with knives tossed perilously in the air. What you do get is the pure, simple classicism of Japanese cooking at its finest.

Honors & awards: Atlanta Journal & Constitution, Critic's Top 10 Restaurants, 1995; *Zagat;* and many, many more. Reviews and commentary on a national level include *USAToday* for chef Kochi Chiba, one of two referenced in the article, 2000.

KURT'S

Zone 4   Lenox/Chamblee
4225 River Green Parkway, Duluth
(770) 623-9413

Continental	
★★★	
Moderate	
Quality 85	Value C

Reservations:	Accepted
When to go:	Any time
Entree range:	$14–25.50
Payment:	All major credit cards
Service rating:	★★★
Friendliness rating:	★★★
Parking:	Self, on site
Bar:	Full service, with excellent imported unusual beers, after-dinner sips and grappas
Wine selection:	Extensive selection with many German wines and unusual choices. Kurt's 23 list is a long selection of wines available at $23; it changes frequently depending on market availability
Dress:	Casual
Disabled access:	Yes
Customers:	Corporate clients during the week and neighbors on the weekends
Dinner:	Monday–Saturday, 6–10 P.M.

Atmosphere/setting: This simple white frame structure among suburban Atlanta's business buildings exudes a remarkable serenity. Two separate operations thrive here, under the leadership of one family. Vreny's Biergarten (see page 294) occupies the back of the house and extends onto an outdoor patio. Kurt's dining room, open only for dinner, is the building's main dining space, although there also are numerous private dining rooms. The surrounding green space is being consumed by new construction, but the restaurant is still an oasis of tranquility.

House specialties: House-made country pâté; house-made spätzle with Black Forest ham; schnitzel; crabmeat Grenobloise; veal India with shrimp and curry; snails baked in small potatoes; Hungarian goulash soup; house-made apple strudel.

Other recommendations: Steaks; lobster; all fish dishes; soups.

Summary & comments: For about three decades, Kurt Eisele has had his stamp on numerous restaurants in Atlanta. Today, this is very much a family operation, with Kurt, Vreny and son Alexander all sharing duties. A smoking room with humidor is specially ventilated for cigar smoking and is isolated from the rest of the restaurant. Kurt is rightfully proud of his wine cellar.

La Grotta Ristorante

Zone 3 Buckhead/Sandy Springs	Northern and Regional Italian
Peachtree House Condominium	★★★★★
2637 Peachtree Road, NE	Very Expensive
(404) 231-1368	Quality 98 Value C

Zone 4   Lenox/Chamblee
Crowne Plaza Ravinia Hotel, 4355 Ashford Dunwoody Road
(770) 395-9925

Reservations:	Essential
When to go:	Any time
Entree range:	$17–28.95
Payment:	Major credit cards
Service rating:	★★★★★
Friendliness rating:	★★★★★
Parking:	Valet only at Buckhead; valet (free with validation) or self, on site at Ravinia
Bar:	Separate, full service, and after-dinner drink list at Buckhead; no separate bar, but full service at Ravinia
Wine selection:	Extensive and well selected, from Italy, California, and France
Dress:	Jacket preferred, tie optional at Buckhead; smart casual at Ravinia
Disabled access:	Excellent, via elevator to the lower level
Customers:	Sophisticated locals, glitterati, politicians, and folks who enjoy good food and wine
Lunch:	Ravinia: Monday–Friday, 11:30 A.M.–2 P.M.; no lunch at Buckhead
Dinner:	Buckhead: Monday–Saturday, 6–10:30 P.M.; Sunday, closed
	Ravinia: Monday–Saturday, 5:45–10 P.M.; Sunday, closed

Atmosphere/setting: Elegant, warmly lit, quiet, and refined, La Grotta in Buckhead demands respect but does so without intimidating. The staff is proper but warm. Much business gets conducted here, but so does much romance. At Ravinia, the atmosphere is contemporary, as floor-to-ceiling glass looks out on a lush garden. Tables are well spaced, conversation easily enjoyed, and the space is

(continued)

very good for business dining. This outfit also handles banquets especially well.

House specialties: Beautiful veal, quail, seafood, and fresh pasta dishes with traditional sauces have ensured this landmark restaurant its happy repeat clientele. Veal Mediterraneano (lunch menu and appetizer at dinner); orecchiette with lobster sauce at Ravinia.

Other recommendations: City's best gnocchi; panna cotta; tiramisu.

Summary & comments: The two restaurants are very different in both atmosphere and menu, but both deliver. The original La Grotta on Peachtree Road is very old world, very sophisticated, very long on attentive, correct service. The Ravinia La Grotta is more casual, more fun, and serves food that tastes like it comes from the trattoria tradition.

Honors & awards: AAA Four Diamond Award, 1994–2000; *Atlanta* magazine, Best Stalwart Italian, 1984–2000; DiRoNa Distinguished Restaurant of America, 1996-2001. *Atlanta Journal & Constitution,* three stars and Top 50, 2000.

LA PAZ

Mexican/Southwestern
★★★
Moderate

Quality 90   Value B

Zone 2   Northwest Atlanta
2950 New Paces Ferry Road, NW
(770) 801-0020

250 Cinema View Way, Woodstock
(770) 591-1073

Zone 3   Buckhead/Sandy Springs
Abbotts Village Shopping Center, 1605 Jones Bridge Road, Alpharetta
(770) 521-0506

Reservations:	During the week
When to go:	Any time, but can be crowded at the prime times
Entree range:	$8–14
Payment:	Major credit cards
Service rating:	★★★
Friendliness rating:	★★★
Parking:	Self, on site
Bar:	Full service
Wine selection:	Decent, with several by the glass
Dress:	Casual
Disabled access:	Yes
Customers:	Locals and visitors
Brunch:	Sunday, 11:30 A.M.–3 P.M.
Lunch:	Monday–Friday, 11:30 A.M.–2:30 P.M.
	Woodstock does not serve lunch Monday–Friday
Lunch/Dinner:	Woodstock: Saturday, noon–11 P.M., Sunday, noon–10 P.M.
Dinner:	Sunday–Thursday, 5–10 P.M.; Friday and Saturday, 5–11 P.M.;
	Woodstock: Tuesday–Thursday, 5–10 P.M.; Friday, 5–11 P.M.; Monday, closed

Atmosphere/setting: At the original Sandy Springs location, one finds the feeling of a classic border cantina, with iron railings on the upstairs balcony, an expansive bar, and an atmosphere that suggests bandoleros could come swaggering in at any moment. Other locations reflect varying aspects of vernacular Mexican architecture: The Vinings location is in an old church, so the interior suggests a chapel; another incorporates stone into a structure that recalls a Mexican hacien-

(continued)

209

da. More than just restaurants, these individual units are designed to reflect aspects of Mexican art and culture.

House specialties: Tortilla soup (with bits of avocado, vegetables, and chicken floating in a crystal clear broth); really tasty chile con queso with spinach; guacamole (made fresh three times a day); seafood.

Other recommendations: Aged tequilas and a wide variety of margaritas; homemade sangría (both red and white).

Summary & comments: Four locations in Atlanta include the original on Roswell Road in Sandy Springs, but that location's menu has been changed to produce a more homestyle, regional Mexican cuisine (see Changing Places, page 19). At the Vinings location there's a generous-sized private room in the street-level space that once was "South of La Paz," a store featuring Mexican artifacts, art, and crafts. That inventory will be transferred to the other restaurant locations. Owner Tom Nickoloff is passionate about Mexican culture and cuisine, and makes frequent trips to Mexico to source good products and to learn more about it. The restaurants feature organically grown coffee from the state of Chiapas, and Nickoloff's support of this industry not only recognizes the quality of the coffee, but also helps support the local economy and promote awareness of the severe deforestation that state has suffered.

La Tavola Trattoria

	Italian
	★★★★
	Expensive
	Quality 95 Value B

Zone 5   Northeast Atlanta
992 Virginia Avenue, Virginia-Highland
(404) 873-5430

Reservations:	Accepted, and recommended for weekends
When to go:	Any time
Entree range:	$10.95–23.95
Payment:	Major credit cards
Service rating:	★★★★
Friendliness rating:	★★★★
Parking:	Valet and lot across the street
Bar:	Full service
Wine selection:	Excellent, with emphasis on Californian and Italian, well arranged into useful sections. Some 25 are available by the glass out of a total of 110. Dessert wines also are available
Dress:	Casual nice
Disabled access:	Easy
Customers:	Neighbors
Brunch:	Sunday, 11 A.M.–3 P.M.
Dinner:	Sunday–Thursday, 5:30–11 P.M.; Friday and Saturday, 5:30 P.M.–midnight

Atmosphere / setting: Tiny, busy, jammed, and quite high energy without being overly noisy, this neighborhood trattoria has a lot going for it. Patrons don't bother to gussy up for this establishment, which attracts them with a comfortable space that's nicely (but not garishly) lit; tables spaced so dating couples can focus on each other; and charming service.

House specialties: Manicotti; mussels (fat, clean and sweet); tuna; duck ragù risotto (occasional special); veal chop (occasionally available); sea scallops on polenta; pastas.

Other recommendations: Mascarpone cheesecake; rum raisin bread pudding.

Summary & comments: A tiny slip of a space tucked into a Virginia-Highland historic commercial area, this little restaurant has been a hit despite starting off to unhappy reviews. The neighbors obviously disagreed with the critics, who now recognize the kitchen's maturity.

Honors & awards: *Atlanta Journal & Constitution* two stars and Top 50, 2000; *Jezebel* magazine, Top 100 Restaurants, 2000.

LE GIVERNY BISTRO

Zone 5 Northeast Atlanta	French
1355 Clairmont Road, Decatur	★★★
(404) 325-7252	Moderate
	Quality 89 Value B+

Reservations: Recommended
When to go: Any time, although dinner menu is more
                        interesting
Entree range: $10–18
Payment: Major credit cards
Service rating: ★★★★
Friendliness rating: ★★★★
Parking: Self, on site, ample
Bar: Beer and wine only
Wine selection: French and American, good selections appropri-
                        ately priced, with about half the list by the glass
Dress: Casual
Disabled access: Through the rear of the building
Customers: Locals, especially retirees, at lunch, and some
                        business people; at dinner, a younger, more hip
                        crowd from the academic community
Lunch: Monday–Friday, 11:30 A.M.–2 P.M.
Dinner: Monday–Saturday, 5:30–10 P.M.

Atmosphere/setting: A small spot in a neighborhood strip center, Le Giverny offers a comfortable, intimate dining experience. Tables are adorned simply with white tablecloths, and posters of Monet's work on the walls link the theme of the restaurant back to its name. Table conversation is easy because the noise level is very subdued. Additional dining space and a bar were recently added a few steps up from the main dining room.

House specialties: House-made country pâté; mussels; fresh fish and steak dishes; chocolate pâté.

Other recommendations: Specials, such as sea bass and mussels on linguine in a light cream/white wine sauce; lamb shank.

Summary & comments: Rémy Kerba, Frenchman, and his Bulgarian wife, Milena, own and operate the place, so it has a definite family feel. Steady, visible improvements in the food and its presentation have marked this neighborhood restaurant from its earliest days. Three-course fixed-price menus range from $18–27, very good deals indeed. Kerba makes no bones about cooking homestyle French food—not the fancy stuff. Don't expect wild presentations or cuisine artistique.

Le Saint Amour

Zone 5 Northeast Atlanta	French
1620 Piedmont Avenue, NE	★★★★
Morningside	Expensive
(404) 881-0300	Quality 92 Value C

Reservations: Accepted, and advised for weekends
When to go: Any time, but it's more restful at dinner
Entree range: $15–24
Payment: Major credit cards
Service rating: ★★★★★
Friendliness rating: ★★★★★
Parking: Lot
Bar: Full service
Wine selection: Limited and mostly French, but good choices
Dress: Casual dressy
Disabled access: Ramp to front door
Customers: Older patrons, folks who enjoy talking while
                        dining, devotees of French food
Lunch: Monday–Friday, 11:30 A.M.–2:30 P.M.
Dinner: Monday–Saturday, 6–10:30 P.M.

Atmosphere / setting: A modest former residence was turned fully on its ear to suggest a house in Provence. Painted a Mediterranean coral color outside, its interior spaces are painted different colors—pale blue, yellow—banded in white trim. The furnishings are deliberate potluck—nothing matches except the chairs at each table. It works.

House specialties: Escargots; foie gras; sweetbreads; salads; seafood; duck confit; rack of lamb; Dover sole Normande; lobster.

Other recommendations: Soufflés for dessert—really superb.

Entertainment & amenities: A vocalist self-accompanied on the piano.

Summary & comments: Owner Noëlle Thomas, from Paris, opened this restaurant 1997. She has cooked for François Mitterand, the late president of France. Noëlle has successfully captured the whimsy and warmth that characterize the small and excellent restaurants of Provence. Vincent Marquet from the south of France is the new chef. Lunch is the same menu as dinner, but with a couple of extra specials.

Honors & awards: WHERE/Atlanta magazine, *Knife & Fork, Intown,* and *Atlanta* magazine all have published good articles about the restaurant.

Little Szechuan

Chinese/Szechuan
★★★★
Inexpensive

Quality 95   Value A+

Zone 4   Lenox/Chamblee
Northwoods Plaza, 5091-C Buford
Highway, NE at Shallowford Road
(770) 451-0192

Reservations:	Accepted
When to go:	Any time
Entree range:	$7–20
Payment:	VISA, MC
Service rating:	★★★★
Friendliness rating:	★★★★
Parking:	Self, on site
Bar:	Beer (wonderful Chinese beers) and wine only
Wine selection:	Limited
Dress:	Casual
Disabled access:	Yes
Customers:	Loads of Chinese families and adventurous Occidentals
Lunch:	Monday, Wednesday–Saturday, 11:30 A.M.–3 P.M.; Sunday, noon–3 P.M.
Dinner:	Monday, Wednesday–Sunday, 5–9:30 P.M.; Tuesday, closed

Atmosphere/setting: Freshly renovated, bright, attractive but simply decorated, Little Szechuan is a no-frills, clean, family-oriented restaurant that no one should miss. "Better look at menu first," advises the concerned waiter when non-Asians appear. It's good advice, because this is serious, no-foolin' Chinese food at its best.

House specialties: String beans; shrimp egg foo yong; kung pao squid; sautéed sweet pea leaves; shrimp with young garlic; house special tofu; Szechuan beef brisket in hot sauce.

Other recommendations: The adventurous should try pig tripe dishes and chicken roll (tofu skin stuffed with minced pork, chicken, and shrimp). Also good soft-shell crab.

Summary & comments: No egg rolls or fortune cookies here. Lunch specials are very inexpensive and outstanding. This simply is one of the city's best Chinese restaurants. Period.

Honors & awards: Many recognitions in local press, including local Chinese language press, have honored this excellent restaurant. *Atlanta Journal & Constitution,* Top 50, 2000; *Creative Loafing,* Best Chinese, 2000.

214

Loca Luna

Zone 8   Downtown East
114 6th Street, NE, Midtown
(404) 875-4494

	Tapas
	★★
	Inexpensive
	Quality 88 Value A

Reservations:	Accepted for parties of six or more
When to go:	Weekdays (weekends are jammed)
Entree range:	$5–7
Payment:	AMEX, MC, VISA
Service rating:	★★★
Friendliness rating:	★★★★★
Parking:	On-site but shared so it's tight
Bar:	Full service
Wine selection:	Limited but well chosen
Dress:	Casual to funky
Disabled access:	Yes
Customers:	20- and 30-somethings with plenty of attitude and energy
Brunch:	Sunday, 11 A.M.–3 P.M.
Lunch:	Tuesday–Friday, 11:30 A.M.–2:30 P.M.
Dinner:	Tuesday-Thursday, 5–11 P.M.; Friday–Saturday, 5 P.M.–12:30 A.M. (bar stays open on weekends)

Atmosphere/setting: This is a wild and crazy kind of place, one that you wouldn't take your mom to unless she were a wild and crazy kind of mom. The decor tilts to thatched roof and tropical, with suggestions of off-beat Latin American beach resorts that might attract a hip crowd.

House specialties: Paella; fried calamari; grilled ribs with Sherry vinaigrette; moqueca soup; chicken skewers; beef kabob; tres leches dessert.

Other recommendations: Beef carpaccio; tacos; Catalan pan amb tomat (bread with tomato); batatas bravas (spicy potatoes).

Entertainment & amenities: A six-piece Brazilian band plays every Friday and Saturday, getting folks up and dancing to lively Gypsy King songs. A five-piece band plays Andean music Thursdays, and live Latin music rules Tuesdays and Thursdays.

Summary & comments: You wouldn't expect a crazy joint like this to pay much attention to the food, but the kitchen does nothing like the kind of bar food one usually finds. Drawn from all over the world, but with emphasis on Hispanic and Latin dishes, these tapas could stand on their own in a more sedate circumstance. Round up a gang, don your favorite tropical shirt, and enjoy the music.

Honors & awards: Atlanta magazine, Best Place to Get Crazy, 1999.

215

Mambo Cuban Restaurant

Cuban	
★★★	
Moderate	
Quality 88	Value C

Zone 5   Northeast Atlanta
1402 N. Highland Avenue, NE
Virginia-Highland
(404) 876-2626

Reservations:	Accepted
When to go:	Any time
Entree range:	$9.95–18.95
Payment:	Major credit cards
Service rating:	★★★
Friendliness rating:	★★★★
Parking:	Self, on the street or at nearby (and usually full) parking lot
Bar:	Beer and wine only
Wine selection:	Medium-long, well-selected list with many Latin American and Spanish wines by the glass
Dress:	Very casual
Disabled access:	Yes
Customers:	Neighbors
Dinner:	Sunday–Thursday, 5:30–10 P.M.; Friday and Saturday, 5:30–11 P.M.

Atmosphere/setting: Dark, a bit cavernous, but always relaxed and full of fun, Mambo sings with that irrepressible Latin rhythm. Co-owner (with wife and chef, Lucy Alvarez) Hilton Joseph gives the front of the house that salsa flair.

House specialties: Paella; black paella; ropa vieja; and especially Chinese-Latino dishes, Lucy's specialty.

Other recommendations: Flan; Three Milks Cake, a Latin specialty; fire-cracker steak (stuffed with peppers); Buena Vista chop (a monster pork chop).

Summary & comments: Ask about Lucy's classes in Cuban and Chinese-Latino dishes, occasionally taught at the restaurant. Wine dinners are becoming frequent, with one being held every three months or so. For these dinners, Cuban food is paired with wines from all over the world. Proprietor Hilton Joseph says Malbec from Argentina is becoming very popular with his patrons. Lately, he's gotten reservations from as far away as Beverly Hills.

Honors & awards: *Hispanic* magazine, One of 50 Best Hispanic Restaurants in the Nation, since 1991; *Atlanta* magazine, Best of Atlanta, Cuban, annually; *Creative Loafing,* Best Cuban, 2000; *Fortune* magazine cited Mambo as a place to savor good Cuban food, 1999.

216

Marra's Grill:
Fresh Seafood and
Great Steaks

Seafood/Steaks
★★★
Moderate
Quality 88   Value C

Zone 5   Northeast Atlanta
1782 Cheshire Bridge Road, NE
(404) 874-7374 or (404) 874-7363

Reservations:	Recommended
When to go:	Any time
Entree range:	$12.95–22.50
Payment:	Major credit cards
Service rating:	★★★
Friendliness rating:	★★★
Parking:	Valet
Bar:	Full service
Wine selection:	Very good, with several by the glass, and a very good half-bottle list
Dress:	Nice casual or business attire
Disabled access:	Yes
Customers:	Locals, conventioneers, and out-of-towners (often brought by the locals)
Dinner:	Monday–Thursday, 6–10 P.M.; Friday and Saturday, 6–11 P.M.; Sunday, 5:30–10 P.M.

Atmosphere/setting: Begun in a small former residence, the restaurant has expanded out the back like a telescope. Well-spaced tables and banquette seating make conversation easy; the energy level is dynamic, but not overwhelming. Pleasing fish-themed art, bright with vibrant colors, adorns the walls.

House specialties: The strong suit is the fish grilled over an open-fire wood grill. House-smoked salmon done over fruitwood; taramosalata; macadamia nut Georgia trout fillet with peach amaretto sauce; whole Dover sole filleted tableside.

Other recommendations: Desserts, such as Southern Comfort chocolate pecan pie.

Summary & comments: Founded in 1981 by Gene Marra, who has since gone on to other assignments, the restaurant is now in the hands of a nurturing couple from eastern Europe. Owners Jerry and Vera Bures came to Atlanta after the Russian invasion of their homeland and have been involved in the Atlanta food scene for nearly 30 years. Chef Dan Noble gives the menu a touch of his native California.

Honors & awards: Wine Spectator, Award of Excellence, annually for the last decade; *Zagat* 2001 (Best Seafood Value).

MARY MAC'S TEA ROOM

Zone 8 Downtown East	Southern
224 Ponce de Leon Avenue, NE	★★
at Myrtle Street, Midtown	Inexpensive
(404) 876-1800	Quality 83 Value B

Reservations:	Not accepted, except for parties of ten or more if space permits
When to go:	Early for lunch, or between 2–5 P.M.; after 8 P.M.;
Entree range:	$9–14
Payment:	Cash only (ATM on site)
Service rating:	★★★★★
Friendliness rating:	★★★★★
Parking:	Self, on site
Bar:	Separate, full service
Wine selection:	Limited
Dress:	Casual
Disabled access:	Excellent
Customers:	Out-of-towners, celebrities, politicians (especially when the legislature is in session), students
Lunch:	Monday–Saturday, 11 A.M.–4 P.M.; Sunday 11 A.M.–3 P.M.
Dinner:	Monday–Saturday, 5–8:30 P.M.

Atmosphere/setting: Bright, lively, and down-home casual, the dining room has a drill for ordering that's ages old: pick up a pencil and fill out your form. A waitress will call you "honey" or maybe "sugar" and take the form, returning promptly with your plate laden with huge portions. Politicians love this place; it's a power-lunch spot when the legislature's in session. In true Southern fashion, lunch is called dinner and dinner is supper.

House specialties: Fried chicken; cornbread dressing and gravy; vegetables (sweet potato soufflé, greens); barbecue; meat loaf; peach cobbler.

Other recommendations: Chicken pot pie; fried shrimp and oysters; roast beef; country-fried steak; roast pork; banana puddin'.

Entertainment & amenities: A pianist performs in the evenings.

Summary & comments: Now more than 50 years old, Mary Mac's is an Atlanta institution. In the middle of the sophisticated urban setting, the visitor immediately senses what Southern hospitality and food are all about. Recently, owner John Ferrell added a grill to expand the restaurant's offerings.

Honors & awards: Creative Loafing, Best Southern Food, Readers' Choice, 2000; *Gourmet* magazine, America's Best Restaurants family dining, 2000.

McKendrick's

Zone 4   Lenox/Chamblee
Park Place Shopping Center
4505 Ashford Dunwoody Road
(770) 512-8888

Steak	
★★★★	
Very Expensive	
Quality 88	Value D

Reservations:	Strongly recommended
When to go:	Any time
Entree range:	$15–50
Payment:	Major credit cards
Service rating:	★★★
Friendliness rating:	★★★
Parking:	Self, on site; valet
Bar:	Full service
Wine selection:	Long, wide-ranging list with a few by good ones by the glass
Dress:	Business casual
Disabled access:	Yes
Customers:	Mostly male business patrons
Lunch:	Monday–Friday, 11:30 A.M.–2:30 P.M.
Dinner:	Monday–Thursday, 5:30–10:30 P.M.; Friday and Saturday, 5:30–11 P.M.; Sunday, 5:30–10 P.M.

Atmosphere/setting: Dark burnished woods and warm, dim lighting enhance a medium-high energy atmosphere for this guy-comfortable steak emporium. The decor is restful, lacks glitter, and relies on fine black-and-white photographs for its embellishment.

House specialties: Steak of all kinds; game (terrific buffalo steak when available); duck; veal chop; grilled fish.

Other recommendations: Barbecued shrimp; vegetables.

Summary & comments: A serious, masculine place, McKendrick's is better for celebrating that great business deal than for popping the question. The marvelous house-baked bread has been restored—hoorah!

Honors & awards: *Atlanta Journal & Constitution,* Top 10 New Restaurants, 1996; *Atlanta* magazine, Best Suburban Steak House, 1996.

McKinnon's Louisiane

Zone 3 Buckhead/Sandy Springs	Creole/Cajun
3209 Maple Drive, NE	★★★
(404) 237-1313	Moderate
	Quality 88 Value B

Reservations:	Essential on weekends or during conventions
When to go:	Any time
Entree range:	$13–19
Payment:	Major credit cards
Service rating:	★★
Friendliness rating:	★★★
Parking:	Self, on site, but scarce
Bar:	Full service
Wine selection:	Decent, with some by the glass
Dress:	Nice casual
Disabled access:	Yes
Customers:	Lots of regulars, but lots of out-of-towners, too
Dinner:	Every day, 6–10 P.M.

Atmosphere/setting: Two main dining spaces plus an entertainment-focused lounge/bar area are tucked into this popular Atlanta restaurant.

House specialties: Crab cakes; stuffed eggplant; all seafood; bread pudding; crème brûlée; blackened amberjack with hot peppered shrimp; Cajun popcorn.

Other recommendations: Absolutely perfect deep-fried shrimp, oysters, and crawfish tails.

Entertainment & amenities: Piano bar Friday and Saturday.

Summary & comments: This Atlanta institution, which marked its 29th year in 2001, was brought into being by a former stockbroker-turned-restaurateur. Founding proprietor Billy McKinnon has moved to his native Brunswick to retire (sort of), while Bill Glendenning and Aziz Mehram, longtime associates at the restaurant, are at the helm. McKinnon remains as a partner.

220

MIRAGE

Zone 3   Buckhead/Sandy Springs
Abernathy Square, 6631 Roswell Road
at Abernathy Road
(404) 843-8300

Persian/Vegetarian
★★★
Moderate

Quality 90   Value B

Reservations:	Accepted
When to go:	Any time
Entree range:	$6.95–18.95
Payment:	Major credit cards
Service rating:	★★★★
Friendliness rating:	★★★
Parking:	Lot
Bar:	Beer and wine
Wine selection	Limited, but with good choices that serve the food well
Dress:	Casual dressy
Disabled access:	Easy
Customers:	Mostly American, lots of vegetarians, neighbors chiefly
Lunch/Dinner:	Monday–Thursday, 11 A.M.–10 P.M.; Friday and Saturday, 11 A.M.–11 P.M.; Sunday, noon–10 P.M.

Atmosphere/setting: This simply decorated shopping mall space doesn't go overboard with Persian atmospherics; emphasis is on the food, and the fast and friendly service. Tables are well spaced, and noise levels accommodate easy private conversation.

House specialties: Combination tenderloin, fish, and chicken with rice and salad, plenty for two people; shrimp kabob; rack of lamb; eggplant dishes.

Other recommendations: House-made ice creams (pistachio, saffron, and rosewater); vegetarian dishes; superbly cooked Basmati rice.

Entertainment & amenities: Occasional belly dancing, live Persian band.

Summary & comments: A recently added private room handles up to 60 for a banquet.

Honors & awards: Atlanta Journal & Constitution, two stars and Top 50, 2000; *Atlanta* magazine, Best Persian, 2000.

Mi Spia

Zone 4   Lenox/Chamblee
Park Place Shopping Center
4505 Ashford Dunwoody Road
Dunwoody
(770) 393-1333

California Italian
★★★
Moderate

Quality 88   Value C

Reservations:	Accepted; highly recommended for lunch
When to go:	Any time
Entree range:	$14.95–24.95
Payment:	Major credit cards
Service rating:	★★★
Friendliness rating:	★★★
Parking:	Tight during busy hours
Bar:	Full service
Wine selection:	Extensive, lots of Californian and Italian
Dress:	Nice casual
Disabled access:	Yes
Customers:	At lunch, business customers; at dinner, business customers, neighbors
Lunch:	Monday–Friday, 11:30 A.M.–2:30 P.M.
Dinner:	Monday–Thursday and Sunday, 5–10 P.M.; Friday and Saturday, 5–11 P.M.

Atmosphere/setting: High ceilings, comfortable and well-spaced tables, and pleasantly warm lighting are among the visual amenities in this suburban dining room. The garden room, now fully enclosed, is the most popular space. A large bar visually conducts patrons into the dining room, and it's a good spot for enjoying a pre-dinner sip. The noise level is moderate.

House specialties: Intriguing starters; wood-grilled, prosciutto-wrapped shrimp on soft polenta with tomato fondue; salmon with honey balsamic glaze; angel hair pasta with tomatoes, garlic, basil, and oregano; all sorts of fish dishes; pork loin chops in whole grain mustard.

Other recommendations: Tiramisu.

Summary & comments: Outdoor dining in nice weather makes this a real break from work for nearby office workers. The rich, faux-Tuscan interior throws off appealing, warm tones, making everyone look wonderful. This one is handy for unwinding after a shopping spree at nearby Perimeter Mall.

Honors & awards: WHERE/Atlanta magazine, finalist Best Ambiance, 1998; finalist Most Memorable Fine Dining and Most Memorable Meal, 1998, Most Delightful Restaurant Bar Winner, 1998; finalist Most Delightful Restaurant Bar, 1999; winner Most Outstanding Service, 2000; *Zagat.*

Mumbo Jumbo

	American/Continental
Zone 7 Downtown West	★★★★
89 Park Place, near Woodruff Park	Expensive
(404) 523-0330	
	Quality 95 Value C

Reservations:	Accepted
When to go:	Any time
Entree range:	$18–28
Payment:	Major credit cards
Service rating:	★★★
Friendliness rating:	★★★★
Parking:	Park (at your cost) in the lot at Park Place
Bar:	Huge bar, full service
Wine selection:	Excellent and wide-ranging with most choices coming from France and California, from good values to impressive selections at hefty (but fair) prices
Dress:	Nice casual
Disabled access:	Yes, street level
Customers:	Business-suited conventioneers and locals in after-work casual
Lunch:	Monday–Friday, 11:30 A.M.–2:30 P.M.
Dinner:	Every day, 5:30–11 P.M. (light fare menu, 2:30–5:30 P.M.; 11:30 P.M.–2:30 A.M.)

Atmosphere/setting: Transforming a raucous nightclub into a posh cutting-edge restaurant and designing food to match takes vision. Enter and the long bar awaits you to the left. To the right is ample bar seating, where a bar menu is offered between lunch and dinner, and after dinner into the late night. To the rear, a fireplace warms in cold weather and amply spaced seating beckons. Noise levels can be very high at busy times, making table conversation difficult.

House specialties: Truffled chicken salad (lunch); Mumbo Gumbo; pasta puttanesca with lobster tails; whole fish; antipasto with bresaola and similar unusual offerings; braised dishes (rabbit and short ribs) in winter; desserts, such as homemade yogurt with honey, white grape raisins, and Kit Kat. This menu changes at least seasonally, if not more often.

Other recommendations: Sardinian flat bread with Vella dry Jack cheese and black truffle oil; short-rib ravioli with foie gras sauce; dishes with ramps (spring special when chef Doty finds them wild near his parents' home in Virginia (ramps

(continued)

223

are a wild garlicky onion that grow in Appalachia); Barcelona-style tapas Friday evenings.

Entertainment & amenities: La Hora Alegre, a Spanish-themed Friday evening happy hour featuring Latin deejays. Bands and live music appear upstairs in the private party space. Occasionally, there's live music in the dining room, such as a jazz combo.

Summary & comments: Since the last edition of this book in 1997, Mumbo Jumbo has undergone some ownership changes, but the kitchen remains under the firm governance of Chef Shaun Doty, now one of the owners along with Tom Cook, who is also an owner of Nathaniel's, and Brent Persall. If the club is operative upstairs, its pulsating beat can disturb dinner table conversation below, so if that's an issue, check as to the goings on upstairs when making reservations.

Honors & awards: Since becoming Mumbo Jumbo's executive chef, Shaun Doty has been named a Rising Star of American Cuisine by the James Beard Foundation and has appeared on numerous television shows; *Playboy* magazine, one of America's Best Bars, 2000; *Zagat,* Top 40 for Most Popular and Décor, 2000; *Atlanta Business Chronicle,* Top 25, 1999; *Atlanta* magazine, Best of Downtown, annually.

Murphy's

	California American
Zone 5 Northeast Atlanta	★★★
997 Virginia Avenue, NE	Inexpensive/Moderate
Virginia-Highland	
(404) 872-0904	Quality 90 Value C

Reservations:	Priority seating on weekends (dinner only)
When to go:	Any time
Entree range:	$9–25
Payment:	Major credit cards
Service rating:	★★★★
Friendliness rating:	★★★★
Parking:	Valet
Bar:	Full service
Wine selection:	Extensive and carefully chosen
Dress:	Casual
Disabled access:	Yes
Customers:	Neighbors from the upscale, restoration-aware, in-town community
Lunch/Dinner:	Monday–Thursday, 11 A.M.–10 P.M. Friday, 11 A.M.–midnight
Dinner:	Saturday and Sunday, 4:30 P.M.–midnight
Brunch:	Saturday and Sunday, 8 A.M.–3 P.M. (light fare menu 3–4:30 P.M.)

Atmosphere/setting: Whether sitting at the bar for a quick dessert and coffee, or at one of the comfortable tables in the main dining room for a meal, you'll always enjoy the restaurant's busy but not noisy ambiance. This intersection (Virginia and N. Highland avenues) is the heart of the district, with snappy businesses of all kinds run by hip young entrepreneurs. Young waiters are brisk but friendly, and wine knowledge is a cut above the ordinary.

House specialties: Brunch egg dishes, including omelets and frittatas; grilled fish and chicken; lobster bisque; all soups are excellent; crab cakes; smoked pork chop; Toll House pie; bonzo cake.

Summary & comments: A significant part of this neighborhood's redevelopment and gentrification process has been Murphy's, originally located elsewhere in Virginia-Highland and now more prominently centered at the busy Virginia and N. Highland avenues intersection. Murphy's commitment to the neighborhood has paid off. This is a good take-out spot if you're composing an impromptu picnic. The bakery does wonderful tarts, muffins, cookies, and all manner of outstanding desserts, even a to-go crème brûlée. Wine is sold at the retail part of this operation.

Honors & awards: *Creative Loafing,* Best Brunch, 1993–1996; *Zagat.*

NAVA

Zone 3 Buckhead/Sandy Springs	Southwestern American
Buckhead Plaza	★★★
3060 Peachtree Road, NW	Expensive
near W. Paces Ferry Road	
(404) 240-1984	Quality 88 Value D

Reservations:	Accepted
When to go:	Early or late in the meal service
Entree range:	$15–25
Payment:	Major credit cards
Service rating:	★★★
Friendliness rating:	★★
Parking:	Valet
Bar:	Separate, full service
Wine selection:	Extensive, mostly American, with some good by-the-glass offerings
Dress:	Nice to dressy casual and business attire
Disabled access:	Yes
Customers:	Glitzy denizens of Buckhead, media types and film stars, out-of-towners
Lunch:	Monday–Friday, 11:30 A.M.–2:30 P.M.
Dinner:	Monday–Thursday, 5:30–11 P.M.; Friday and Saturday, 5:30 P.M.–midnight; Sunday, 5:30–10 P.M.

Atmosphere/setting: A fortune has been spent transforming this interior into a treasure trove of Southwestern American art, complete with kachina dolls in every nook.

House specialties: Corn-crusted snapper; masa chicken soup; yellow-fin tuna; pork tenderloin with poblano peppers and tamarind glaze; grilled flank steak fajitas.

Other recommendations: Green chile masa taco; grilled vegetable quesadilla.

Summary & comments: Appetizers are the most interesting dishes at this multilevel, show-stopping restaurant. That makes it easy to assemble a lunch of light treats, combining, for instance, soup and quesadilla or salad.

Honors & awards: Esquire magazine, One of Top 25 New Restaurants, 1995; Pastry Chef Kirk Parks won the 1997 Brandy & Benedictine annual chocolate award for his chocolate mousse and chocolate cube with crushed chocolate chip cookies; *Gourmet* magazine, Gold Medal New Restaurant, 1996; *Restaurant Hospitality* magazine, Kevin Rathbun selected Best and Brightest Rising Star, 1996; AAA Three Diamond Award, 1997; *Atlanta* magazine, Best Taste of the Southwest, 2000.

Nickiemoto's

Zone 8   Downtown East
990 Piedmont Avenue
at 10th Street, Midtown
(404) 253-2010

Pan Asian	
★★★	
Inexpensive/Moderate	
Quality 90	Value A

Reservations:	Not accepted
When to go:	Any time
Entree range:	$6.75–19.95
Payment:	Major credit cards
Service rating:	★★★★
Friendliness rating:	★★★★
Parking:	Self, on site
Bar:	Full service
Wine selection:	Modest, with good selections
Dress:	Casual
Disabled access:	Easy
Customers:	Neighbors, hip young folks from Midtown's apartments and condos
Lunch/Dinner:	Monday–Thursday, 11:30 A.M.–11 P.M.; Friday, 11:30 A.M.–midnight; Saturday, noon–midnight; Sunday, noon–11 P.M.

Atmosphere/setting: This classy, gleaming, hip dining room features lots of brushed metal and open spaces, with generous fenestration. Look out onto the busy Midtown intersection, or in good weather dine on the sidewalk patio and savor the activity along with your lunch. Weekends, Midtown buzzes with young folks jogging, walking, and in-line skating. It's the place to be, and Nickiemoto's sits right at its heart. And the sushi bar sits at the heart of Nickiemoto's.

House specialties: Sushi; whole sizzling catfish; stir fries; moo shus; steamed dumplings; ginger crème brûlée.

Other recommendations: Spicy rare beef salad; Vietnamese-style summer rolls.

Entertainment & amenities: Drag show on Monday nights called "Drag-a-Maki."

Summary & comments: Assembling all the flavors of Asia into a cohesive whole is not easy, but chef William Yu makes it all make sense—and taste good. No dish ever seems out of balance or weird. Yu makes Asian flavors seem American while not losing their authenticity. Nice work.

Honors & awards: Citysearch, nominated for Best Sushi Restaurant in Atlanta, 2000; *Midtown Gazette,* Best Sushi in Midtown, 2000.

227

Nikolai's Roof

Continental/French
★★★★★
Very expensive
Quality 96   Value C

Zone 7   Downtown West
Hilton Atlanta Hotel
255 Courtland and Harris Streets, NE
(404) 221-6362

Reservations:	Required
When to go:	Any time
Entree range:	$73 per person, fixed price
Payment:	Major credit cards
Service rating:	★★★★★
Friendliness rating:	★★★★
Parking:	Valet or self, validated
Bar:	Full service
Wine selection:	Extensive, mostly French and Californian
Dress:	Business attire to black tie
Disabled access:	Yes, using elevators
Customers:	The well heeled, the power shakers
Dinner:	Every day, 6–9 P.M.

Atmosphere/setting: Opulence with a view is how best to describe this dowager dining establishment. The seats are plush, the flatware and china first rate, making this a "pamper-me" kind of place.

House specialties: Piroshkis, which this restaurant introduced to the city; beef tenderloin; game; fish; white truffles in season.

Other recommendations: Caviar; whatever soufflé is done the evening of your visit, but hope and pray it's the warm almond.

Summary & comments: The pseudo-Russian nonsense originally purveyed here, with Cossack-garbed waiters reciting the dishes, has (mercifully) given way to a more professionally trained staff that deftly brings the delights of classic French fare to the table. Young, vivacious chef Johannes Klapdohr has a sophisticated way with this cooking, giving it a lightness and intensity of flavor that's totally contemporary.

Honors & awards: For more than two decades, this has been one of the city's most recognized restaurants: Ivy Award, 1982; Mobil Travel Guide, Four Stars, 1988–2000; AAA Four Diamond Award, 1991–2000; DiRoNA Award, 1992–2000; among others.

228

Noche

<table>
<tr><td>Zone 5   Northeast Atlanta</td><td rowspan="6">Southwestern/American
★★★
Expensive

Quality 88   Value C</td></tr>
<tr><td>1000 Virginia Avenue, NE</td></tr>
<tr><td>at N. Highland Avenue</td></tr>
<tr><td>Virginia-Highland</td></tr>
<tr><td>(404) 815-9155</td></tr>
</table>

Reservations:	Accepted before 7:30 P.M.
When to go:	Any time
Entree range:	$13–22
Payment:	Major credit cards
Service rating:	★★★
Friendliness rating:	★★★
Parking:	Valet
Bar:	Full service
Wine selection:	California rules this list of about 50 wines, roughly half of them available by the glass
Dress:	Casual
Disabled access:	Easy
Customers:	Neighbors and young, hip types from all over metro Atlanta
Dinner:	Monday–Thursday, 5:30–10:30 P.M.; Friday and Saturday, 5–11 P.M.; Sunday, 5–10 P.M.

Atmosphere/setting: Enter off the busy street, and you'll find the bar and kitchen to the left, giving you first a great view of the active culinary crew. Owner Tom Catherall's wife, Leigh, has produced lovely Southwest-style paintings for the restaurant's artwork. Well-spaced table seating fills the back of the space and spills out onto the patio.

House specialties: Barbecued salmon or shrimp on corn masa; mussels in lobster stock with hominy grits and chiles; tortilla soup; chocolate tres leches cake.

Other recommendations: Rabbit, duck, venison, and buffalo short ribs in cold weather; ceviche in summer.

Summary & comments: In the warmer months, the bar opens at 2 P.M. on Sundays. This is the only Tom Catherall–owned restaurant that doesn't serve sushi.

Honors & awards: Atlanta magazine, Best of Atlanta, Best Reason to Visit Virginia-Highland, 1999, Best Place to Sit Cheek-to-Cheek with a High-Energy Bar Crowd, 2000; James Beard invited chef, Don Diem, 2000; A*tlanta Journal & Constitution,* two stars and Top 50, 1999–2000.

Nona's Italian Kitchen

Zone 3 Buckhead/Sandy Springs	Italian
Tower Place, Suite 1025	★★
3365 Piedmont Road, NE	Moderate
(404) 261-1312	Quality 85 Value B

Reservations:	Accepted
When to go:	Any time
Entree range:	$12.95–22.95
Payment:	Major credit cards
Service rating:	★★★★
Friendliness rating:	★★★★
Parking:	Valet
Bar:	Full service
Wine selection:	Excellent, mostly Californian and Italian, with a good selection by the glass and an extensive reserve list of pricier choices
Dress:	Casual
Disabled access:	Elevator
Customers:	Residents of Buckhead
Lunch:	Monday–Friday, 11:30 A.M.–2:30 P.M.
Dinner:	Monday–Thursday, 5–10 P.M.; Friday and Saturday, 5–11 P.M.; Sunday, 5–9 P.M.

Atmosphere/setting: Upstairs in this rather Miami Vice–styled add-on to a major Buckhead office complex, Nona's Italian Kitchen (yes, it should be Nonna, but the guys decided to spell it their way) combines a sophisticated interior design with down-to-earth homestyle Italian cooking. A sweeping sheltered outdoor patio provides a breezy outdoor dining space with a view of Piedmont Road. The noise level within is lively, but not so fearsome as to intimidate conversation.

House specialties: Chicken saltimbocca on baby spinach; roasted red peppers and pancetta salad; eggplant fritters; bucatini with sweet sausage and vodka sauce; spumoni ice cream sandwich.

Other recommendations: House-made pastas; Nona's mussels with saffron-fennel white wine broth; seafood stew; tiramisu; roasted pork loin with garlic mashed potatoes.

Summary & comments: This has become an in spot for residents of Buckhead to dine impromptu, while it has enhanced the lunch opportunities for area businesspeople. Casual but friendly and correct, brisk service makes the meal move along at a good pace.

Honors & awards: Good local press.

Northlake Thai

Eurasian/Thai
★★★★
Moderate
Quality 90   Value A

Zone 5   Northeast Atlanta
3939 LaVista Road (but actually facing
on Montreal Road), Northlake, Tucker
(770) 938-2223

Reservations:	Accepted, and highly advised for weekends
When to go:	Any time
Entree range:	$12–17
Payment:	AMEX, MC, VISA
Service rating:	★★★★★
Friendliness rating:	★★★★★
Parking:	Self, on site
Bar:	Beer and wine only
Wine selection:	Limited, with good selections, but they don't pair all that well with this food
Dress:	Casual nice
Disabled access:	Easy
Customers:	Neighbors, business folks at lunch, couples at night
Lunch:	Monday–Friday, 11 A.M.–2:30 P.M.
Dinner:	Monday–Thursday, 5–10 P.M.; Friday and Saturday, 5–11 P.M.; Sunday, closed

Atmosphere/setting: What started off as a nondescript space acquires warmth from low lighting and distinctive contemporary paintings with only a touch of Asian influence. The atmosphere is relaxed and refined. It's the perfect setting for this food, which isn't heavy on specific Thai dishes, but instead lends Thai flavors to Western-style fare.

House specialties: Herb-crusted rack of lamb in Thai basil sauce; deep-fried sea scallops in rice batter; rice-battered calamari; lemongrass shrimp bisque.

Other recommendations: Sea bass in sweet-and-sour mushroom broth; pastries and chocolate cheesecake for dessert.

Summary & comments: The special set menu ($35) is a nine-course dinner, including five kinds of appetizers. Owner Donald Mui, a native of Hong Kong, grew up in New York, and has worked in restaurants from his teen years. "This really isn't a Thai restaurant," he says, "it's a good restaurant with Thai touches." The result is distinctive fare that's Thai, but with a difference. Unlike many Thai restaurants that offer searingly hot foods, this one tempers the heat factor.

Honors & awards: Atlanta Journal & Constitution, Best Thai in DeKalb Readers' Choice, 2000, Reviewed Two Stars, 1998.

Nuevo Laredo Cantina

Zone 2   Northwest Atlanta
1495 Chattahoochee Avenue
(404) 352-9009

Mexican/Tex-Mex
★★
Inexpensive
Quality 86   Value A

Reservations:	For parties of six or more only
When to go:	Any time
Entree range:	$6.95–12.95
Payment:	Major credit cards
Service rating:	★★★★
Friendliness rating:	★★★★★
Parking:	Self, on site
Bar:	Full service
Wine selection:	Limited, good selections from Spain, but also consider the sangría or a Mexican beer
Dress:	Casual
Disabled access:	Separate entrance next to main door
Customers:	Anglos, lots of families
Lunch/Dinner:	Monday–Thursday, 11:30 A.M.–10 P.M.; Friday 11:30 A.M.–11 P.M.; Saturday, 11:30 A.M.– 10 P.M.; Sunday, closed

Atmosphere/setting: Fancy yourself at one of those roughneck-style border bars, such as the famous Cadillac Bar. That's exactly the model owner Chance Evans chose for his Atlanta cantina. Framed black-and-white photographs on the walls attest to Evans' familiarity with the Cadillac. But this cantina is decidedly family-friendly.

House specialties: Chile relleno; steak Tampiqueño (with beans and pico de gallo); tamales; sopes (corn masa topped with chorizo sausage, sour cream, beans, and pico de gallo); barbecued shrimp Guadalajara style.

Other recommendations: Fajitas; lots of good vegetarian dishes; good guacamole.

Summary & comments: Freshly made border fare can be some of the best food anywhere when it's made right from fresh ingredients. If you're hungry for a taste of Houston, this is where you come.

Honors & awards: Atlanta magazine, Best Mexican Cantina, 1993–1998, Best Buckhead Insider's Cantina, 2000; *WHERE/Atlanta* magazine, Memorable Meals nominated for Most Fun for the Family and Most Meal for the Money, 1998; *Atlanta Journal & Constitution,* Readers' Choice Best Mexican/Tex-Mex Cantina, 1999; *Zagat.*

OH . . . MARÍA!

Zone 3   Buckhead/Sandy Springs
3167 Peachtree Road, NE
at Grandview Avenue
(404) 261-2032

| Authentic Mexican |
| ★★★★★ |
| Moderate |
| Quality 95   Value B |

Reservations:	Highly advised
When to go:	Early or late in the service hours
Entree range:	$14.50–18.95
Payment:	Major credit cards
Service rating:	★★★★
Friendliness rating:	★★★★★
Parking:	On site, but tight
Bar:	Full service and separate from the dining room, with lots of tequila añejo (aged tequila)
Wine selection:	Limited
Dress:	Casual dressy
Disabled access:	Yes
Customers:	Adventurous diners, the young at heart, from Buckhead and around the metro area
Brunch:	Sunday, 11 A.M.–2 P.M.
Dinner:	Monday–Thursday, 5:30–11 P.M.; Friday and Saturday, 5:30 P.M.–midnight

Atmosphere/setting: The interior resembles a stage set from the film Like Water for Chocolate. Antique doors hang on the back wall, the ceiling is draped in the Mexican national colors to celebrate Mexico's REAL independence day in September, and copies of paintings by the great 20th-century Mexican artist Botero line the walls. The warm glow of the interior comes from well-designed lighting, augmented by the flickering light of giant candles against textured adobe-like walls. Entering this restaurant is like stepping back to colonial Mexico, right into the heart of a wealthy hacienda. The separate bar is the perfect spot for a pre-prandial margarita or an after-dinner shot of well-aged tequila.

House specialties: Crema de frijol (a light, beautifully seasoned, creamy bean soup); Huasteca salad (cactus salad with red onions and diced tomatoes); Chicken Oh. . . María! (stuffed with assorted Mexican fruits and covered with almond sauce); arrachera (beef with black beans, cactus, serrano peppers, mushrooms, onions, and pico de gallo with warm corn tortillas—it's the ancestor of fajitas); red snapper Veracruz (stuffed with huitlacoche, the traditional corn fungus, and served

(continued)

with salsa poblano and guajillo pepper rings); cochinita pibil (pork cooked in banana leaf); Three Milks Cake.

Other recommendations: Tamarind red snapper baked in a banana leaf; enchiladas filled with chicken in red mole sauce; Encantos de María, a dessert of flour tortilla flakes layered with cinnamon and sugared apples, covered with cajeta (a kind of caramel sauce) and sprinkled with fresh pecans. Great kids menu and vegetarian dishes.

Entertainment & amenities: Mariachi music, excellent but a mite energetic, lends character but makes table conversation a bit difficult.

Summary & comments: Do not expect a basket of tortilla chips and a cup of salsa on the table. When the restaurant first opened, some disappointed guests got up and left when not finding what they thought of as "Mexican" food. This isn't border buffet time. This is the real thing. The Martínez-Obregón family—siblings Marco, Luis, and Lucero—named this restaurant after their mother, and they cut their restaurateur teeth on Zócalo, which they launched on a shoestring. There aren't any chips and salsa to be had there, either.

Honors & awards: Knife & Fork, 1999; *Atlanta Journal & Constitution,* three stars and Top 50, 2000; *Atlanta* magazine, Best Mexican, 2000.

Pacific Rim Bistro

Zone 8 Downtown East	Asian
SunTrust Plaza Garden Office	★★★
303 Peachtree Center Avenue	Moderate
(404) 893-0018	Quality 90 Value B

Reservations:	Accepted
When to go:	Any time
Entree range:	$15.95–25.95
Payment:	Major credit cards
Service rating:	★★★
Friendliness rating:	★★★
Parking:	Parking garage, free with validation
Bar:	Full service
Wine selection:	Limited, also premium sakes
Dress:	Casual dressy
Disabled access:	Easy
Customers:	Downtown businesspeople, conventioneers, out-of-towners, even visiting Europeans
Lunch:	Monday–Friday, 11:30 A.M.–3 P.M.
Dinner:	Every day, 5–10:30 P.M.

Atmosphere/setting: The glass-and-wood contemporary space provides a welcome respite from the street's frantic rhythms. Settle in at the sushi bar or at the libations bar and give the traffic a chance to get out of your way. The ambiance is so soothing you'll have no need of a second drink to achieve mellowness. Well-spaced booths and tables assure comfortable conversation, and there's streetside dining for good weather.

House specialties: Satays; sushi/sashimi; lobster three ways; wasabi steak (grilled, marinated 12-ounce New York strip with wasabi in a brown sauce on top); duck with Chinese seasonings; deep-fried Hanoi bay scallops with brown sauce.

Other recommendations: Wanchi shrimp (crispy-fried in a honey coating with walnuts on top).

Summary & comments: This contemporary bistro reflects what's best in American cooking today: a gathering of influences from East and West, brought together with taste and discretion.

Honors & awards: Good local reviews, including *Atlanta Journal & Constitution,* Top 100, 2000.

Pano's & Paul's

Zone 3 Buckhead/Sandy Springs	Continental
1232 W. Paces Ferry Road, NW	★★★★
at Northside Drive	Very expensive
(404) 261-3662	Quality 94 Value C

Reservations:	Essential
When to go:	Any time
Entree range:	$16–32
Payment:	Major credit cards
Service rating:	★★★★★
Friendliness rating:	★★★★★
Parking:	Self, on site
Bar:	Separate with lounge, full service
Wine selection:	Extensive, ranging across the winegrowing regions of the world, with about a dozen good ones by the glass
Dress:	Suits, silk dresses, and glitter
Disabled access:	Easy
Customers:	The well-heeled; Old Atlanta
Dinner:	Monday–Friday, 6–11 P.M.; Saturday, 5:30–11 P.M.; Sunday, closed

Atmosphere/setting: A major change since this guide's last edition in 1997 is the complete revision of the decor at this popular Atlanta restaurant. Atlanta restaurant designer Bill Johnson tossed out the heavy fabrics and the studied opulence. Gone, too are the semi-curtained banquettes that once were prized spots for question popping, replaced by simple—and uncurtained—dining shells.

House specialties: Foie gras; soft-shell crab. Cold jumbo lobster tail fried in a light batter and served with Chinese honey mustard is a house standard.

Other recommendations: Lemon-roasted chicken with crisp, celery-potato cake; sautéed gulf red snapper fillet; lobster bisque.

Entertainment & amenities: Piano light classics and popular music Thursday, Friday, and Saturday evenings.

Summary & comments: Among other changes at Pano's and Paul's is the departure of Pano's partner Paul Albrecht for his own restaurant in the Florida.

Honors & awards: Wine Spectator, for the wine list, 1996; one of Atlanta's 10 best Continental restaurants by many publications; frequent DiRoNA Award winner; Mobil Four and Three Stars, 1986–2000; *WHERE/Atlanta* magazine, Memorable Meals Best Fine Dining, 1997 and 1999; *Atlanta Homes & Lifestyles,* Best Burgundy Wines, 1999; *Atlanta* magazine, Best Makeover and Best Restaurateur for Pano Karatassos, 2000; *Gourmet* magazine, America's Top Tables, 1996-1999; *Zagat.*

Park 75 Restaurant

<table>
<tr><td>Zone 8   Downtown East</td><td>New American</td></tr>
<tr><td>Four Seasons Hotel</td><td>★★★★</td></tr>
<tr><td>75 14th Street, NE, Midtown</td><td>Very Expensive</td></tr>
<tr><td>(404) 881-9898</td><td>Quality 90   Value B</td></tr>
</table>

Reservations:	Accepted
When to go:	Any time
Entree range:	$20–32
Payment:	Major credit cards
Service rating:	★★★★★
Friendliness rating:	★★★★★
Parking:	Valet
Bar:	Full service, separate, with comfortable seating
Wine selection:	Not extensive, but well selected and wide-ranging
Dress:	Casual dressy
Disabled access:	Yes
Customers:	Hotel guests and neighbors
Brunch:	Sunday, 11 A.M.–2 P.M.
Lunch:	Every day, 11 A.M.–2 P.M.
Dinner:	Monday–Saturday, 5–10 P.M.

Atmosphere/setting: A grand marble staircase sweeps up to the restaurant/ bar/terrace level. Cool marble surfaces create an elegant, reserved ambiance. Very stylistic paintings of formal gardens line the walls. Everything feels like the top of posh, but if you elect to dine in casual attire (but still nice), that's fine, too. The noise level is nicely subdued, making table conversation a delight.

House specialties: Macaroni and cheese with shrimp and crab at lunch; Montana bison tenderloin and plank-cooked cured salmon at dinner; house-made ice creams and sorbets; American dim sum brunch with various little dishes.

Other recommendations: Glorious foie gras; rack of lamb with pastrami-style seasoning; soups; any dish with the day boat scallops; delicious and stylish vegetarian dishes.

Entertainment & amenities: Weekend piano player at the bar.

Summary & comments: The cool, somewhat austere dining room is warmed by subdued lighting. Music from the bar across the terrace wafts in, but never overwhelms table talk. If attending nearby performances, such as at Woodruff Arts Center, check out the pre-theater dinner for $35, served from 5:30–7 P.M. Also, there's a tasting menu ($42) and a vegetarian menu ($38).

Honors & awards: Mobil four Stars; *Atlanta* magazine, Best Power Breakfast, 2000; *Zagat,* One of the Top Two for New American Cuisine, 2000; *Atlanta Journal & Constitution,* kudos to the spring pea soup by dining critic John Kessler.

PASCAL'S BISTRO

Westpark Walk, 217 Commerce Drive
Peachtree City
(770) 632-0112

Eclectic	
★★★	
Moderate	
Quality 88	Value B

Reservations:	Accepted
When to go:	Any time
Entree range:	$9.95–16.95
Payment:	Major credit cards
Service rating:	★★
Friendliness rating:	★★★★
Parking:	On site
Bar:	Full service, in a good-sized, slightly separated space
Wine selection:	A small list of well-selected wines, with many of them by the glass
Dress:	Casual dressy
Disabled access:	Yes
Customers:	Neighbors, including families and couples on dates, and out-of-towners from nearby hotels
Lunch:	Monday–Friday, 11 A.M.–2 P.M.
Dinner:	Monday–Thursday, 5–9 P.M.; Friday and Saturday, 5–10 P.M.; Sunday, closed

Atmosphere/setting: The clean, nearly all white interior of this double-space mall enterprise has been warmed up by nice lighting and friendliness. A curved front allows lots of window-side table seating. The noise level is subdued, allowing patrons to enjoy pleasant table conversation.

House specialties: At dinner: medium-rare blackened tuna with orange-butter sauce; New York strip with Gorgonzola sauce; seafood pasta; crème brûlée; baked Brie with pecans in phyllo dough; honey-glazed apple pie with vanilla sauce.

Other recommendations: Smoked salmon pâté (seasonal); crab cakes. Four pastas at lunch with chef standing behind the pasta bar to customize sauces.

Summary & comments: Frenchman Pascal LeCorre, from Bordeaux, and his wife Karen ditched the chill of Colorado after she visited her sister in warmer Peachtree City. He cooked at the local country club to get used to the local market, then found the location he wanted and made his move. Lunch is $5.95, and comes with a salad and garlic bread.

Honors & awards: Good notices in The *Atlanta Journal & Constitution,* 2000; *Atlanta* mgazine, Best Reason to go to Peachtree City, 2000.

238

Pastificcio Cameli

Zone 6   Southeast Atlanta
1263 Glenwood Avenue, SE
East Atlanta Village
(404) 622-9926

Italian
★★
Moderate

Quality 88   Value B

Reservations:	Accepted
When to go:	Any time
Entree range:	$10–19
Payment:	Major credit cards
Service rating:	★★★★
Friendliness rating:	★★★★
Parking:	On street only
Bar:	Beer and wine only
Wine selection:	Italian and American selections, including several good and unusual ones by the glass
Dress:	Casual
Disabled access:	Easy
Customers:	Cross section of Atlantans, younger couples and some older patrons
Dinner:	Tuesday–Thursday, 5–10 P.M.; Friday and Saturday, 5–10:30 P.M.; Sunday, 5–9 P.M.

Atmosphere/setting: A hip, contemporary interior has been installed in this early 20th-century commercial space. High ceilings, hardwood floors, and brick walls add lots of texture. There's not too much fabric to attenuate noise, but it seems not to disturb table conversation. No matter your age, you'll feel young in here.

House specialties: Handmade pastas; hand-crafted sauces; house-made bread.

Other recommendations: Steak; house-made desserts; tiramisu.

Summary & comments: The Cameli brothers, Joseph and George, have hit on two winners, this neighborhood trattoria and a pizza joint, Cameli's Gourmet Pizza Joint (see Best Pizza, page 38).

Honors & awards: Citysearch, nominated for Best Italian Restaurant, 2000; *Atlanta* magazine, Best of East Atlanta, 1999.

PATTAYA SEAFOOD RESTAURANT

Thai/Seafood	
★★	
Moderate	
Quality 86	Value C

Zone 2   Northwest Atlanta
Terrell Mill Village Shopping Center
1433 Terrell Mill Road, SE, Marietta
(770) 226-8884

Reservations:	Accepted
When to go:	Any time
Entree range:	$7.50–14.95
Payment:	Major credit cards
Service rating:	★★★★
Friendliness rating:	★★★★★
Parking:	Self, on site
Bar:	Beer and wine only
Wine selection:	Fairly limited, but with at least a few decent selections to go with this food
Dress:	Casual
Disabled access:	Easy
Customers:	Mostly the neighbors
Lunch:	Monday–Friday, 11 A.M.–2:30 P.M.
Dinner:	Every day, 5–10 P.M.

Atmosphere/setting: Some framed photos of Thailand are about the only reference to the home country. The simple decor doesn't focus on overdone Asian treatments, and nobody bothers with any kind of costume. It's a serious place for good food, though, whether you're seeking Thai food or seafood. Noise levels are moderate, making table conversation easy.

House specialties: Tamarind snapper; almond trout; yellow penang curries; massaman curry; yum seafood salad.

Other recommendations: Seafood soup; basil noodles with any meat; Thai basil roll.

Summary & comments: Owners/chefs Rick Asdavut and Song Apirutvarakul, both from Bangkok, keep the lid on the pots in the kitchen. Opened in 1997, the restaurant has made its mark.

Honors & awards: *WHERE/Atlanta* magazine, Memorable Meals award for Thai food, 1998–99; *Atlanta Journal & Constitution,* Good and Cheap, 2000; lots of other positive local press.

PENANG

<table>
<tr><td></td><td>Malaysian</td></tr>
<tr><td>Zone 5   Northeast Atlanta</td><td>★★★★</td></tr>
<tr><td>Orient Center Shopping Center</td><td>Moderate</td></tr>
<tr><td>4897 Buford Highway, Suite 113</td><td></td></tr>
<tr><td>Chamblee</td><td>Quality 95   Value A</td></tr>
<tr><td>(770) 220-0308</td><td></td></tr>
</table>

Reservations:	Accepted, and highly recommended for large parties
When to go:	Any time
Entree range:	$10–30
Payment:	Major credit cards
Service rating:	★★★★
Friendliness rating:	★★★★
Parking:	On site
Bar:	Beer, sake, and wine only
Wine selection:	Limited
Dress:	Casual
Disabled access:	Yes, easy
Customers:	Malaysians and non-Asians eager for value and fine dining
Lunch/Dinner:	Sunday–Thursday, 11 A.M.–11 P.M.; Friday and Saturday, 11 A.M.–11:30 P.M.

Atmosphere/setting: Located in a shopping center devoted to Asian cuisine and businesses, this bright, busy restaurant attracts a mix of dating couples and families. Guys gather in the semiprivate alcoves to swap jokes and stories while sharing dishes of familiar fare. Over these private areas a house deity in her royal chariot beams down on the gathered patrons. Lively but not overly noisy, the restaurant has an energetic feel to it.

House specialties: Curried chicken; satay; sarang burong (chicken, shrimp, snow peas, baby corn, and mushrooms); seafood (fried fish in assam sauce); tofu dishes.

Other recommendations: Pork leg with mushrooms; sautéed jumbo shrimp with lemon grass and chili paste in coconut curry; fried squid.

Summary & comments: Chinese "Mother of Mercy" sits over a thatched separate space that can seat up to 30 people. Many of the dishes are derived from Malaysian home cooking and add a new dimension to Atlanta's ethnic dining scene.

Honors & awards: Atlanta magazine, Best Malaysian Restaurant, 2000; *Zagat,* 2001; *Atlanta Journal & Constitution,* two stars and Top 50, 2000.

POONA

	Indian
Zone 5 Northeast Atlanta	★★★
1630 Pleasant Hill Road, NW	Moderate
Duluth	
(770) 717-1053	Quality 90 Value A

Reservations:	Accepted
When to go:	Any time
Entree range:	$8–13; combination dinners $27.95 for two
Payment:	Major credit cards
Service rating:	★★★
Friendliness rating:	★★★★
Parking:	Self, on site
Bar:	None
Wine selection:	Decent, especially for an Asian restaurant
Dress:	Nice casual
Disabled access:	Yes
Customers:	Indians and non-Indians from the area
Lunch:	Monday–Friday, 11:30 A.M.–2:30 P.M.; Saturday and Sunday, noon–3 P.M.
Dinner:	Every day, 5:30–10:30 P.M.

Atmosphere/setting: Warmly lit, glowing butter walls are arched and shaped to hold dining spaces. Indian art hangs from the walls, but the spaces are not over-decorated. Atmosphere is quiet and serene.

House specialties: Well-prepared classics: chicken tikka; lamb vindaloo; excellent samosas; shrimp; an extensive list of vegetarian dishes.

Other recommendations: Especially good chickpeas and potato dishes.

Summary & comments: Atlanta's Indian community does not give the city's Indian restaurants rave reviews, but this one is consistently mentioned as one of the best, with careful preparation of classical dishes. No pork dishes here; these folks are Islamic. Lunch buffet is still $5.95! A great deal.

Honors & awards: Creative Loafing Gwinnett edition, Best of Gwinnett, 1994 and 1996; *Atlanta Journal & Constitution,* Best Indian Restaurant/Gwinnett 1999 and 2000.

242

Pricci

Zone 3 Buckhead/Sandy Springs	Italian
500 Pharr Road, N W, at Maple Drive	★★★★
(404) 237-2941	Expensive
	Quality 90 Value C

Reservations: Accepted
When to go: Any time
Entree range: $13–26.50
Payment: Major credit cards
Service rating: ★★★★
Friendliness rating: ★★★★
Parking: Valet
Bar: Separate, full service
Wine selection: Extensive Italian list, with some California selec-
                       tions, and many good wines by the glass
Dress: Nice, dressy casual
Disabled access: Yes
Customers: Locals, upscale residents of Buckhead
Lunch: Monday–Friday, 11 A.M.–5 P.M.
Dinner: Monday–Thursday, 5–11 P.M.; Friday and Satur-
                       day, 5 P.M.–midnight; Sunday, 5–10 P.M.

Atmosphere/setting: Patrick Kuleto (designer of sleek San Francisco establishments) did both the Buckhead Diner (see page 131) and this tony emporium
of Italian cooking. Sleek lines and shiny surfaces don't temper the noise level,
which creates high-energy feeling the restaurant imparts.

House specialties: Homemade pastas; risotto; wood-oven grilled pizzas;
tiramisu; osso buco.

Other recommendations: Vitello tonnato (occasional special); seafood soups
and stews (caciucco) alla Toscano.

Summary & comments: Pricci can be very diet sensitive if you request lightly prepared food. Parchment steamed sea bass with vegetables and fresh herbs is
just one delicious example. A southern California native, Chef Marc Sublette
took over this kitchen in 1999, keeping the cooking true-to-character.

Honors & awards: *Esquire* magazine, Best New Restaurant, 1992; *Creative
Loafing,* Best Italian/Critics' Choice, 1997–98; *Atlanta Homes & Lifestyles,* Top Five
Restaurants, Best Chocolate Dessert, and Best Italian Wine List, 1999; Mobil
Three Stars, 1994–99; *Wine Spectator,* Award of Excellent, 1993–2000.

PRIME

Zone 3   Buckhead/Sandy Springs
Lenox Square Shopping Center
3393 Peachtree Road, NE
(404) 812-0555

Steaks/Sushi	
★★★★	
Expensive	
Quality 92	Value C

Reservations:	Accepted
When to go:	After 1 P.M. for lunch, and on either side of the hours 7–8 P.M. for dinner
Entree range:	$18.50–28.50
Payment:	Major credit cards
Service rating:	★★★
Friendliness rating:	★★★
Parking:	Valet (mall) and lot
Bar:	Full service
Wine selection:	Extensive, about 250 labels, with about 60 by the glass, some sake
Dress:	Business casual
Disabled access:	Elevator across from the restaurant; access from mall front entrance
Lunch:	Monday–Friday, 11:30 A.M.–2:30 P.M.; Saturday 11:30 A.M.–3 P.M.
Dinner:	Monday–Thursday, 5–10 P.M.; Friday and Saturday, 5–11 P.M.; Sunday, 4–10 P.M.

Atmosphere/setting: The ambiance feels Asian Contemporary with sophisticated lighting, a long sushi bar, and plush banquette seating to complement the well-spaced tables. Located in a busy shopping mall, the space goes far to make you forget your aching feet. It's good for business dining as well as romance.

House specialties: Sushi; prime steaks; veal chop; tuna steak; smoked salmon.

Other recommendations: Surf 'n' turf; jalapeño cheese stone-ground grits; cottage fries; spinach, crème brûlée; ginger cake with sautéed apples.

Entertainment & amenities: Jazz saxophone nightly.

Summary & comments: The real meal deal: $10 rib eye, filet, and New York strip steaks are a special offered nightly from 5–6:30 P.M.; dollar sushi rules on Sundays. Owner Tom Catherall claims to be the first non-Japanese restaurateur to sell sushi in a nontraditional circumstance.

Honors & awards: *Atlanta* magazine, Best Surf 'n' Turf, 2000, power dining and other categories, 1996–2000; *Wine Spectator,* kudos for sushi-steak tandem, 1998; lots of positive local and national press.

Queen of Sheba

Ethiopian	
★★★★	
Inexpensive	
Quality 88	Value A

Zone 5   Northeast Atlanta
1594 Woodcliff Drive, NE, Suite G
(404) 321-1493

Reservations:	Not accepted
When to go:	Any time
Entree range:	$8–15.99
Payment:	Major credit cards
Service rating:	★★★
Friendliness rating:	★★★★
Parking:	On site
Bar:	Full service
Wine selection:	Very brief
Dress:	Casual
Disabled access:	At door
Customers:	Former denizens of east Africa especially
Lunch/Dinner:	Monday–Thursday, 11 A.M.–11 P.M.; Friday and Saturday 11 A.M.–2 P.M.

Atmosphere/setting: Friendly, welcoming, warmly lit but not dim, this restaurant is rigorous about being open to all comers. Creating a feeling of home, there is an area set up to suggest Ethiopian decor, with low casual tables and drums.

House specialties: House-made enjera (the spongy bread Ethiopia is famous for) used to scoop up tasty morsels; "tibs" (cubes of lean beef sautéed with garlic and green peppers); doro wat (chicken simmered in spicy sauce and served with hard-boiled egg—an Ethiopian classic).

Other recommendations: Yebog wot (slow-cooked lamb braised in red pepper sauce; veggie combo.

Entertainment & amenities: Live music from Ethiopia Friday and Saturday.

Summary & comments: Nebyou Tefera, who has been a graduate student at the Georgia Institute of Technology, possesses considerable ability to make folks from other cultures feel welcome. The place also serves as a gathering spot for expatriate Ethiopians. If you want to give the kids some exposure to the culture and cuisine of this part of the planet, Queen of Sheba is the place to be.

Honors & awards: Atlanta magazine, Top 50, 1998–1999, Best African, 2000.

245

R. Thomas Deluxe Grill

Zone 3   Buckhead/Sandy Springs
1287 Peachtree Road, NE
(404) 872-2942 or (404) 881-0246

American
★★★
Inexpensive
Quality 85   Value C

Reservations: Not accepted
When to go: Any time, but it's very popular for lunch and
                         late at night
Entree range: $9–13.95
Payment: Major credit cards
Service rating: ★★
Friendliness rating: ★★
Parking: Self, on site behind the building
Bar: Beer and wine only
Wine selection: Limited but well chosen with certified organic
                         wine by the bottle
Dress: Scruffy to nice casual
Disabled access: Seating is on outdoor sheltered space
Customers: Business types at lunch, lots of locals around the
                         clock
Open: Almost 24 hours; Monday–Friday,
                         closes from 6–9 A.M.

Atmosphere/setting: A heated outdoor cafe with juice bar and a relaxed ambiance, it's popular for brunch on Sunday.

House specialties: Omelets; stuffed baked potatoes; fresh juices and smoothies; vegetarian fare that's "Body Ecology" approved (very little oil, certified organic produce, also sold in vegetarian retail stores around town).

Other recommendations: Breakfast dishes of all kinds; Bloody Marys with sake; mimosas; all grilled items; really good hamburgers.

Summary & comments: This is a good spot to bring kids who enjoy burgers, salads, and malteds. Staff tends to ignore single diners, spending more time on large parties—a real annoyance. Owner Richard Thomas is proud of his insistence on organic produce and free-range chicken. He's even received recognition from Earth Tones, an environmental organization that honors the restaurant's refusal to use earth-unfriendly detergents.

Honors & awards: *Creative Loafing,* Best Patio, 1990–1995; *Atlanta* magazine, Best Juice Bar, 1995; and many other press kudos.

Rockin' Rob's B-B-Q

Zone 5 Northeast Atlanta	Barbecue
1479 Scott Boulevard, Decatur	★★★★
(404) 378-6041	Inexpensive
	Quality 95 Value A

Reservations:	Not accepted
When to go:	Any time
Entree range:	$5.95–12.95
Payment:	AMEX, MC, VISA
Service rating:	★★★★
Friendliness rating:	★★★★
Parking:	On site
Bar:	Beer only
Wine selection:	None
Dress:	Very casual
Disabled access:	Easy
Customers:	Everybody—students, neighbors, fellow music lovers—everybody
Lunch/Dinner:	Monday–Saturday, 11 A.M.–9 P.M.

Atmosphere/setting: The rustic, slightly down-at-the heel look of the place fits the food and the fun. A whiff of burning wood and smoking meat greets you as you step from your car, then becomes more intense as you enter the door. Framed *Rolling Stone* magazine covers combine with hunting trophies and plenty of Marilyn Monroe and Elvis Presley memorabilia to craft a definite guy interior. But women don't feel unwelcome or hustled. This is a serious 'cue joint, make no mistake, and first owner and 'cue man Rob Aldridge makes sure of it.

House specialties: Beautiful smoked pork ribs; smoked beef brisket; pulled pork sandwiches; barbecued chicken; Brunswick stew.

Other recommendations: Freshly brewed sweetened iced tea made the right way; excellent side dishes (macaroni 'n' cheese, slaw, and greens especially); hot dog topped with Brunswick stew—a neat variation on the classic chili dog.

Entertainment & amenities: A mix of live music—blues to bluegrass—on Friday nights.

Summary & comments: This is a relative newcomer in the barbecue department, but the quality should give it major staying power.

Honors & awards: None so far, it's just a year old, but they'll be coming. The *Atlanta Journal & Constitution* has taken positive note of the high quality of the stew and 'cue.

Roman Lily Cafe

	Contemporary American
Zone 5 Northeast Atlanta	★★★
668 Highland Avenue, NE	Moderate
Old Fourth Ward	
(404) 653-1155	Quality 90 Value A

Reservations:	Recommended
When to go:	Any time
Entree range:	$9–15
Payment:	MC, VISA
Service rating:	★★★★
Friendliness rating:	★★★★★
Parking:	On street, lot behind the strip building
Bar:	Beer and wine
Wine selection:	Small but well-selected list that goes with the food
Dress:	Just how casual CAN you get?
Disabled access:	Easy
Customers:	From all over the place
Breakfast/Lunch:	Tuesday–Saturday, 8 A.M.–3 P.M.
Dinner:	Tuesday–Saturday, 5:30–10:30 P.M.

Atmosphere/setting: This tiny place is rimmed with the nostalgic mementos of a romantic past, including an antique tricycle attached by its wheels to the rough brick wall. Patrons have a full view of the open kitchen, which stays busy throughout the meal service hours. In good weather, sit outdoors on the patio for a splendid view of the downtown city skyline.

House specialties: Turkey poblano meat loaf with jalapeño tequila gravy; spinach/asparagus ravioli with dill/tarragon pesto; pastas (fresh made by a good supplier and sauced most inventively); scallops on baked polenta; banana bread with caramelized bananas and locally made vanilla bean ice cream.

Other recommendations: Good sandwiches at lunch and dinner; housemade soups; croissant with warm cinnamon apples; biscuits and sausage with jalapeño tequila gravy; sweet and white potato pancakes for breakfast.

Summary & comments: Calavino Donati, a native of Wisconsin, opened this funky neighborhood bistro on New Year's Eve of 1998. Named in honor of her grandparents, Roman and Lillian, who were from Tuscany, the restaurant reaches into her Italian background. Grandmother even made banana bread, a special treat that she used to spoil her little granddaughter.

Honors & awards: "I hardly pay attention to those at all," says Donati. *Atlanta* magazine, One of Atlanta's Best Little Restaurants, 2001.

The Rib Ranch

Texas-style Barbecue

★★★

Inexpensive

Quality 85   Value A

Zone 3   Buckhead/Sandy Springs
25 Irby Avenue, NW, at Roswell Road
one block north of W. Paces Ferry Road
(404) 233-7644

Zone 2   Northwest Atlanta
2063 Canton Highway at Sandy Plains Road, Marietta
(404) 422-5755

Reservations:	Not accepted
When to go:	Any time
Entree range:	$4–17.95; beef ribs for 3 people ($25.95)
Payment:	VISA, MC
Service rating:	★★★
Friendliness rating:	★★
Parking:	Self, across the street
Bar:	Beer only, long necks, no draught
Wine selection:	None
Dress:	Scruffy casual to business attire
Disabled access:	Ramp to the front, but tables are tightly packed
Customers:	Locals
Lunch/Dinner:	Monday–Saturday, 11 A.M.–11 P.M.; Sunday, noon–10 P.M.

Atmosphere/setting: A shack that hums with activity in the middle of sophisticated Buckhead brings serious barbecue to the urbane. Don't glitter in here. Elbows on the table is manners at the Rib Ranch. The Marietta location is owned by another member of the family and is styled completely different. It's larger, modern, and doesn't dwell on the "shack" atmosphere of the Buckhead location.

House specialties: Beef ribs; baby-back ribs; some good side dishes, such as the greens, onion rings, Brunswick stew, and chili.

Other recommendations: Grilled smoked chicken; sausage; smoked turkey.

Summary & comments: The huge plate of Texas-style beef ribs will easily feed two hungry honchos. Fries are about the only thing not done from scratch, but the mac 'n' cheese isn't stellar even if made from scratch. Other side dishes are quite good, however.

Honors & awards: Lots of kudos in the local press.

Ruth's Chris Steak House

Steak	
★★★★	
Expensive	
Quality 90 Value C	

Zone 3   Buckhead/Sandy Springs
Renaissance Plaza
50 E. Paces Ferry Road, NE
(404) 365-0660

Zone 3   Buckhead/Sandy Springs
5788 Roswell Road, NE, Sandy Springs
(404) 255-0035

Zone 7   Downtown West
Embassy Suites Hotel, 267 Marietta Street, NE
(404) 223-6500

Reservations:	Accepted, recommended especially for weekends
When to go:	Any time
Entree range:	$17.95–35
Payment:	Major credit cards
Service rating:	★★★★★
Friendliness rating:	★★★★★
Parking:	Valet at Buckhead and Downtown; lot at Sandy Springs
Bar:	Full service
Wine selection:	Award-winning list
Dress:	Casual dressy to business attire
Disabled access:	Easy
Customers:	Depending on the season and the location, lots of corporate and convention businesspeople, with locals weighing in during the summer
Breakfast:	Monday–Friday, 6–9:30 A.M.; Saturday, Sunday, and holidays 7–10:30 A.M. (Downtown)
Lunch:	Monday–Friday, 11:30 A.M.–3 P.M. (Buckhead); 11 A.M.–3 P.M. (Downtown)
Dinner:	Monday–Saturday, 5–11 P.M., Sunday 5–10 P.M. (Buckhead and Sandy Springs); Every day, 3–11 P.M. (Downtown)

Atmosphere/setting: The Buckhead location is situated in a high-rise office building set off by a fine Henry Moore sculpture. The contemporary and sophis-

(continued)

ticated interior is especially dramatic at night. In Sandy Springs, the restaurant occupies a freestanding building that has housed several restaurants; it's more suburban steakhouse in feel. Downtown's location has generous fenestration that provides a splendid view of Atlanta's skyline, from Midtown to Downtown.

House specialties: Hand-cut 22-ounce bone-in rib-eye steak; tournedos with shrimp; fish.

Other recommendations: Steak with Gorgonzola sauce when you can convince somebody to order it.

Summary & comments: Breakfast at the Downtown location is $9.50 for the buffet if you're not a hotel guest. It's also a quiet and delightful spot for a Sunday-lunch outing. In winter, you can watch ice skaters on the rink at Centennial Olympic Park. The distinguishing feature of these steaks is the way they're served on a searing hot plate, so the consumer can finish them off by cutting a bite and searing it on the plate.

Honors & awards: *Wine Spectator,* Award of Excellence, 1997, 1998, 2000; Ivy Award, 1998; *WHERE/Atlanta,* Memorable Meal Awards, Most Memorable Meal, 1997, Service, 1998.

SAGE ON SYCAMORE

Zone 5   Northeast Atlanta
121 Sycamore Street, Decatur
(404) 373-5574

Eclectic/American	
★★★	
Moderate	
Quality 88	Value C

Reservations: Not accepted
When to go: Any time
Entree range: $8–22
Payment: Major credit cards
Service rating: ★★★
Friendliness rating: ★★★★
Parking: On street
Bar: Full service
Wine selection: Extensive list but a work in progress that's
                        constantly getting updated; many by-the-glass
                        choices, and plenty of well-priced bottle selec-
                        tions that go with this food; emphasis on
                        California wines
Dress: Casual
Disabled access: Yes
Customers: Decatur's young and restless denizens, sometimes
                        including the funkier folks
Brunch: Sunday, 11 A.M.–3 P.M.
Lunch: Monday–Friday, 11:30 A.M.–2:30 P.M.
Dinner: Sunday–Thursday, 5:30–10 P.M.; Friday and
                        Saturday, 5:30–11 P.M.

Atmosphere/setting: A historic strip of stores in downtown Decatur has been carefully renovated, and several good restaurants have found niches in them. Among them is Sage on Sycamore by Rémy Kerba, who also owns Le Giverny (see page 212). At Sage, Kerba takes advantage of the textured old brick walls to craft a warm space that seems lively without overwhelming diners with noise. The slightly separated bar area enables folks gathered for drinks to have fun without encroaching on the dining room. The young cleintele is a lot of fun.

House specialties: Vermont goat cheese and blue crab cake with roasted red pepper coulis; grilled pear and watercress salad with walnuts and crumbled blue cheese; for vegetarians, a vol-au-vent of vegetables and tofu; mascarpone-stuffed French toast (brunch).

Other recommendations: Sage ceviche in a blue tortilla timbale; fresh squeezed

(continued)

orange juice mimosas at brunch; whatever cheesecake the kitchen happens to make for dessert, but especially the apricot.

Entertainment & amenities: Soft live jazz Monday and Wednesday nights.

Summary & comments: After a rocky start, the food improved quickly, and Sage became well established as a good neighborhood dining experience. Decaturites stroll in for after-work drinks and leisurely savor brunch on Sunday. Walk from here to the historic courthouse, or take in a concert on the square. It makes for a special evening.

Honors & awards: Historic Decatur Preservation Award, 2000.

Sa Tsu Ki

Zone 5   Northeast Atlanta
3043 Buford Highway, NE
(404) 325-5285

Japanese
★★★★
Inexpensive
Quality 95   Value B

Reservations:	Not accepted
When to go:	Any time
Entree range:	$11–18
Payment:	Major credit cards
Service rating:	★★★★
Friendliness rating:	★★★★
Parking:	Self, on site
Bar:	None
Wine selection:	Limited
Dress:	Nice casual
Disabled access:	Yes
Customers:	Lots of Japanese, making one feel in an authentic spot
Dinner:	Sunday–Thursday, 5:30–10 P.M.; Friday and Saturday, 5:30–10:30 P.M.

Atmosphere/setting: Set back from a busy highway and with strip joints for neighbors, this fine Japanese restaurant goes about its business as if nothing nearby could bother it. A freestanding building, it is a world of soji screens and busy Japanese patrons enjoying quite authentic fare. Noise levels are moderate, and the place feels quite soothing.

House specialties: Beef tataki; salt-grilled fish; shabu shabu; sukiyaki.

Other recommendations: Deep-fried shrimp heads; excellent sushi and sashimi; soft-shell crab.

Summary & comments: The Japanese patrons enjoy their cigarettes, so if smoke is a problem, insist on sitting deep in the nonsmoking area. Ventilation isn't great, and there can be some drifting smoke. If you're dining solo, the sushi bar is a fun spot to sit and carry on a conversation with the animated chefs. This is a good Japanese restaurant in which to introduce the young set to this cuisine, as it's not so formal as some and seems less intimidating. The staff takes great care with children.

254

Savu

Zone 4 Lenox/Chamblee	Asian Contemporary
W Atlanta Hotel	★★★
111 Perimeter Center West	Expensive
(770) 396-6800	Quality 88 Value C

Reservations:	Accepted
When to go:	Any time
Entree range:	$19–27
Payment:	Major credit cards
Service rating:	★★
Friendliness rating:	★★★★
Parking:	Valet and on-site
Bar:	Full service
Wine selection:	Downright skimpy, but many go well with the food, and many are offered by the glass; the Pacific Echo Brut Rosé is a fine value that goes well with much of this food; look under "Alternative White" for several appropriate selections
Dress:	Casual dressy
Disabled access:	Yes
Customers:	Hotel guests, Dunwoody residents, occasional curious diners from other parts of town
Breakfast:	Every day, 6:30–11 A.M.
Brunch:	Sunday, 11:30 A.M.–2:30 P.M.
Lunch:	Every day, 11:30 A.M.–2:30 P.M.
Dinner:	Every day, 5:30–11 P.M.

Atmosphere/setting: Enter the lobby set alight with votive candles on nearly every surface. In a way, you wonder if you're in church or at a séance. The cool, contemporary space leads from the renovated hotel's lobby to the equally cool, contemporary decor. The noise level is most subdued, making it a delight to share table conversation.

House specialties: Sesame chicken salad; lobster Indochine (on rice noodles with curry); crispy shrimp and noodles; Christine's Candy Bar (dark chocolate, macadamia nut brittle, vanilla and raspberry sauces); Pousse-Café (mascarpone semi-freddo, with white and dark chocolate truffle, butter cake, and java chocolate sauce); open-faced artichoke fondue omelet (brunch and lunch).

(continued)

SAVU *(continued)*

Other recommendations: Vegetarian selections from the wok—especially the crispy spinach, the stir-fry sesame citrus noodles, and the wok sautéed vegetables; the sizzling whole fish; crispy Beijing duck; salt & pepper oysters; barbecued spare ribs; frozen lemon soufflé.

Entertainment & amenities: The last Thursday of the month features jazz in the patio area.

Summary & comments: The food is quite good here, but the service, while friendly, often is third-rate from a professional perspective. What a shame to have a waiter who doesn't know not to pour the wine up to the rim of the glass or who can't present a bottle of wine and open it properly.

Honors & awards: *Jezebel* magazine, Top 100, July 2000; *Knife & Fork.*

SEEGER'S

Zone 3   Buckhead/Sandy Springs
111 W. Paces Ferry Road, NW
(404) 846-9779

Contemporary	
★★★★★	
Very expensive	
Quality 98	Value C

Reservations:	Essential
When to go:	Any time
Entree range:	Fixed-price five-course "a la carte" menu $64 per person without wines; $80 for chef's tasting menu without wines; additional $55 with wines
Payment:	Major credit cards
Service rating:	★★★★★
Friendliness rating:	★★★
Parking:	Lot in back, a difficult up-hill walk for older folks, no valet parking (tsk, tsk)
Bar:	Full service
Wine selection:	Extraordinary, with depth and breadth; good values as well as expensive choices (more than 1,000 labels)
Dress:	Casual dressy
Disabled access:	Wheelchair parking in front
Customers:	The well-heeled, thus an older crowd, often from Buckhead, plus visitors from all over the planet seeking out this brilliant, cutting-edge cuisine
Dinner:	Monday–Saturday, 6–10 P.M.

Atmosphere/setting: The once modest residential bungalow was taken literally down to its foundation and rebuilt by Atlanta restaurant designer Bill Johnson. Minimalism rules, not only in the design, but also in the food presentations. Hard surfaces are not softened by any fabric, making sound bothersome for some folks, but table conversation seems unproblematic. Sitting at the loft tables upstairs may ameliorate this problem somewhat.

House specialties: The menu changes daily, so "house" specialties do not occur, strictly speaking. Count on superb fish and game; farmstead cheeses of the finest quality; "private stock" ostera and beluga caviar; foie gras.

Other recommendations: Scallops; sweetbreads; any of the desserts.

Summary & comments: Chef Gunther Seeger came to Atlanta's attention at the Dining Room, Ritz-Carlton, Buckhead, from Germany. His star is truly

(continued)

international, as well it should be. This is a restaurant for the adventurous, for any-one seeking revolutionary cooking ideas. Don't come here looking for a steak and a spud; that's not what this is about. This chef stays uncompromisingly on the edge and doesn't care who thinks what about it. Bottled water, either sparkling or still, is $3.50 per person, no matter how much is ordered. Party menus can be multicourse set menus with paired wines.

Honors & awards: *Esquire* magazine, Restaurant of the Year, 1998; *Atlanta Journal & Constitution,* four stars and Top 50, 2000; *Zagat,* 2001; *Atlanta* magazine, Best Restaurant/Best Chef, 2000; *Relais & Chateaux Relais Gourmands,* 2001; Mobil Five-Star, 2000 and 2001.

Seoul Garden Restaurant

Zone 5 Northeast Atlanta	Korean/Japanese
5938 Buford Highway, Doraville	★★★
(770) 452-0123	Inexpensive/Moderate
	Quality 90 Value C

Reservations:	Accepted
When to go:	Any time
Entree range:	$7.99–14.99 (some dishes for two run higher)
Payment:	Major credit cards
Service rating:	★★★★
Friendliness rating:	★★★★★
Parking:	Self, on site
Bar:	Some spirits available
Wine selection:	Limited
Dress:	Nice casual
Disabled access:	Yes
Customers:	Koreans and Japanese, young couples on dates at dinner; lunchtime sees a lot of non-Asians
Lunch/Dinner:	Monday–Saturday, 11 A.M.–2 A.M.; Sunday, 11 A.M.–midnight

Atmosphere/setting: Once a chain steakhouse, Seoul Garden seems almost forbidding from the outside. But within, it's bright and cheerful, as is the staff. Young couples flirt and giggle at the sushi bar, while the wait staff patiently answers questions.

House specialties: Table barbecued ribs and beef (bulgogi; short ribs); traditional Korean dishes (simmered beef ribs); chef's specials (Korean seafood pancake); barbecued chicken.

Other recommendations: Daily lunch boxes with both Korean and Japanese dishes are inexpensive (about $6) and very popular with non-Asian customers. The sushi is excellent, and the sushi box is just $7.95.

Summary & comments: Spend a rainy night in Georgia here, as I did, and experience Korean hospitality and friendliness. The sushi bar attracts young couples in avid conversation while they savor this very good sushi and sashimi.

Sia's

	Eclectic American
Zone 3 Buckhead/Sandy Springs	★★★
Shops at St. Ives Shopping Center	Expensive
10305 Medlock Bridge Road	
Duluth	Quality 90 Value B
(770) 497-9727	

Reservations: Recommended
When to go: Any time
Entree range: $16.50–28.50
Payment: Major credit cards
Service rating: ★★★★★
Friendliness rating: ★★★★★
Parking: On site
Bar: Full service
Wine selection: Extensive
Dress: Casual dressy
Disabled access: Easy
Customers: Neighbors, but also others from throughout the
                        metro Atlanta area
Lunch: Monday–Friday, 11:30 A.M.–2 P.M.
Dinner: Monday–Saturday, 5–10:30 P.M.; Sunday, closed

Atmosphere/setting: An unusual circular-shaped design, set off by brushed chrome and cherry wood, features high ceilings done in tangerine and cobalt blue. The feeling is contemporary but warm. Tables are well spaced, and the noise level does not interrupt table conversation. The 50-seat private dining room, centered by a warming fireplace, often is used for overflow dining. This is fine dining at its best brought to the 'burbs.

House specialties: Lemon crab cream cheese fritters with Indonesian syrup; crispy calamari; roasted duck and cabbage crispy roll with sambal syrup; braised pork and Brie quesadilla.

Other recommendations: Chilean sea bass; pork tenderloin; terrific side dishes.

Summary & comments: Southwestern and Asian touches imbue all this cooking. Owner Sia Moshk, a native of Iran, brought more than two decades' restaurant experience with him to this endeavor. He also is a committed and active member of the community, often chairing charity events, such as Share our Strength.

Honors & awards: *Atlanta* magazine, Best New Restaurant Outside the Perimeter, 1999, Best Reason to go to Duluth, 2000; *Atlanta Journal & Constitution,* three stars and Top 50, 2000.

SoHo

Zone 2   Northwest Atlanta
Vinings Jubilee Shopping Center
4200 Paces Ferry Road, NW
(770) 801-0069

Reservations:	Recommended
When to go:	Any time
Entree range:	$15–24
Payment:	Major credit cards
Service rating:	★★★★★
Friendliness rating:	★★★
Parking:	Lot
Bar:	Full service
Wine selection:	Excellent, mostly Californian, with 100 choices by the glass
Dress:	Casual dressy
Disabled access:	Easy
Customers:	Business dining at lunch, dating couples in the evening, conventioneers
Lunch:	Monday–Friday, 11:30 A.M.–2:30 P.M.
Dinner:	Monday–Thursday, 5:30–10:30 P.M.; Friday and Saturday, 5:30–11 P.M.; Sunday 5:30–9:30 P.M.

Atmosphere/setting: A large welcoming bar greets patrons as soon as they enter this lively, well-composed space. There's a porch-like area off to the right for dining, and a slightly more subdued noise level makes that spot extra enjoyable. Lots of windows admit good natural light, making the spaces bright and energetic.

House specialties: Chicken tortilla soup; Chilean sea bass with Asian barbecue sauce; General Joey's Asian calamari with ginger soy glaze; French-cut pork chop with buttermilk mashed potatoes and apple fig chutney.

Other recommendations: Seared elk loin with raspberry mustard glaze and apricot walnut risotto; chocolate bread pudding.

Summary & comments: Chef Joseph Ahn has a gift for not only bringing refined Asian touches to many of these dishes, but also American and European notes. The menu is a stimulating tangle of dishes he's inherited from his predecessors, such as the chicken tortilla soup, and those he's known for himself, such as the calamari.

Honors & awards: Atlanta magazine, Best Wine Bar, 2000; *Zagat,* 2001; *Community Profiles,* Our Favorite 52 Restaurants, 2000; *Jezebel* magazine, Top 100, 2000.

Son's Place

Zone 5   Northeast Atlanta
100 Hurt Street, NE, Inman Park
(404) 581-0530

Southern
★★
Inexpensive
Quality 80   Value C

Reservations:	Accepted
When to go:	Any time
Entree range:	$4.75–5.75
Payment:	No credit cards
Service rating:	★★
Friendliness rating:	★★★
Parking:	Limited, on site
Bar:	None
Wine selection:	None
Dress:	Very casual to business attire
Disabled access:	Yes
Customers:	Police officers, businesspeople, students—everybody
Breakfast:	Monday–Friday, 7–10:30 A.M.
Lunch:	Monday–Friday, 11 A.M.–4 P.M.; Saturday and Sunday, closed

Atmosphere/setting: Bright, pretty and cheerful, Son's Place is right next door to the original Deacon Burton's and takes its name from the fact that owner Lenn Storey swears he's the late and beloved Deacon's son. The lively establishment seems to have won the war for the loyalty of the Deacon's former customers.

House specialties: Fried chicken; ribs (Friday); catfish and whiting (Tuesday and Friday); baked pork chops (Tuesday or Wednesday); meat loaf (Thursday).

Other recommendations: Sweet potato pie; pound cake; homemade lemonade with seeds still in it!

Summary & comments: Call it "soul food" if you must (in fact, it's Southern food through and through), this cooking is what everybody in the South grew up on, and Lenn Storey prepares it in the same old-fashioned way Deacon Burton did. The frying chickens are soaked first overnight in salted seasoned water, then fried in soybean oil. The same black cast-iron frying pans that the Deacon used at the original location are the ones used here. Mrs. Beverly Storey, Lenn's wife, does all the cakes.

Honors & awards: Creative Loafing, Best Soul Food, 1996; *Gourmet* magazine, America's Best Restaurants for the skillet-fried chicken, 2000.

262

SOTO JAPANESE RESTAURANT

	Japanese
	★★★★
Zone 3 Buckhead/Sandy Springs	Expensive
Peachtree Piedmont Crossing	
Shopping Center	Quality 95 Value C
3330 Piedmont Road, NE	
(404) 233-2005	

Reservations:	Accepted and highly recommended
When to go:	Any time
Entree range:	$7.50–15
Payment:	Major credit cards
Service rating:	★★★
Friendliness rating:	★★★★
Parking:	On site
Bar:	Beer and wine only
Wine selection:	There are good wines, but only a few that go with the food
Dress:	Casual
Disabled access:	Easy
Customers:	Asians, but lots of appreciative and adventurous Occidentals from all over the metro area
Dinner:	Monday–Thursday, 6–11:30 P.M.; Friday and Saturday, 6 P.M.–12:30 A.M.

Atmosphere/setting: Little about this restaurant's interior screams Japanese restaurant. The wait staff isn't done up in obi sashes. But at the rear of the dining room, bent over his work, bespectacled youthful master sushi chef and owner Sotohiro Kosugi works diligently if slowly with his team.

House specialties: Sea scallop minced and blended with smelt fish roe and fresh mango served in an orange cup; sea urchin in sashimi squid; live flounder (when available); exquisite, inventive rolls; ginger ice cream.

Other recommendations: Sashimi-style Salmon ceviche; shima agi carpaccio with soy truffle sauce.

Summary & comments: Don't expect fast food here; it won't happen. Service, notoriously slow, has gotten better, but still seems to move at a trickle. Sit at the sushi bar if you can to keep better track of your dinner. Freshness is a prime consideration at this restaurant, so if you have favorites, get there early.

Honors & awards: Food and Wine magazine, Top 10 Chefs, 1997; *Zagat,* 2001; *Atlanta Journal & Constitution,* three stars and Top 50, 2000; *Atlanta* magazine, Best Japanese/Best Sushi, 2000.

Sotto Sotto

Zone 5   Northeast Atlanta
313 N. Highland Avenue, NE
Inman Park
(404) 523-6678

Italian	
★★★★	
Moderate	
Quality 95	Value A

Reservations:	Essential
When to go:	Early or late in the dinner service
Entree range:	$13–22
Payment:	Major credit cards
Service rating:	★★★
Friendliness rating:	★★★★★
Parking:	On the street and not easy to find, but one manages
Bar:	Full service
Wine selection:	All Italian (except for a couple of Champagnes), and with excellent choices; a good bunch by the glass; assembled with the food in mind
Dress:	Casual dressy
Disabled access:	Easy
Customers:	Everybody who likes good Italian food from neighborhood denizens to Buckhead types
Dinner:	Monday–Saturday, 5–11 P.M.

Atmosphere/setting: This old brick commercial space takes on warmth and character in its rehabilitated state, providing an intimate, romantic, and exciting venue for this clever little Italian bistro. The noise level is pretty high, sometimes making table conversation difficult. Dating couples, singles, women out for all-girl dinners, and even families find their way here nonetheless. Just prepare to be elbow to jowl with your neighbor.

House specialties: Vitello tonnato (veal with tuna sauce and capers); spaghetti alla bottarga (with Sardininan sundried mullet roe, lemon, and parsley); wood-roasted whole fish; handmade pasta; panna cotta (vanilla-scented cooked cream set with unflavored gelatin).

Other recommendations: Antipasto misto for the table; mussels; scallops with truffled white beans and arugula; risotto; bresaola (air-dried beef) with arugula, celery, and Parmigiano.

Summary & comments: Chef/owner Riccardo Ullio was born in Italy but grew up in nearby Conyers. His Georgia Tech education in environmental engineering, complete with master's degree, became meaningless after a trip back

(continued)

to Italy with his fiancée, MaDora, now his wife. Returning to Atlanta, he set about becoming a chef and restaurateur. Sotto Sotto opened to rave notices and has stayed packed from day one. In fact, at first the little bistro's popularity nearly overwhelmed its young staff. Those were some exhausted folks! But they've gotten it figured out. The upshot is, on weekday nights, it's as jumpin' a joint as anything in Buckhead. So plan ahead well. In 2000 Ullio opened adjacent Fritti (see New Places, page 9), a fine new pizza and casual dining place.

   Honors & awards: *Atlanta Journal & Constitution,* 3 stars and Top 50, 2000.

South City Kitchen

Southern
★★★★
Expensive
Quality 93   Value C

Zone 8   Downtown East
1144 Crescent Avenue, NE, Midtown
(404) 873-7358

Reservations:	Highly recommended
When to go:	Early in the service shift
Entree range:	$12.95–24.95
Payment:	Major credit cards
Service rating:	★★★★
Friendliness rating:	★★★★
Parking:	Some in the back, on street, nearby paid parking
Bar:	Separate, full service
Wine selection:	Extensive and excellent, American, with many good ones by the glass
Dress:	Jeans casual to business attire
Disabled access:	Not to the interior; patio dining in good weather, but access to restrooms is impossible
Customers:	Business patrons at lunch, locals in casual duds for brunch, all kinds at dinner
Brunch:	Sunday, 11 A.M.–3:30 P.M.
Lunch:	Monday–Saturday, 11 A.M.–3:30 P.M.
Dinner:	Monday–Thursday, 5–11 P.M.; Friday and Saturday, 5 P.M.–midnight; Sunday, 5–10 P.M.

Atmosphere/setting: The clean, bare surfaces do nothing to mitigate the noise level, so be prepared to endure a fair amount of high-energy atmosphere. A lot of work went into rescuing this former Midtown residence, whose walls are adorned with art from a local gallery.

House specialties: Crab cakes; crab hash with poached eggs; she-crab soup; catfish Reuben; sautéed shrimp and scallops over stone-ground grits with garlic cream gravy; chocolate pecan pie; fried green tomatoes with herbed goat cheese; buttermilk fried chicken.

Other recommendations: Crawfish and tasso pasta; fried oysters salad; pork tenderloin.

Honors & awards: *Atlanta* magazine, Best Reason to go to Midtown, 1999–2000; Chef Jay Swift invited to prepare a James Beard dinner, 2000; *Jezebel* magazine, Top 20, 2000; *Wine Spectator,* Award of Excellence, 2000; *Jezebel* magazine, Top 100 (no. 11), 2000.

Spiced Right

	Barbecue
	★★★
	Inexpensive
	Quality 90 Value B

Zone 5   Northeast Atlanta
5364 Lawrenceville Highway
Lilburn (I-85 north of city to
Jimmy Carter Boulevard exit, east to
Rockbridge Road, left on Lawrenceville
Highway, less than a half mile on right)
(770) 564-0355

Reservations:	Not accepted
When to go:	Any time
Entree range:	$6.50–11.50
Payment:	Major credit cards
Service rating:	★★★★
Friendliness rating:	★★★★★
Parking:	On site
Bar:	None
Wine selection:	No alcohol
Dress:	Casual
Disabled access:	Ramp to front entrance
Customers:	Locals
Lunch:	Sunday, noon–4 P.M.; Monday–Wednesday, 11 A.M.–4 P.M.
Lunch/Dinner:	Tuesday–Saturday, 11 A.M.–9 P.M.

Atmosphere/setting: This little nondescript structure houses one of the metro area's best barbecue joints. Just inside the entry is a display of some of the trophies Steve Lelle and Bill Stansell have won in barbecue competitions. The very sight of them gives patrons great confidence that they're about to taste some of the best 'cue they'll ever put in their mouths. Wood tables and a steam table for the lunch buffet set the stage for simple fare that's memorable right down to the perfect sweet iced tea.

House specialties: Ribs, ribs, and more ribs.

Other recommendations: Really good barbecued chicken; chopped pork; Brunswick stew; cornbread.

Summary & comments: Lelle and Stansell emphasize wood-cooked 'cue, explaining to uninitiated patrons about the red smoke ring on the outside of the meat. This is the hallmark of real 'cue, as they lecture on their menus, and they're right!

Honors & awards: Too many to count.

Stringer's Fish Camp

	Southern/Seafood
Zone 4 Lenox/Chamblee	★★★
3384 Shallowford Road, NE	Inexpensive
near Buford Highway	
(770) 458-7145	Quality 85 Value C

Reservations:	Accepted for parties of eight or more
When to go:	Any time
Entree range:	$11–15
Payment:	VISA, MC
Service rating:	★★★
Friendliness rating:	★★★★
Parking:	Self, on site
Bar:	Beer and wine
Wine selection:	Unexciting and limited
Dress:	Scruffy casual
Disabled access:	Yes
Customers:	Locals (usually colorful)
Lunch:	Monday–Friday, 11 A.M.–4 P.M.;
Dinner:	Monday–Thursday, 4–9 P.M.; Friday, 4–10 P.M.; Saturday, noon–10 P.M.; Sunday, noon–9 P.M.

Atmosphere/setting: Feeling like a true fish camp, Stringer's takes the prize for preserving a Southern waterfront atmosphere.

House specialties: Gumbo; fried seafood and fish; soft-shell crab; oysters.

Other recommendations: Spicy corn salad; homemade hush puppies.

Summary & comments: The entertainment is provided by the colorful types that frequent the place. The windows are covered with scrawl announcing specials. Oysters, they boast, are served fried, nude, and stewed. Unpretentious food in huge quantities is what draws everyone to Stringer's.

268

Sukothai

	Thai
Zone 2 Northwest Atlanta	★★★
Windy Hill West Shopping Center,	Inexpensive
1995 Windy Hill Road, Suite K	
near Cobb Parkway	Quality 85 Value C
(770) 434-9276	

Reservations:	Accepted
When to go:	Any time
Entree range:	$7–18
Payment:	Major credit cards
Service rating:	★★
Friendliness rating:	★★★
Parking:	Self, on site
Bar:	Beer and wine
Wine selection:	Decent, with some wines that will complement the food, but only a few by the glass
Dress:	Nice casual
Disabled access:	Yes
Customers:	Locals, mostly non-Asians
Lunch:	Monday–Friday, 11:30 A.M.–2:30 P.M.
Dinner:	Monday–Thursday, 6–10 P.M.; Friday and Saturday, 5:30–11 P.M.; Sunday, closed

Atmosphere/setting: One of the prettiest Thai restaurants in the city, Sukothai battles its shopping-center location with faux-aged walls and subdued lighting. The tables are well spaced, and the subdued (but not dim) lighting keeps everything feeling warm.

House specialties: Larb (spicy mint and meat salad); pad thai; tom yum goong and tom kha gai soups; Sukothai salad (shrimp, squid, lettuce, and spicy lime dressing).

Other recommendations: All curries; duck; lamb; soup of the day.

Summary & comments: The place for Thai food in Cobb County, this one has been popular among devotees of Thai food, who are known to trek here from all parts of town.

Honors & awards: Zagat, 2001.

Sundown Cafe

Zone 5   Northeast Atlanta
2165 Cheshire Bridge Road, NE
between LaVista/Lindberg and
Piedmont Road
(404) 321-1118

Southwestern	
★★★	
Moderate/Expensive	
Quality 93	Value C

Reservations:	Not accepted
When to go:	Early in the service shift
Entree range:	$11–15; specials to $11–19
Payment:	Major credit cards
Service rating:	★★★★
Friendliness rating:	★★★★★
Parking:	Self, all around the building
Bar:	Separate, full service
Wine selection:	Moderately limited
Dress:	Nice casual
Disabled access:	Yes, with ramp
Customers:	Mostly locals
Lunch:	Monday–Friday, 11 A.M.–2 P.M. (taquería)
Dinner:	Monday–Thursday, 5:30–10 P.M.; Friday and Saturday, 5:30–11 P.M.; Sunday, closed

Atmosphere/setting: The clever, faux-stucco interior makes you feel like you just took a short plane ride to the American Southwest. The place gets busy, but the noise level stays well within the comfort zone.

House specialties: Handmade tortillas; about five homemade salsas; green chile stew; wonderful turnip greens; divine chocolate chimichanga with tequila sauce.

Other recommendations: Specials include crab cakes, margaritas, mashed ancho potatoes with jalapeño gravy (divine with Eddie's Pork); posole (during the holidays to New Year's).

Summary & comments: This lunchtime taquería was one of the first in Atlanta, starting a craze that shows no signs of abating. This is a good place for kids to enjoy different kinds of dishes; they love the tacos.

Honors & awards: Creative Loafing, Best Southwestern, 1995, Best Salsa and Best Southwest, 1996; *Atlanta* magazine, Best Southwestern and other bests, 1996–2000; *Zagat.*

270

SURIN of Thailand

Zone 5   Northeast Atlanta
810 N. Highland Avenue, NE
(404) 892-7789

Thai
★★★
Inexpensive/Moderate
Quality 88   Value A

Reservations:	Not accepted
When to go:	Any time
Entree range:	$7.95–14.95
Payment:	Major credit cards
Service rating:	★★★★
Friendliness rating:	★★★★★
Parking:	Difficult; small lot behind the restaurant, on street
Bar:	Full service
Wine selection:	Limited but well selected
Dress:	Casual
Disabled access:	Easy
Customers:	Residents of Virginia-Highland
Lunch/Dinner:	Monday–Thursday, 11:30 A.M.–10:30 P.M.; Friday and Saturday, 11:30 A.M.–11:30 P.M.; Sunday, noon–10:30 P.M.

Atmosphere/setting: Blue awnings shade generous windows that look out onto a busy intersection in this bustling in-town neighborhood. Within, pressed tin ceilings attest to the building's age (early 20th century). The spare decor is relieved by simple photos of Thailand, a few decorative elements, and a banner heralding Buddha suspended in the middle of the space. Closely packed tables fill quickly with young couples and young families.

House specialties: A host of unique dishes: spicy papaya salad with sun-dried beef and sticky rice; roast red curry duck; Thai catfish; soft-shell crab with asparagus sauce.

Other recommendations: Homemade ice creams—durian(!), mango, and coconut.

Summary & comments: This is a distinctive Thai restaurant, with dishes that go beyond the norm. The same and similar dishes are served at Harry House's and Surin Techarukpong's other restaurant Harry & Son's, just up the street. If Surin of Thailand is packed, you can get the same fare plus sushi at 820 N. Highland Avenue, NE, (404) 873-2009, and often this location is not as busy.

Honors & awards: Atlanta Journal & Constitution, Readers' Choice Best Thai Restaurant Atlanta, 1999, Best Thai Restaurant Fulton County, 2000; *Creative Loafing,* Readers' Choice Best Thai Restaurant, 1999-2000; *Atlanta Business Chronicle,* Readers' Choice Best Thai, 2001.

Swallow at the Hollow

Zone 3 Buckhead/Sandy Springs	Southern/Barbecue
1079 Green Street, Roswell	★★
(678) 352-1975	Inexpensive/Moderate
	Quality 88 Value B

Reservations:	Not accepted
When to go:	Early in the lunch and dinner service
Entree range:	$5.95–17.95
Payment:	AMEX, MC, VISA
Service rating:	★★★
Friendliness rating:	★★★
Parking:	On site
Bar:	Beer and wine only
Wine selection:	Very limited
Dress:	Casual
Disabled access:	Yes
Customers:	Mostly neighbors and families, sometimes out-of-staters who've driven here just to find the restaurant
Lunch:	Wednesday–Saturday, 11 A.M.–2:30 P.M.
Dinner:	Wednesday–Thursday, 5–10 P.M.; Friday–Saturday, 5–9:30 P.M. (but open until midnight for songwriter's night); Sunday, 5–9 P.M.

Atmosphere/setting: With its characteristic wide veranda across the front, possibly original tin roof, and weathered rough-textured siding, this generously welcoming structure might have once been somebody's home. Inside, line up in front of the bar to place orders. Grab a brew (the wines aren't much) and head to find a table. Strangers gather at the long tables, and waitresses manage to keep checks separate. You might find yourself elbow-to-elbow with new friends.

House specialties: Chopped barbecued pork and pork ribs; house-made sausage; house-made bread-and-butter pickles; barbecued pizza (dinner only).

Other recommendations: Cole slaw; Brunswick stew; biscuits; macaroni and cheese made with Parmesan cheese; banana pudding.

Entertainment & amenities: Live music on songwriters' nights on Friday and Saturday, when writers from Nashville's Blue Bird Café showcase original work. A house band performs Wednesday and Sunday.

Summary & comments: Doreen and Paul Dorster, with backing from Bill Greenwood at Green's on Green Street (see page 188), opened this very successful

(continued)

272

establishment only about a year ago. It stays packed, so plan your arrival accordingly. Even though the ribs are precooked then grilled, thus lacking a smoky taste, they're tender (not flabby) and very good. Everything is made on site. It's great for family dining, but the adults won't find their palates insulted. Vegetarians fear not: Try the pot-cooked portobello sandwich with smoked Gouda and fried green tomatoes.

Honors & awards: *Atlanta* magazine, several recognitions; *Knife & Fork; Atlanta Journal & Constitution,* 2 stars and Top 50, 2000.

Tamarind

Zone 8   Downtown East
80 14th Street, at Spring Street
Midtown
(404) 873-4888

	Thai
	★★★★
	Moderate
	Quality 94 Value C

Reservations:	Accepted
When to go:	Any time
Entree range:	$10.95–21
Payment:	AMEX, VISA, MC
Service rating:	★★★★
Friendliness rating:	★★★★
Parking:	On site
Bar:	Beer and wine only
Wine selection:	Quite good for an Asian restaurant
Dress:	Casual
Disabled access:	Ramp
Customers:	Admiring patrons from all over town
Lunch:	Monday–Friday, 11:30 A.M.–2:30 P.M.
Dinner:	Monday–Thursday, 5:30–10 P.M.; Friday, 5:30–11 P.M.; Saturday, 5–11 P.M.; Sunday, 5–10 P.M.

Atmosphere/setting: Perched precariously on the corner of a busy urban intersection, the restaurant is an oasis of calm and repose. Step within and feel secure and welcomed. The contemporary design is appointed with Asian touches here and there, but not overrun. Noise levels are moderate, permitting comfortable table conversation.

House specialties: Curries; seafood; lamb with basil and chili; soups.

Other recommendations: Panang curries; green curries. Will modify spice level to suit each patron's palate.

Summary & comments: This is by all measures the city's top Thai restaurant, bringing Thai cooking to the level of fine dining with commensurate service. The decor points up the contemporary nature of this kind of cooking, with its lightness and intensity of flavor.

Honors & awards: Zagat, 1998–2001; *Atlanta Journal & Constitution,* two stars and Top 50, 2000; *Atlanta* magazine, Best Thai, 2000; lots of positive local press.

TEN DEGREES SOUTH

Zone 3   Buckhead/Sandy Springs
4183 Roswell Road
(404) 705-8870

South African	
★★★	
Moderate	
Quality 88	Value B

Reservations:	Not required but recommended, especially on weekends
When to go:	Any time
Entree range:	$13.95–19.95
Payment:	Major credit cards
Service rating:	★★★
Friendliness rating:	★★★★★
Parking:	On site
Bar:	Full service
Wine selection:	Extensive, all South African
Dress:	Casual dressy
Disabled access:	Yes
Customers:	The neighbors, some from South Africa, but mostly locals
Dinner:	Every day, 5:30–10:30 P.M.

Atmosphere/setting: A small former residence set well back from the road is ably divided into two small, cozy, warmly lit spaces that invite romantic dining. The low noise level enables comfortable table conversation. The entrance leads to a welcoming bar for pre-dinner gathering.

House specialties: Sosaties (skewers of beef filet in curry sauce); bobotie (ground curry-flavored beef topped with savory custard); grilled calamari steak; Di's Delight (sponge cake with fruits).

Other recommendations: Bredie (South African lamb stew); chicken or chicken livers with peri-peri sauce (hot!).

Summary & comments: A unique dining experience, Ten Degrees South lets you explore the rich diversity of South African food and wine. The wine list is entirely South African, except for Champagnes and sparkling wines.

TEN EAST WASHINGTON

10 East Washington Street
Newnan
(770) 502-9100

Continental
★★
Moderate
Quality 85   Value C

Reservations:	Accepted
When to go:	Any time
Entree range:	$13–20
Payment:	Major credit cards
Service rating:	★★★★
Friendliness rating:	★★★★★
Parking:	Self, on the street
Bar:	None; beer and wine available
Wine selection:	Limited but decent and well priced
Dress:	Nice casual
Disabled access:	Yes
Customers:	Locals
Dinner:	Tuesday–Saturday, 5:30–9:30 P.M.; Sunday and Monday, closed

Atmosphere/setting: Bright, with well-spaced tables, a moderate noise level, and comfortable seating, this endeavor by Czech-born George Rasovsky brings casual fine dining to an antebellum metro Atlanta–area town. Located off the downtown square, the restaurant sits in the heart of Newnan's business district.

House specialties: Crab cakes Savannah; seafood Provençal served over pasta; grilled tenderloin of lamb with port wine, rosemary, and shallots; seared duck breast with cranberry coulis.

Other recommendations: Crème caramel (oh lá lá, but skip the whipped cream and other needless garnishes); nightly European and Czech specials such as schnitzel and sauerbraten.

Summary & comments: Make dining here an excursion affair after visiting some of the town's antebellum houses when they're on tour or after a visit to the Powers Crossing Country Fair, held Labor Day weekend. Newnan is about an hour south of Atlanta via I-85 (Exit 7).

THai CHili

Thai	
★★★★	
Moderate	
Quality 90	Value B

Zone 5   Northeast Atlanta
Briarvista Shopping Center
2169 Briarcliff Road, NE
at Lavista Road
(404) 315-6750

Reservations:	Limited
When to go:	Any time
Entree range:	$9.25–16.95
Payment:	Major credit cards
Service rating:	★★★
Friendliness rating:	★★
Parking:	On site, ample
Bar:	None
Wine selection:	Limited, but with at least one good choice for Asian food
Dress:	Casual
Disabled access:	Easy
Customers:	Neighbors from surrounding residential area
Lunch:	Monday–Friday, 11 A.M.–2:30 P.M.
Dinner:	Sunday–Thursday, 5–10 P.M.; Friday and Saturday, 5–11 P.M.

Atmosphere/setting: This small space is pleasantly embellished with Thai art, but spares the over-decorating that afflicts so many ethnic restaurants. The wait staff is friendly and appropriately garbed, but not in outlandish costuming that sometimes adorns staffers in Thai restaurants. This is a serious restaurant where food comes first.

House specialties: Thai curry; larb; Thai chili noodles.

Other recommendations: The spicy chef's specials, especially the catfish and vegetarian dishes—many based on tofu.

Summary & comments: This tiny restaurant put itself on the map as one of the best Thai restaurants in the city just about from the moment its doors opened. Chef Robert Khankiew has earned his reputation (formerly at Surin of Thailand, see page 271) as a gifted interpreter of Thai cuisine.

Honors & awards: Frequent kudos in local press, some of which consider this one Atlanta's best Thai restaurant.

Thelma's Kitchen

	Southern
	★★
	Inexpensive
	Quality 88 Value C

Zone 7   Downtown West
Roxy Hotel, ground floor
768 Marietta Street, NW
(404) 688-5855

Reservations:	Not accepted
When to go:	Any time
Entree range:	$5.99–9.25
Payment:	Cash or travelers' checks
Service rating:	★★★★
Friendliness rating:	★★★
Parking:	Self, on street
Bar:	None
Wine selection:	None
Dress:	Very casual
Disabled access:	Easy
Customers:	Regular patrons from surrounding businesses, occasional tourists
Breakfast/Lunch:	Monday–Friday, 7:30 A.M.–4:30 P.M.; Saturday, 7 A.M.–3 P.M.; Sunday, closed

Atmosphere/setting: Reinstalled in the very modest and slightly restored Roxy Hotel, the restaurant had to move to make way for Centennial Park, a feature of the 1996 Olympic Games. This setting is much brighter and airier than the old one, with high ceilings, lots of white paint, faux ivy creeping up the latticed walls separating the kitchen from the steam tables, and plenty of natural light. Food is still dispensed from steam tables, with freshly made portions coming out at regular intervals. The servings are huge.

House specialties: Fried catfish; fried chicken; mashed potatoes and gravy; macaroni and cheese; black-eyed peas; butter beans; collard and turnip greens; country-fried steak; beef tips; okra cakes (when available).

Other recommendations: Desserts: Super-rich pecan pie; chocolate-frosted yellow cake; sweet potato pie; chocolate cake.

Summary & comments: Anyone looking for authentic "soul food" or Southern food need look no further, for Thelma's is its temple.

Honors & awards: Plenty of local press and lots of satisfied patrons from all walks of life. *Zagat,* 1999; *Travel & Leisure,* America's Top 50 Restaurants, 1999.

278

THOMAS MARKETPLACE RESTAURANT

Southern	
★★★	
Inexpensive	
Quality 90	Value A

Zone 6   Southeast Atlanta
State Farmers Market
16 Forest Parkway, Forest Park
(404) 361-1367

Reservations:	Accepted
When to go:	Any time
Entree range:	$5.50–14
Payment:	Major credit cards
Service rating:	★★★★
Friendliness rating:	★★★★
Parking:	Self, on site in the market parking lot
Bar:	None
Wine selection:	None
Dress:	Casual
Disabled access:	Easy
Customers:	Market managers, vendors, anybody looking for a good meal
Open:	Every day, 6 A.M.–9 P.M.

Atmosphere / setting: A cavernous but comfortable space with murals on one wall suggesting both Europe and the New World is set with well-spaced booths and tables. Waitresses are the old-fashioned sorts who may call you "honey" as they take your order and pat your arm in reassurance that food is on the way.

House specialties: Fried green tomatoes ($4.25); fried chicken; fresh vegetables; house-smoked turkey and ham; barbecue; seafood; steaks.

Other recommendations: Desserts, especially homemade cobblers with fresh fruit as often as possible.

Summary & comments: Nothing could be more down-home Southern than this restaurant smack in the middle of the freshest possible produce. The restaurant moved here a few years back when its original location went up in smoke; now it's firmly established here, although this move was supposed to be temporary. Now, happily, it's permanent, meaning there are lots of fresh vegetables immediately available for supplying the restaurant's hungry customers.

TibuRon GRillE

Zone 5 Northeast Atlanta	Eclectic American
1190 N. Highland Avenue, NE	★★★★
Virginia-Highland	Moderate
(404) 892-2393	Quality 90 Value C

Reservations:	Not accepted
When to go:	Any time
Entree range:	$16.50–22
Payment:	Major credit cards
Service rating:	★★★★
Friendliness rating:	★★★★
Parking:	On site
Bar:	Full service
Wine selection:	Excellent, with many unusual and special labels
Dress:	Casual dressy
Disabled access:	Yes
Customers:	The neighbors from the surrounding Morning-side/Virginia-Highland residences
Dinner:	Every day, 6–10 P.M.

Atmosphere/setting: The walls are faux treated to create the look and feel of a Tuscan trattoria. Lighting is warm, and intimacy enhanced. Outside, the patio invites al fresco dining. It's a perfect spot for a nice date.

House specialties: Hickory-grilled asparagus with soy vinaigrette; grilled ostrich fillet; Georgia shrimp and grits.

Other recommendations: Honey-lacquered duck with Stilton grits; hickory-grilled filet mignon.

Summary & comments: Atlanta neighborhoods are blessed with little out-of-the-way spots such as this charming, warm bistro. But the best is that in addition to atmosphere, Tiburon Grille wins for its food, service, and superior wine list—one that goes far beyond what other such bistros offer. Dine outdoors on the patio in the back if at all possible.

280

TIERRA

	Latin American
Zone 8 Downtown East	★★★
1425-B Piedmont Avenue, NE	Expensive
near Monroe Drive	
(404) 874-5951	Quality 93 Value B

Reservations:	Accepted, advised on weekends
When to go:	Any time
Entree range:	$10.95–19.50
Payment:	Major credit cards
Service rating:	★★★★
Friendliness rating:	★★★★★
Parking:	On site
Bar:	Beer and wine only
Wine selection:	Spanish and Latin American selections, a short list, but good values and good quality
Dress:	Casual dressy
Disabled access:	Easy
Customers:	Neighbors and adventurous diners
Dinner:	Tuesday–Thursday, 6–10 P.M.; Friday and Saturday, 6–11 P.M.; Sunday 5–9 P.M.

Atmosphere/setting: Tiny Tierra (about 40 seats) sports a cover of brushed silver clouds, intense (but not intrusively so) red-orange walls, Latin music on the sound system, and a fine patio with heaters for cool weather. Patrons can carry on intimate table conversation without straining to hear. The place is lively but not crushingly noisy.

House specialties: Black bean soup; Peruvian ceviche; Pionono (plantain filled with picadillo); mussels in pasilla pepper broth; pupusas; Argentine tenderloin (sauces vary, but chimichurri is popular): grilled pork medallions with warm fruit compote and chipotle mashed potatoes.

Other recommendations: Fresh vegetables; light caldos (broths) with either seafood or chicken; mole poblano chicken lasagna; Tres Leches Cake (Three Milks Cake); glorious fig tart.

Summary & comments: Ticha and Dan Krinsky draw to their tables adventurous diners seeking new taste experiences. The cooking crosses nationalistic lines in Latin America, but they blend among cuisines. So a Brazilian dish is authentically presented, for instance, without intrusion from some other cuisine.

Honors & awards: *Atlanta* magazine, Best New Cuisine, 1999, Best Travelogue, 2000; *Zagat,* 2000–2001; *Atlanta Journal & Constitution,* two stars and Top 50, 2000.

TomTom, a Bistro and Sushi Bar

Mediterranean/Fusion
★★★★
Moderate

Quality 90   Value C

Zone 3   Buckhead/Sandy Springs
Lenox Square, Plaza Level
3393 Peachtree Road, NE
(404) 264-1163

Reservations:	Accepted for parties of eight or more
When to go:	Any time
Entree range:	$12–20
Payment:	Major credit cards
Service rating:	★★★★
Friendliness rating:	★★★
Parking:	Self, on site in the mall parking lot
Bar:	Separate bar, full service
Wine selection:	Mostly American wine list, with about 35 wines by the glass
Dress:	Nice casual
Disabled access:	Easy
Customers:	Shoppers, both locals and visitors
Brunch:	Sunday, 11:30 A.M.–3 P.M.
Lunch:	Monday–Saturday, 11:30 A.M.–4 P.M.
Dinner:	Monday–Thursday, 4–10 P.M.; Friday and Saturday, 4–11 P.M.; Sunday, 3–9 P.M.

Atmosphere/setting: High-energy, art-filled (the chef's wife, Leigh, did many of the paintings), and warm-toned, TomTom a bistro is ideal for curing post-shopping stress disorder. Relaxed, comfortable, modern, and approachable.

House specialties: Grilled tuna; barbecued salmon over white cheese grits; whole deep-fried catfish with Asian seasonings; hot chili seafood.

Other recommendations: Pizzas and pastas; roast chicken or lamb with mashed potatoes; haricots verts.

Summary & comments: Patio dining is fun in good weather. Owner Tom Catherall, himself a Scot by birth, believes sushi has become as American as pasta; as a result, he has added it to the menus of most of his restaurants.

Honors & awards: Discovery Channel, Great Chefs series, 1996; *Atlanta* magazine, Best Bistro, 1993–1996; *WHERE/Atlanta* magazine, Memorable Meals Award nominated for Best Service, 1999.

TOULOUSE

Zone 3   Buckhead/Sandy Springs
Peachtree Walk (in rear)
2293 Peachtree Road, NE
(404) 351-9533

American
★★★★
Moderate
Quality 88   Value C

Reservations:	Accepted
When to go:	Any time
Entree range:	$11–16.95 (except $21.95 for the filet mignon)
Payment:	Major credit cards
Service rating:	★★★★
Friendliness rating:	★★★★★
Parking:	Self, on site
Bar:	Full service
Wine selection:	One of Atlanta's outstanding wine lists, wide-ranging, enhanced by committee tastings
Dress:	Nice casual
Disabled access:	Via a ground-floor elevator
Customers:	Everybody, from out-of-towners to locals
Dinner:	Sunday–Thursday, 5:30–10 P.M.; Friday and Saturday, 5:30–11 P.M.
Brunch:	Sunday, 11:30 A.M.–2 P.M.

Atmosphere/setting: Located behind a strip shopping center, with a view of the parking lot and little else, warmly lit Toulouse feels great inside. Paintings by Athens, Georgia–based artist Steve Penley warm the brick walls with their rich colors. With its open bar, open kitchen, generous seat spacing, and limited outdoor balcony dining in nice weather, this is a restaurant that successfully overcame a less-than-ideal hidden location.

House specialties: Roast chicken; lamb shank (seasonal); fish; steak; house-made breads and ice creams.

Other recommendations: Grilled vegetable plate; crème brûlée; potato soup; apple tart with homemade cinnamon ice cream (worth eating all by itself!).

Summary & comments: Entrees are matched with wine suggestions, all available by the glass, making the diner's wine choosing an easy proposition. It also takes the heat off the eager young staff to make learned wine decisions for quizzical patrons. Owner George Tice is a master at getting diners to try wines besides chardonnay and cabernet sauvignon, although there are plenty of these to be had. The entire restaurant is nonsmoking except for the balcony seating.

Honors & awards: Santé magazine, Excellence in Restaurant Wine and Hospitality, 2000, one of five bistros so honored nationwide.

Udipi Café

<table>
<tr><td></td><td>South Indian</td></tr>
<tr><td>Zone 5   Northeast Atlanta</td><td>★★★</td></tr>
<tr><td>1850 Lawrenceville Highway</td><td>Inexpensive</td></tr>
<tr><td>Suite 700, Decatur</td><td></td></tr>
<tr><td>(404) 325-1933</td><td>Quality 90   Value B</td></tr>
</table>

Reservations:	Accepted Friday–Sunday only
When to go:	Any time
Entree range:	$4.50–14.95
Payment:	MC, VISA
Service rating:	★★★★
Friendliness rating:	★★★★
Parking:	Self, on site
Bar:	None
Wine selection:	None
Dress:	Casual
Disabled access:	Easy, street level
Customers:	Indians from all over and young couples on budgets, families
Lunch/Dinner:	Monday–Thursday, 11:30 A.M.–9:30 P.M.; Friday–Sunday, 11:30 A.M.–10 P.M.

Atmosphere / setting: The huge dining room almost has a dining hall feeling to it. Decor is minimal, with strings of colored lights and the occasional Indian-themed art on the walls. Tables are lined up in rows, rather institutionally, instead of being set at interesting angles to break up the space. Best seats are the booths that line the walls. The focus definitely is on the activity in the kitchen, not on the frills in the dining room.

House specialties: Dosai (thin crepes with special fillings, such as potatoes and onions); lentil pancakes with vegetables; chana batura (a large puffy bread with chick peas); rasmalai (sweet cottage cheese in rose water-flavored condensed milk).

Other recommendations: Potato bonda (a fried potato dumpling with two dipping sauces; the world's crispest pappadums; Baigan Bartha (eggplant curry); pachadi (yogurt with cucumber, onions, and cilantro leaves—like a raita).

Summary & comments: Udipi is a coastal city in Southeast India that is famous for its vegetarian cooking. The city and its cuisine are the inspiration for this very popular restaurant, founded in 1998.

Honors & awards: Atlanta Journal & Constitution, two stars Top 50, 2000; *Atlanta* magazine, Best Place to Take a Vegetarian, 2000.

284

Van Gogh's

Zone 3   Buckhead/Sandy Springs
Crabapple Square Shopping Center
70 West Crossville Road, Roswell
(770) 993-1156

Continental	
★★★	
Moderate/Expensive	
Quality 90	Value C

Reservations:	Accepted
When to go:	Weekdays, and early dinner if you don't want to wait
Entree range:	$13–26
Payment:	Major credit cards
Service rating:	★★★
Friendliness rating:	★★★
Parking:	Valet and self, on site
Bar:	Separate, full service
Wine selection:	Extensive and excellent, with many by the glass; ask about the wine of the month
Dress:	Nice casual to business attire
Disabled access:	Easy
Customers:	Neighbors
Lunch:	Monday–Saturday, 11:30 A.M.–2:30 P.M.; limited menu, 2:30–5 P.M.
Dinner:	Every day, 5–10 P.M.

Atmosphere/setting: This serene space offers several separate dining rooms, warm and flattering lighting, and well-spaced tables. Brick walls showcase art from one of the owner's brothers, who owns Alpha Omega Galleries in Roswell. The noise level is moderate, making dining very comfortable.

House specialties: Crab cakes; grilled portobello mushroom/veggie sandwich (lunch) and appetizer; steak carpaccio; sea bass; veal special (occasional). Menu changes monthly.

Other recommendations: Pork tenderloin loin; rack of lamb (just watch out for any sauces as some combinations of flavors can be a bit odd); stir fries at lunch; seafood chowder.

Summary & comments: Wait times on the weekends can be excruciating (understandable, since it's one of the best restaurants in the 'burbs), so plan to dine early or late on those days or make sure to have a reservation.

Honors & awards: Creative Loafing and *Atlanta* magazines, Best Restaurant in Roswell, 1995; *Wine Spectator,* Award of Excellence, 1995–2000.

The Varsity

Zone 8   Downtown East
61 North Avenue, NE, at Spring Street
Midtown   (404) 881-1706

Zone 5   Northeast Atlanta
1085 Lindbergh Drive, NE at Cheshire Bridge Road
(404) 261-8843

Zone 5   Northeast Atlanta
6045 Dawson Boulevard at Jimmy Carter Boulevard, Norcross
(770) 840-8519

Zone 2   Northwest Atlanta
2790 Town Center Drive at Mall Boulevard, Kennesaw
(770) 795-0802

Reservations:	Not accepted
When to go:	Any time
Entree range:	$3.75–5.45
Payment:	Cash only
Service rating:	★★★★
Friendliness rating:	★★★★★
Parking:	Self, on site
Bar:	None
Wine selection:	None
Dress:	As casual as you can
Disabled access:	Easy, street level
Customers:	Everyone from presidents to street people downtown; business types for lunch, couples and families for dinner at the suburban locations
Open:	North Avenue: Sunday–Thursday, 9 A.M.–11:30 P.M.; Friday and Saturday, 9:30 A.M.–12:30 A.M.
	Lindbergh: Monday–Thursday, 10 A.M.–11 P.M.; Friday and Saturday, 10 A.M.–midnight; Sunday, 11 A.M.–11 P.M.
	Norcross: Monday–Thursday, 10 A.M.–10 P.M.;

(continued)

Friday and Saturday, 10 A.M.–11 P.M.,
Sunday, 11 A.M.–10 P.M.
Kennesaw: Sunday–Thursday, 10 A.M.–10 P.M.;
Friday and Saturday, 10 A.M.–11 P.M.

Atmosphere/setting: The four locations vary widely in ambiance, but the most atmospheric is the original spot downtown. It's total 1950s. The most exciting cultural experience, especially for your out-of-town guests, is to do it the right way, by parking and letting the curbhop take your order. Inside, is another trip right down memory lane.

House specialties: Chili dog (homemade chili); toasted pimiento cheese sandwich; orange frosty; onion rings.

Other recommendations: Fried pies done the right way; french fries cut on the premises from whole, unpeeled potatoes—they actually taste like potato! The best.

Entertainment & amenities: At Northside Drive, the best people-watching in town.

Summary & comments: The photo line-up at the Northside location is a who's who: From presidents Carter, Bush Sr., and Clinton, to Elvis Presley and comedian Nipsy Russell, who used to work here as a carhop. Curb service is available at North Avenue and at Varsity Jr. only.

Honors & awards: So many. *Creative Loafing,* Best Onion Rings and Best Hot Dog, 1999; *WHERE/Atlanta,* Memorable Meals finalist Most Meal for the Money, 1997, Most Fun for the Family winner, 1999; *Atlanta* magazine, Best Hot Dog Panel's Choice, 1996, Best Curb Service, 2000.

Veni Vidi Vici

Zone 8   Downtown East
41 14th Street, NE, at Spring Street
Midtown
(404) 875-8424

Classic Italian	
★★★★★	
Moderate/Expensive	
Quality 98	Value B

Reservations:	Required
When to go:	It is easier to be seated for lunch than for dinner
Entree range:	$13–25.50
Payment:	Major credit cards
Service rating:	★★★★
Friendliness rating:	★★★★
Parking:	Valet
Bar:	Separate bar, full service
Wine selection:	Extensive, all Italian, and many well priced, with a few good selections by the glass
Dress:	Dressy casual to formal
Disabled access:	From parking deck, on the second floor, but very difficult to find, badly needs better signage. Turn left at the end of the second floor ramp
Customers:	Locals, film stars, business and political figures
Lunch:	Monday–Friday, 11:30 A.M.–4 P.M.
Dinner:	Monday–Thursday, 4–11 P.M.; Friday 4 P.M.–midnight; Saturday, 5 P.M.–midnight; Sunday, 5–10 P.M.

Atmosphere/setting: A stylish dining establishment in a parking garage—what will they think of next?

House specialties: Small plates (piatti piccoli) with tasty morsels; braised artichoke bottoms in salsa verde; prosciutto on pear; spiedini (deep-fried skewer of rock shrimp and Fontina cheese); roast suckling pig; fresh and imported dried pastas; rotisserie meats (duck!).

Other recommendations: Balsamic chicken; linguine with white or red clam sauce; scallops, no matter how they're served; all desserts, especially crostata di mandorle (almond chocolate bars) with fresh blackberry compote; panna cotta.

Entertainment & amenities: Occasional jazz trio (Wednesday and Sunday 6:30–9:30 P.M.)

Summary & comments: Begun by Marcella Hazan in 1990, the restaurant came under the firm direction of Pano Karatassos and Paul Albrecht's group of restaurants (see Buckhead Diner, page 131; Pricci, page 343; Pano's and Paul's, page

(continued)

288

230; Atlanta Fish Market, page 107; BluePointe, page 117, Chops/The Lobster Bar, page 144, and Buckhead Bread Company and Corner Café, page 22) in 1994. Chef Michael Persichetti has worked in lots of Italian restaurants in New York. Mary Anne Selby is the outstanding pastry chef.

Honors & awards: Mobil Travel Guide, Three Stars (1994–1999); AAA Four Diamond Award; Wi*ne Spectator,* Award of Excellence, 1993–2000; DiRoNA Award, 1996–2000; *Gourmet* magazine, Best Restaurant, based on a national survey of advertising executives, 1996; *Zagat; Atlanta Homes & Lifestyles,* Top Five Restaurants, Best Chocolate Dessert, and Best Italian Wine List, 1999; *Jezebel* magazine, Top 15 Atlanta restaurants, 2000.

Villa Christina

Zone 4 Lenox/Chamblee	Contemporary Italian
Perimeter Summit	★★★
4000 Summit Boulevard	Moderate/Expensive
off Ashford Dunwoody Road	Quality 90 Value C
(404) 303-0133	

Reservations:	Accepted
When to go:	Any time
Entree range:	$13–24
Payment:	Major credit cards
Service rating:	★★★★
Friendliness rating:	★★★★
Parking:	Self, on site; valet complimentary (both lunch and dinner)
Bar:	Full service
Wine selection:	Extensive
Dress:	Nice casual
Disabled Access:	Yes
Customers:	Corporate clientele at lunch as well as some at night; dating and wedded couples during the week
Lunch:	Monday–Friday, 11:30 A.M.–2 P.M.
Dinner:	Monday–Thursday, 6–9:30 P.M.; Friday and Saturday, 6–10:30 P.M.; Sunday, closed

Atmosphere/setting: One of the most beautiful dining spaces in the entire city, the street-level restaurant is filled with fine local contemporary art, some of it especially executed for the space. Built to accommodate the dining needs of those office-tower denizens who labor in posh spaces above and around this building.

House specialties: Pasta; veal chop; roasted rack of lamb; portobello mushroom appetizer; angel hair pasta á la Toscana; filet mignon; white bean minestrone; good salads from classic Caesar to filet salad.

Other recommendations: Desserts, which are architecturally composed to reflect the artful quality of the space. Happily, however, they also taste great. Case in point: the bittersweet chocolate torte.

Summary & comments: While most patrons have business on the brain, romantic dining should not be overlooked here. Table 41 overlooks the waterfall, making it a fine spot for amorous conversation. Outdoor dining takes advantage of exquisitely landscaped grounds. Banquet and special-event spaces are stellar,

(continued)

290

including a stone gazebo for weddings. "Date Night" is offered twice a month (the second and last Fridays of the month). One of the banquet rooms becomes a kids' zone, where little guests (ages 1–10) dine on chicken nuggets or pizzas while the parents dine downstairs. The room is full of stuffed animals, cots if they get a little sleepy, and games. Caregivers are certified by a local hospital. Cost is just $10 per child. This program has been wildly popular. The kids may even get a tour of the kitchen to see how the chefs cook the food. Most of the time the kids are running around enjoying one big pajama party. Parents often book the next night before leaving the restaurant. Manager Adam Ghali has a little one of his own, so he knows what they need. Monthly regional wine tastings are also held. Chef Timothy Sprigg recently replaced Chef Darryl Evans (he went on to head up Spice—see New Places, page 17).

Honors & awards: *Esquire* magazine, One of 25 Best New Restaurants, 1995; *Restaurant & Hospitality,* Top of the Table, Grand Award winner, 1996; Citation by the Italian government as one of the 12 best modern Italian restaurants in the United States, 2000.

VININGS INN

Zone 2   Northwest Atlanta
3011 Paces Mill Road, Vinings
(770) 438-2282

New American	
★★★	
Expensive	
Quality 85	Value C

Reservations:	Accepted, advised for weekends
When to go:	Any time (but weekends between 7–8:30 P.M. it's packed)
Entree range:	$14–26
Payment:	Major credit cards
Service rating:	★★★★
Friendliness rating:	★★★★
Parking:	Valet
Bar:	Full service
Wine selection:	About 120 wines come mostly from California and other U.S. states; about 25 are offered by the glass
Dress:	Casual dressy
Disabled access:	Ramp; check in with valet
Customers:	Business folks at lunch; dating couples at dinner; neighbors mostly but folks from all over the metro area, too
Lunch:	Monday–Saturday, 11:30 A.M.–2:30 P.M.
Dinner:	Monday–Saturday, 5:30–10 P.M.

Atmosphere / setting: This more than 130-year-old former residence is an assembly of cozy spaces for intimate dining in the evening and business dining at lunch. Decor is rustic comfortable, governed by simplicity. A pair of fireplaces chases winter's chill. Noise levels are not intrusive, so table conversation is comfortably accomplished.

House specialties: Crab cakes; peach barbecued prawns; salmon; Bob's barbecue; veal chop.

Other recommendations: Soups, which vary daily.

Entertainment & amenities: Live jazz, rhythm 'n' blues, vocals, guitar—always live music—Tuesday–Thursday; weekends a band of some kind. Upstairs the Attic Bar, with its outdoor deck, is a quaint and cozy spot to reconnoiter, savor a glass of wine, and enjoy a good view of the old Vinings area.

Summary & comments: Rich Selsor and Tom Turrentine launched their now four-restaurant group from this well-established entity, in which they joined forces in 1995. This one differs from the others, all built in recent years, thanks to its unique historical position.

292

Vinny's on Windward

Zone 4   Lenox/Chamblee
5355 Windward Parkway, W.
Alpharetta
(770) 772-4644

Italian	
★★★★	
Expensive	
Quality 90	Value C

Reservations:	Accepted
When to go:	Any time
Entree range:	$12.95–25.95
Payment:	Major credit cards
Service rating:	★★★★
Friendliness rating:	★★★★
Parking:	Valet available as well as self-parking on site
Bar:	Full service, separate bar is a nice gathering spot
Wine selection:	Excellent, heavily Italian but with some California offerings; the dessert wine list is outstanding
Dress:	Casual
Disabled access:	Easy
Customers:	Business folks at lunch, neighbors at dinner
Lunch:	Monday–Saturday, 11 A.M.–3 P.M.
Dinner:	Monday–Thursday, 5–10:30 P.M.; Friday and Saturday, 5–11:30 P.M.; Sunday, 5–10 P.M.
Appetizer menu:	Every day, 11 A.M.–closing

Atmosphere/setting: A freestanding building with a slight Tuscan feel to it, Vinny's presents an inviting atmosphere with a slightly industrial look, almost like a renovated warehouse or factory. Substantial is how it feels, with lots of sturdy materials like brick, wood, and granite. Brick-lined walls glow with warm light, with arches separating spaces. The generous bar space sits to the rear.

House specialties: Tomato ciabatta bread soup; sea bass; crab cakes; individual pizzas; salads; rack of lamb; breads from company-owned Theo's Brother's Bakery.

Other recommendations: Game; crème brûlée (flavors vary); braised dishes.

Summary & comments: Of the three restaurants owned by Chris and Michele Sedgwick, this one is the top of the lot. New executive chef Brian Kibler plans on adding braised bison short ribs and other innovative dishes, but the Italian cast will remain firmly in place. The wine list, devoted as it is to Italian selections, rivals some of the in-town wine lists for its adventurous selections. Imported grappa to conclude the meal is another fine touch. Not too long ago, a restaurant of this caliber this far from the city's gastronomic center would have been unthinkable.

Honors & awards: *Zagat,* 2001, *Wine Spectator,* Award of Excellence, 1997–2001.

293

Vino!

	Eclectic
Zone 3 Buckhead/Sandy Springs	★★★
The Peach Shopping Center	Moderate
2900 Peachtree Road, NW	
at Delmont Drive	Quality 85 Value C
(404) 816-0511	

Reservations:	Accepted
When to go:	Any time
Entree range:	$17–23
Payment:	AMEX, MC, VISA
Service rating:	★★★★
Friendliness rating:	★★★★
Parking:	Self, on site
Bar:	Full service
Wine selection:	Excellent, with interesting varieties; lots by the glass, a reserve list, and the ability to explore
Dress:	Casual
Disabled access:	Easy
Customers:	Neighbors from Buckhead; some visitors
Lunch:	Monday–Friday, 11:30 A.M.–3 P.M.
Dinner:	Monday–Thursday, 5–9:30 P.M.; Friday and Saturday, 5–10:30 P.M.; Sunday, closed

Atmosphere/setting: A tiny slip of a space at the corner of this busy shopping center, Vino! draws couples gathering at the intimate bar after work and before dinner; guests attending wine tastings and dinners; and the occasional guest from a nearby hotel. While the urban bustle churns outside, the interior feels like a moment somewhere on the Mediterranean.

House specialties: Pâté; paella; lobster appetizer with Grand Marnier basil butter; tapas (mixed spiced nuts, anchovies); sautéed trout with apple butter.

Other recommendations: Fish; lamb; duck with raspberry sauce (occasional); French chocolate pudding; cheese course.

Summary & comments: Ofelia Santos' splendid little restaurant is good for quiet lunches, but it comes alive in the evenings as it fills with devoted patrons.

Honors & awards: Wine Spectator, Award of Excellence, 1999, 2000; *Zagat; Atlanta* magazine, One of 10 Best Chocolate Desserts, 2000.

Violette

<table>
<tr><td></td><td>French</td></tr>
</table>

Zone 5   Northeast Atlanta
2948 Clairmont Road, NE
(404) 633-3363

French
★★★
Moderate/Expensive

Quality 90   Value B

Reservations:	Accepted
When to go:	Any time
Entree range:	$9–15
Payment:	Major credit cards
Service rating:	★★★
Friendliness rating:	★★
Parking:	Self, on site
Bar:	Full service
Wine selection:	French and Californian, with some good ones by the glass
Dress:	Nice casual
Disabled access:	Easy
Customers:	Neighbors and other locals
Lunch:	Monday–Friday, 11:30 A.M.–2 P.M.
Dinner:	Monday–Saturday, 5:30–10:30 P.M.

Atmosphere/setting: The original Violette occupied a freestanding building that once was a bank. Then owner Guy Luck, a native of Alsace, built a spanking-fresh structure that has a lot more room and atmosphere than the first one. Neighbors love gathering at the bar for drinks before heading home as much as they love sticking around for dinner. Businesspeople take advantage of some of the best inexpensive lunchtime dining one can find. Dining on the outside patio area in nice weather puts you in touch with lovely surrounding trees.

House specialties: Traditional bistro comfort fare: steak au poivre or Roquefort; pâtés; chicken with tarragon; quiche; pork with green peppercorns; salads and soups.

Other recommendations: Salmon rilletes; crème brûlée; pear tart.

Entertainment & amenities: Live piano at dinner Friday and Saturday; live jazz Monday–Thursday 5:30-8:30 P.M.

Summary & comments: If you want a special dish prepared, "We can do it," answers the chef with aplomb and alacrity. This is one of the best value lunches in Atlanta, and dinner falls into that category as well. Other restaurants charge huge money for a simple coq au vin, but here it goes for $8.95.

The Vortex Bar & Grill

American
★★
Inexpensive
Quality 88   Value C

Zone 8   Downtown East
878 Peachtree Street, NW
between 7th and 8th Streets
Midtown
(404) 875-1667

Zone 5   Northeast Atlanta
438 Moreland Avenue, Little Five Points
(404) 688-1828

Reservations:	Not accepted
When to go:	Any time
Entree range:	$5.75–6.95
Payment:	Major credit cards
Service rating:	★★★
Friendliness rating:	★★
Parking:	Limited, on street in Midtown; pay parking across the street; good-size free lot at Little Five Points
Bar:	Full service
Wine selection:	Limited, but decent
Dress:	Funk casual
Disabled access:	Yes
Customers:	Locals, on weekends the Buckhead/Little Five Points sets respectively
Lunch/Dinner:	Monday–Saturday, 11 A.M.–2 A.M.; Sunday, 11 A.M.–midnight

Atmosphere/setting: Positively wacky, this popular establishment chooses an Edvard Munch skull for its logo, forming the entrance to the Moreland Avenue location and decorating the menus of both. The interior is awash in flotsam and jetsam, hanging from the ceilings and falling off the walls. Noisy, busy, fun.

House specialties: Burgers of all kinds, especially the Blue 'Shroom Bacon Burger—for when calories don't count.

Other recommendations: Hot dogs; salads; and for the vegetarian a choice of veggie burgers made from either rolled oats or black beans.

Summary & comments: More than 100 varieties of beer, including several good nonalcoholic beers, and at least 50 single-malt Scotch whiskeys add to the joys of being at the Vortex.

Honors & awards: Lots of positive press comments. *Atlanta Journal Constitution,* Best Burger, and Top 50, 2000; *Creative Loafing,* Best Burger, 2000.

296

Vrney's Biergarten and German Grille

	German
	★★★
	Inexpensive/Moderate
	Quality 88 Value B

Zone 4   Lenox/Chamblee
4225 River Green Parkway, Duluth
(770) 523-9413

Reservations:	Not accepted
When to go:	Any time
Entree range:	$9.50–13.50
Payment:	Major credit cards
Service rating:	★★★★
Friendliness rating:	★★★★★
Parking:	On site (no valet)
Bar:	Full service, lots of good imported beers
Wine selection:	Inexpensive, with one Riesling by the glass; "Kurt's 23" list (23 wines all sold for $23) changes frequently to take advantage of market availability
Dress:	Casual
Disabled access:	Yes
Customers:	Mostly neighbors, but others seeking German cooking
Dinner:	Tuesday–Saturday, 4–10 P.M.

Atmosphere/setting: A white frame house holds two restaurants: Vreny's, which focuses on German food, and adjacent Kurt's, a Continental restaurant (see page 206), at the front. Vreny's itself is a comfort kind of place, with twirling fans and a ceiling adorned with flags from Germany, Switzerland, and other nations. Outside, a patio beckons in good weather, making this a very pleasant place to savor this hearty fare.

House specialties: Spätzle; schnitzel; goulash soup; sausages; maultaschen (a beef-filled ravioli); apple strudel.

Other recommendations: House-made country pâté; soups; fresh-baked German pretzels; Black Forest cake.

Summary & comments: Grab a stein of good imported German beer (some of these are rarely seen) and a plate of good wursts, and you'll get to the heart of good German food.

Watershed

Zone 5 Northeast Atlanta	American/Southern
406 W. Ponce de Leon Avenue	★★★★
Decatur	Moderate/Expensive
(404) 378-4900	Quality 95 Value C

Reservations:	Not accepted
When to go:	Early in the service
Entree range:	$14–20
Payment:	Major credit cards
Service rating:	★★★★
Friendliness rating:	★★★★★
Parking:	On site
Bar:	Beer and wine only
Wine selection:	Extraordinary! Also does retail sales of wine, and any bottle available on the shelves may be purchased and opened in the restaurant
Dress:	Casual
Disabled access:	Easy
Customers:	Young, upwardly mobile residents of the surrounding neighborhoods, and many from around the city eager for this splendid food
Lunch:	Monday–Saturday, 11 A.M.–3 P.M.
Tea:	Monday–Saturday, 3–5 P.M.
Dinner:	Monday–Saturday, 5–10 P.M.

Atmosphere/setting: In what was once a single-bay garage, Indigo Girl Emily Saliers and three of her good friends launched a very special place that was not really designed to become a fine dining establishment. But it is one. The four partners have grown in assurance and reputation, and the place has shown remarkable progress since its founding.

House specialties: Fried chicken (Tuesday only) done the traditional right way; old-fashioned Southern pimiento cheese; awesome egg and white truffle chicken salads on great breads; chocolate cake.

Other recommendations: Pasta dishes; white bean hummus; chocolate macaroons; superior soups, especially New England cod chowder and vegetarian cauliflower.

Summary & comments: Former Governor's Mansion Chef Scott Peacock (also associated with Edna Lewis) handles the kitchen in this dynamic establishment. He takes such pains with the fried chicken, soaking it overnight in salted

(continued)

water then in buttermilk, before it's coated and fried. Its popularity is such that it sells out quickly, so make a point of getting there early if you care to sample it. Vegetarians will dine gloriously here. The excellent Egg Farm Dairy cheeses are among the featured American artisan cheeses on the cheese tasting plate. Watershed also operates as a wine bar, with exquisite mostly American wines (but some Australian, Italian, and French, too) available by the bottle and by the glass. But it's also a retail store, so if you want to order take-out and grab a bottle of wine to go, that's also an option. The interior is set up like a real enoteca.

Honors & awards: The awesome fried chicken made the cover of the March 2000 *Food and Wine* magazine. *Atlanta Journal & Constitution,* Top 10 Newcomers, 1999 and three stars and Top 50, 2000; *Creative Loafing,* Best New Restaurant, 1999; *Creative Loafing,* Best of Atlanta, Desserts, 1999; *Atlanta* magazine, Best Chocolate Cake and Best Wine Bar, 1999, Best Taste of the South (Fancy), 2000; *Gourmet* magazine, Top 5, 2000.

YEN JING

Zone 5   Northeast Atlanta
Koreatown Shopping Center, A-6
6302 Buford Highway, NE
(770) 454-6688

Chinese/Korean
★★★★★
Inexpensive

Quality 95   Value A

Reservations:	Not accepted
When to go:	Any time, but the dinner menu is the interesting one
Entree range:	$7.95–24.95
Payment:	Major credit cards
Service rating:	★★★★
Friendliness rating:	★★★★
Parking:	On site
Bar:	Beer and wine only
Wine selection:	Very limited, beer or sake are best choices
Dress:	Casual dressy
Disabled access:	Yes
Customers:	Locals, especially Koreans of Chinese descent
Lunch:	Every day, 11:30 A.M.–3 P.M.
Dinner:	Every day, 3–11 P.M.

Atmosphere/setting: A certain subdued, if standardized, opulence rules in this restaurant, devoted to Chinese cooking with a Korean twist. Occupying the end unit of the small Koreatown, Yen Jing feels authentic, yet works for a wide audience.

House specialties: Pig "funckle" with brown sauce; dumplings; handmade noodles; seafood dishes; special tofu dishes.

Other recommendations: Spicy dishes; sea cucumber (if you like the stuff); mussels with black bean sauce.

Summary & comments: This is a family-operated enterprise, with the kids speaking good English while the parents struggle and smile. The family is of Chinese descent, but reared in Korea, thus creating an Asian/Fusion cuisine on eastern turf. The family's grandmother walked from China to Korea! Today, the restaurant looks toward a decade of good business. It attracts gourmands who enjoy adventurous dining and enjoys lots of respect from Atlanta's Asian community.

Honors & awards: *Knife & Fork* and lots of other positive local press.

Zócalo

Zone 8   Downtown East
187 10th Street, NE,
at Piedmont Avenue
(404) 249-7576

<table>
<tr><td colspan="2">Authentic Mexican</td></tr>
<tr><td colspan="2">★★★</td></tr>
<tr><td colspan="2">Inexpensive</td></tr>
<tr><td>Quality 95</td><td>Value A</td></tr>
</table>

Reservations:	Not accepted
When to go:	Any time
Entree range:	$9.50–19.25
Payment:	Major credit cards
Service rating:	★★★
Friendliness rating:	★★★★★
Parking:	Limited, on site
Bar:	Full service
Wine selection:	Chilean, Spanish, Californian, with some by the glass; house-made sangría (both red and white)
Dress:	Very casual
Disabled access:	Excellent, with ramp to deck
Customers:	Neighbors, locals, and other area restaurateurs
Brunch:	Sunday, 10:30 A.M.–2:30 P.M.
Lunch:	Monday–Friday, 11:30 A.M.–2:30 P.M.
Lunch/Dinner:	Saturday, 11:30 A.M.–midnight; Sunday, 2–10 P.M.
Dinner:	Monday–Thursday, 5:30–11 P.M.; Friday, 5:30 P.M.–midnight

Atmosphere/setting: Bright colors, artful and whimsical forms, outdoor dining on a sheltered (and heated, in cold weather) deck have been popular with the neighbors ever since the restaurant opened.

House specialties: Cochinata pibil (a Yucatecan dish featuring seasoned pork tenderloin cooked in banana leaf); black bean cakes; rajas (poblano peppers with onions and corn); enchiladas verdes; flan.

Other recommendations: Steak with eggs and tomatillo salsa with chipotle; crepas de mole blanco (crepes stuffed with chicken breast and rich white mole sauce); quesadilla camarón cielo e infierno (sautéed shrimps "heaven and hell" in a flour tortilla with asadero cheese and chipotle pepper salsa); vegetarian specialties.

Summary & comments: Dynamic, cheerful Lucero Martínez-Obregón dispenses authentic Mexican dishes with style and flair. Don't talk to her about any of the staples of Mexican-American cooking. She's not interested. But when it comes to classical Mexican food, the real thing, she's ready to perform and she's rigorous about authenticity.

Honors & awards: *Atlanta* magazine, Best Mexican Brunch, 1996; *Creative Loafing,* Best Tequila Bar, 2000, *Atlanta Journal & Constitution,* Top 50, 2000.

Zyka

Zone 5   Northeast Atlanta
1677 Scott Boulevard, Decatur
(404) 728-4444

	Indian
	★★★
	Inexpensive
	Quality 90 Value A

Reservations:	Not accepted
When to go:	Any time
Entree range:	$3.99–4.99
Payment:	Major credit cards
Service rating:	★★★★
Friendliness rating:	★★★★★
Parking:	On site
Bar:	None
Wine selection:	None
Dress:	Casual
Disabled access:	Yes
Customers:	Local members of the Indian community swarm all over this place, enticing non-Indian guests to explore this rich and varied cuisine
Lunch/Dinner:	Sunday and Tuesday–Thursday, noon–10:15 P.M.; Friday and Saturday, noon–10:45 P.M.; Monday, closed

Atmosphere/setting: There's not much in the way of Indian ambiance in this almost school cafeteria–style place. You place your order and pay for it at the cash register. They won't even LET you leave a tip, because it's completely self-service. You carry away trays of steaming delicacies to your table, or boxed to take home.

House specialties: Chicken 65 (boneless chunks anointed with aromatic but mild spices then batter-fried and flavored with green chilies, cilantro, and curry leaves); Hyderabadi Birnani (goat meat and basmati rice); dal Hyderabadi (lentils with tomatoes, cilantro, mint, and cumin); Spanish saffron-flavored ice cream with pistachio nuts and cardamom.

Other recommendations: No bummers here, but especially good is Nehari (beef shanks simmered with ginger, garlic, and spices); classic tandoori chicken; extraordinarily good naan (flat bread); differently styled raita (onions, diced potatoes in yogurt with mint and cilantro—no cucumbers).

Summary & comments: This is Indian food that will please anyone wary of its heat and spicing. The quality of the cooking is peerless. Alcohol cannot be served because of the restaurant's proximity to both a school and a church, so take-out is popular.

Honors & awards: Plenty of positive local press.

302